AF616572

Gandhian Philosophy and Terrorism

Caution to Readers

- **This book is not for sceptics—the people who suffer from pre-conceived negative thought concentrations.**
- **It is for the optimists—the people with significant positive thought dominance who, if situation so demands, are able to take a 180 degree turn—and are ready for trying a new out of box approach.**
- **Hence, the readers are cautioned not to form opinions either about terrorism or the Gandhian Philosophy (GP), before a thorough reading of the book.**
- **A reading through the book is likely to ignite and/or strengthen the readers' confidence in the 'soul force' and its capabilities for conflict resolution, irrespective the side of the terror divide one belongs.**
- **It is important to remember that GP is not a bullet-proof jacket that one could straightway adorn and face the terrorism. The terror infrastructures first have to be crushed through employment of situation specific "Fortified Conventional Strategy," before capsules of GP are employed to stop its regeneration and neutralizing the terror generating environment. Additionally, the GP is highly effective as a preventive against terrorisms of all types.**

Gandhian Philosophy and Terrorism

DR U.V. SINGH

PENTAGON PRESS

Gandhian Philosophy and Terrorism / Dr. U.V. Singh

ISBN 978-81-8274-476-9

First Published in 2011

Published in India by

PENTAGON PRESS
206, Peacock Lane, Shahpur Jat,
New Delhi-110049
Phones: 011-64706243, 26491568
Telefax: 011-26490600
email: rajan@pentagonpress.in
website: www.pentagonpress.in

Published in UK by
PENTAGON BOOKS UK LTD
2-8, Longcroft House,
Victoria Avenue, Liverpool Street,
London England EC2M 4NS

Printed at
New Elegant Printers, New Delhi.

This book is dedicated to
innocent victims of terrorism
irrespective of their religion
and country of origin

The greatest USP of the Gandhian Philosophy is: It does not generate any negative response amongst targeted groups or people.

To some readers, an in depth reading of this book might seem incarnating the 'Terrorism Management Strategy' of the 44th US President, Mr. Barack Obama, a righteous mix of the fortified conventional strategy (FCS)" and the "Gandhian Philosophy (GP)," towards conflict resolution.

Such an imaging, if it emerges in mind of any reader, would be totally contextual. The author has no intention and/or design in this direction.

CONTENTS

ACKNOWLEDGEMENT

The idea of this book arose from an intense discussion that the author had one evening with two of his intellectual friends, Mr. Kartar Hemrajani and Mr. Virendra K. Khaneja, in September 2008, in the shadow of the Batla house counter-terrorism incident, at Jamia Nagar colony of New Delhi, in which two suspected terrorists and a Delhi police officer were killed.

One of my two good friends was in a mental mode to tar the Muslim community with the evil of terrorism. He went to the extent of suggesting that the original promoter of the modern day terrorism was Mahatma Gandhi who had encouraged the Indian Muslim community to unite in favour of the preservation of the institution of Caliphate that the post World War 1 imperialist powers contemplated to abolish. Since my information level on the subject, at that moment, was not deep enough, I said that the subject assertion needed to be examined in depth. Also, it was added that the subject of terrorism and its apparent association with a community, too, was a complex problem.

From subsequent efforts to understand the above contentions, arose the need to examine various manifestations of terrorism, their genesis and spread, and also the motivations of its perpetrators and promoters; a significant majority of whom seemed to belong to the Muslim community.

These efforts and studies gave birth to the idea of bringing out the book, **"Gandhian Philosophy and Terrorism."** The limitations of terrorism's response to the conventional strategies for controlling it, i.e. the inability to apply requisite quantum of force without creating serious side-effects, on one hand, its basic limitation of not being able to address the ideology of terror, on the other, propelled the author to have a deep and analytical look at the Gandhian Philosophy or the GP. And, the obvious question that why the GP had not been examined, assessed and attempted for this purpose, continued to agitate my mind, till some formations of the GP, capable of meeting the challenges in this field were located in the large volume of literature available on it.

During the same period, cross-checking the judiciousness of the idea of doing a book on such a complex subject, with my wisdom-concentrate daughter Udita Singh and my decisively analytical son-in-law, Roberto Ripa, led to cementation in my mind of the likely utility of this project. Without their positive inputs, the intellectual stimulation caused by my two friends, referred to earlier, would have gone as a waste. Hence, I sincerely acknowledge the massive contribution of these four people towards completion of this work.

My deepest appreciation and sincerest thanks, however, go to Mr. Wajahat Habibullah, the Chief Information Commissioner, Government of India, who found time from his busy schedule to go through the manuscript.

Further, my wife, Jyotsna Singh's excellent collection of books on Mahatma Gandhi and his work philosophies came very handy in tackling the subject. My daughter-in-law, Gayatri Singh contributed the idea of the book-cover. And my son, Udayan Singh's silent support and appreciation were perpetually available.

August 2010.

U.V. SINGH

For a Reader in Hurry

Terrorism has given a severe jolt to the civilized world community: It is proving to be a hard nut to crack. Conventional terror management measures, whether in West Asia, Iraq, Afghanistan, Swat valley of Pakistan or in India, are failing to subdue the demon of terrorism. India, particularly, finds itself as a defenceless victim of the Islamic terror emanating from its immediate neighbourhood. While US and NATO forces continue to struggle in dealing with it in Iraq and Afghanistan, several other democratic countries are exhibiting an unusual difficulty, or loss of effective direction, in dealing with it.

In view of terrorism's recent virulence, the present book, in addition to tracing and analyzing its genesis and spread, its various manifestations, and their relationship with democratic and non-democratic, and secular and non-secular systems of governance, attempts to evaluate feasibility of an 'alternate path', the Gandhian Philosophy (GP), in dealing with this menace, not as a lone alternate—but in a wise—mix with the conventional approach towards handling of the evil challenge to the civilized world.

It proposes to iron out the weaknesses of the current conventional approach—converting the same into a "Fortified Conventional Strategy (FCS)" and then developing its yoga with the elements of the GP, turning the by-product into a true Brahmastra against the dreadful menace of terrorism.

Chapter 1 follows a brief introduction to the GP, discusses terrorism's various manifestations, and their peculiarities and severity. It encompasses, in addition to the essential nature and forms of terrorism, its genesis and spread along with its various causatives, stimulants, perpetrators, state and non-state actors, managers, foot-soldiers, financiers, and sympathizers acting with or without design. Negative energies of anger, intolerance, greed, selfishness, desire for dominance, non-inclusiveness, religious mis-interpretations and misinformation, and several other relevant causatives, stimulants and justifications are discussed under this chapter. It lays a stout foundation for multilateral understanding of this peculiar abnormality of human race and its differential emergences, which throw substantial challenges to the established world order.

Secularism and its relationship with terror genesis, as well as, its capacity to contain this demonic force, is analyzed and assessed in the second chapter.

Chapter 3 takes an intense look at the concept and perception of the **"Clash of Civilizations,"** as enunciated by Prof. Samuel Huntington, and various other concepts and formations of Islamic and non-Islamic experts on **"War and Peace"** in Islam—and its share of contributions towards genesis and spread of terrorism.

Further, the role of some countries, which have functioned as the **"Crucibles of Terror"** and **"Universities of Terrorism,"** including that of Saudi Arabia and Pakistan, has been covered herein.

The chapter 4 discusses the complex terror economy—and its various channels of flow of terror supporting funds, along with the nature and variety of its funding agents and their motivations. Along with the funds that fuel the generation and continuity of terrorism, utilization and mis-utilizations of such funds are dealt with in requisite details. The suitability and feasibility of terror funding channels' drying-up, as a measure for crushing the terrorism, too is dwelt upon.

The next two chapters are occupied with (a) the 'conventional approach' towards controlling terrorism, and (b) the 'fortified conventional strategies' (FCS) for cracking and crushing the evil nut of this human cancer.

The last two chapters of the book deal with key perceptions and practices of the **Gandhian Philosophy (GP)** and its application for digging up and destroying roots, shoots and seeds of terrorism, so that it is denied opportunities and environment of its regeneration. Along with the four **Brahmastras** of GP, this chapter elaborates upon the suitability of mixing the GP with FCS in right manner and proportions. The following aspects of the GP are discussed herein for the purpose of examining the foresaid objectivity.

- Scriptural approach towards management of evil and its perpetrators;
- Ahimsa or non-violence as a tool against terrorism;
- Application of Ahimsa in riot-terror management;
- Combined tool of Satyagraha and non-violence;
- Samvada or intense dialogue for mutual trust development;
- Peaceful mass-action as a practice of GP;
- Love, compassion and the healing-touch;
- GP a great tool of re-indoctrination;
- Soul-force for effective countering of terror;
- Inclusiveness as a tool for terror dissipation;
- Constructive programs as a component of the GP;
- Contextual approach as dynamism of GP;
- Optimism as a productive tool of GP
- GP: For wining the battle of hearts and minds;
- Application of GP for management of terrorism;
- Some Brahmastras emerging from the GP;
- GP cements the forces of introspection;
- Islam and the Gandhian Philosophy;
- GP: For taming the wild?
- GP: The holistic approach; and
- GP: Towards a road map for its implementation.

Along with the road map for implementation of the GP at international scale, its efficacy at almost 10 percent of the current costs imposed by the terrorism on the world community, towards the desired target of terror elimination has been stressed. Further, the general scepticism of ignorant and uninformed, towards efficacy of the GP has been attended to, so that readers do not shy away from a spontaneous effort to read and understand the same.

The greatest USP of the Gandhian Philosophy is: It does not generate any negative response amongst targeted groups or people.

Acronyms Employed

ANC	:	African National Congress.
ARC	:	Administrative Reforms Commission.
ATS	:	Anti-terrorist squad.
BJP	:	Bhartiya Janta Party—a political party of India.
CBNI	:	Chip based national identification.
CCD	:	Cooling and cleaning device—a reference to the GP.
CHS	:	Civilized human society.
CIA	:	An intelligence agency of USA.
CEO	:	Chief Executive Officer.
CMI	:	Centre for moral indoctrination.
CRP	:	Conflict resolution potential.
DTP	:	Disturbed thought process.
EDC	:	Economy destruction capacity.
EMI	:	Equated Monthly instalments.
ETA	:	A Basque organization promoting separatism.
FA	:	Failures accumulation-a condition that blocks right decision making..
FAF	:	Means forgetting and forgiving.
FATA	:	North-western region of Pakistan.
FBI	:	Federal Bureau of Investigations USA.
FCS	:	Fortified conventional strategy.
FFI	:	Foreign financial institutions.
FGF	:	Refers to feel good factor.
GP	:	Refers to the Gandhian Philosophy.
GWT	:	Global war on terrorism.
HOV	:	Hawkers of violence.

HMTR : Human male thought requirement.
I&B : Information and Broadcasting.
IFM : Interference free management.
IHWE : International human work environment.
IL : Illogical logic.
IMF : International Monetary Organization.
ISI : Inter Services Intelligence of Pakistan.
IQP : Refers to inadequate quantum of punishment.
IRA : Irish Republican Army.
ITW : Illogical thought warriorism.
J&K : Refers to the Indian state of Jammu and Kashmir.
JMI : Jami Milia Islamia, a university in New Delhi.
JNU : Jawaharlal Nehru University.
LeT : A Pakistani terrorist organization by the name of Lashkar-e-Toiba.
LTTE : Lankan Tamil Tigers Elem.
LCHE : Low cost high efficiency.
NATO : North Atlantic Treaty Organization.
NCFR : Refers to near complete freedom of religion in western society.
NGOs : Means non-governmental organizations.
NIC : Natal Indian Congress.
NSG : National security group.
OBC : Other backward classes.
PDG : Performance deficiency generator.
PLO : Palestinian Liberation Front.
POK : Pakistan occupied Kashmir.
POIT : Perception of Islamic terrorism.
POS : Perception of superiority.
POTA : Prevention of terrorist activities related law that was repealed by the UPA Government.
MAP : Minimum acceptable program.
MCS : Mentally challenged state.
MNC : Multi-national Corporation.
MR : Muslim rage.
MPDS : Multi-party democratic system.

MTP : Mental thought process.
NDA : National Democratic Alliance.
NWFP : North-West Frontier Province; now part of Pakistan.
R&AW : Research and Analysis Wing—an intelligence agency of India.
RACI : Refers to religious and cultural incompatibilities.
RC : Righteous conscience.
RGAT : Refers to the principle of righteous give and take.
RIAT : Religion independent anti-terror agency.
RT : Righteous thinking.
RTO : Road traffic officer.
SGT : Means self-generating traps.
SMT : Superior modern technology.
SOC : Means strength of conviction.
SID : Means secularized intellectual discourse.
TNT : Means the two nations theory which failed to sustain itself.
DOG : Delusions of greatness
LTTE : Lankan Tamil Tigers Elam.
LTP : Logical thought process.
ULFA : United Liberation Front of Assam.
UNESCO : United Nations Educational, Scientific and Cultural Organization.
UNSC : United Nations Security Council.
USPM : Refers to unacceptably severe punitive measures.
USA : United States of America.
UPA : United Progressive Alliance—a political grouping of India.
VHP : Vishva Hindu Parishad.
WMDs : Weapons of mass destruction.

INTRODUCTION

Gandhian Philosophy

Gandhian philosophy (GP) is one of the most significant developments of the 20th century—and the fact that it emerged in the conflict intense environments of the two world wars of this period, and during India's own struggle for independence from British rule, makes it still more significant. For conflicting ideological interests of the West's capitalism, Russian communism, and the pan-Islamism of Muslim world, coupled with India's own politico-economic weaknesses, the world could not benefit from the **Gandhian Philosophy's 'conflict resolution potential'** (CRP), not even to a fraction of its potential in this respect.

> Now, at turn of the first decade of the new century, circumstances offer the terrorism traumatized world community an opportunity to benefit from the GP's immense conflict resolution capabilities.

Presently, the world is suffering from intense bursts of the menace of terrorism, which is behaving like an active volcano—burdening the international community with a huge cost in terms of (a) the loss of human life, and (b) the massive funds diversion towards its attempted control.

The current major international campaigns in the direction of terrorism control, particularly in Iraq, Afghanistan, north-west Pakistan, and in India's own Jammu and Kashmir, are resulting into the loss of several thousand precious human lives, each year. Besides, pockets of active terrorist convulsions in Palestine, Lebanon, Syria, Egypt, Spain, Israel, Chechnya, Balkans, Indonesia, Philippines, Thailand, Bangladesh, Sri-Lanka, and many other countries are multiplying the cost several fold.

In terms of money, its true costs are difficult to calculate but, as a rough assessment, it runs into hundreds of billions US dollars each year. It has contributed substantially towards Pakistan's journey into near bankruptcy. And the US financial crisis, which enveloped almost whole the economically active world with a **'market meltdown'** in September-December 2008, owed a lot to the vast funds wastage and/or diversion towards fighting the evil of terrorism.

Additionally, the indirect costs of countering terrorism such as enhanced security at airports, protection of commercial and political interests, security of political leaders—and conferences and meetings, amongst others, are truly incalculable. The losses of business opportunities and growth as a response to this menace, is almost impossible to calculate. Collectively, they were responsible for a significant part of the heating-up of the international economy and its final collapse in the latter half of 2008.

Forces of terrorism, including its promoters and mentors, seem to love the anti-terrorism measures of inadequate intensity. They behave, more or less, like bacterial infections, which respond to low dosages of antibiotics by becoming more virulent—developing immunity and turning resistant, and more difficult to control—threatening grave consequences to the victim populations.

Perpetrators of terrorism, in the key international theatres of this conflict, are behaving exactly in this manner. They are striking at will—and the countries protecting and supporting these evil forces raise the bogey of sovereignty violation (like Pakistan, Syria and Lebanon), whenever tough inter-state campaigns are launched. Victim nations, particularly India, after each terrorist strike or bomb blasts, issue a variety of statements for countering the menace, which from the angle of the perpetrators of this crime against innocent public, seem nothing but symptoms of weakness of a soft state.

> Inadequacy of response toughness (the quantum of punitive force) is being enjoyed by the terrorists and their supporters.

Only in very insignificant cases in the world, except Chechnya, where Russia employed the needed dose of counter-force, have military means succeeded in effective control and/or suppression of terrorism. In Northern Ireland, violence and counter-violence subsided only after a political settlement was arrived at, between the two warring factions, which had almost exhausted themselves through a long unyielding conflict. Conflict between Israel and its Arab neighbours, because of the types of the means employed, is nowhere near to completion.

Western media always came to the assistance or rescue of terrorism, whenever it got significantly pinned down by Israeli counter-terrorism measures. International assistance, from Islamic as well as non-Islamic countries, to terror perpetrating organizations was never linked effectively to their movement towards reconciliation. And, in several cases, it openly conflicted with the objectivity of conflict resolution.

On the other hand, in South Africa, GP displayed its miraculous effect in significantly evaporating the long-persisting hostilities (most of the time truly inhuman in nature) between the ruling white minority and the local black majority. In his book, **"No Future without Forgiveness," Desmond Tutu** appropriately described the actions taken for reconciliation. Initiated by leading statesmen who themselves made courageous confessions in open courts, people from all walks of life, blacks and whites, were encouraged to come forward and confess their crimes. It had an electrifying effect in cooling tempers and making people to forget and forgive. They wept as they recounted their own crimes and shameful actions. There, the GP was at its functional best. De-stressed and healed, people purged themselves free of the residues of hatred and guilt.

GP has had several distinguished adopters to its credit; the prominent ones being **Khan Abdul Ghaffar Khan** (also known as **Frontier Gandhi**), **Albert Einstein, Martin Luther King Jr.** and **Nelson Mandela**. And in the present times, America's 44th president, the first history maker of the African-American descent, **Mr Barack Husein Obama** is reported to be the newest and brightest adherent of the GP. He hung a portrait of the Mahatma in his Senate office. Barack Obama has always seen Mahatma Gandhi as an inspiration who reminds him about the **'real message of life.'**

Through the power of his own example and his unshakable spirit, Gandhi inspired a whole mass of people to resist oppression, sparking a revolution with an entirely new

technology of non-violence, and freed a nation from long and painful colonial rule.

> "Gandhi's significance is universal. Countless people around the world have been touched by his spirit and example."
>
> "His victory in turn inspired a generation of Americans to peacefully wipe out a system of overt oppression that had endured for a century,"
>
> **"And more recently led to velvet revolutions in Eastern Europe and extinguished apartheid in South Africa,"** the 47 year old Senator was reported to have said in his message on October 2, 2008, for birth day celebrations of Mahatma Gandhi.

In view of the fact that the GP has influenced so many great minds and movements—and the emerging fact that the menace of terrorism cannot be handled effectively by military force alone, **as enough of it cannot be applied for fear of resultant consequences** (particularly in a multi-party vote-bank democracy like India), it is time to deliberate upon the **'Low Cost High Efficiency'** (LCHE) technology contained in the Gandhian philosophy.

GP is a global phenomenon, free from racial, religious and/or territorial limitations. It is also free from requirements of education and financial developments—as it can be applied in a poor and/or rich country, with equal ease. It is not very much a philosophy of governance—but a philosophy of corrective and reformative resistance—and, to be truly effective, it has to be applied from within a suffering community; its applications from outside are not expected to be very effective.

Whenever and where-ever tried, the human life cost component of the Gandhian philosophy has been almost zero, except when its application was not in accordance to its basic formations.

And, almost one-tenth of the financial cost of what is now being incurred on the military options (the war against terror) can suffice to cool down and de-congest the polluted minds of terrorists, their supporters and mentors. The benefit of the cooperation and/or de-escalation that would emerge from the applications of the Gandhian Philosophy will, indeed, be huge and multilateral. As per assessment of the author, this world shall become a much more peaceful and happier place to live in, on application of the Gandhian Philosophy, in requisite doses and in righteous manner.

What is Gandhian Philosophy?

The Gandhian Philosophy forms a '**unique process of conflict resolution**' through intense dialogue, inclusiveness and sharing, collective welfare, wider consensus, and confidence building through linkage of body, mind, and soul of the conflicting elements, or the people who are suffering from active gaps of trust and understanding. It primarily consists of:

- Active multilateral dialogue (Samvada or Sarva-dharma Samvada).
- Sataya (Truth) and Satayagraha in support of what is right and judicious.
- Non-violence or Ahimsa as a tool for response in situations of conflict.
- Following the spiritual path where everything, even non-violence is secondary; unless there is love behind it; unless one loves the person protesting against or attempting to change.
- Non-cooperation (or civil disobedience) with trouble-some elements or the perpetrators of evil.
- Peaceful mass-action for grievance magnification and its eventual resolution.
- Forgiveness—the sprit to forget and forgive.
- Up-liftment of poor and discriminated (dalits) or those having grievance accumulation.
- Self-purification (fasting and dharna) to make the conflict generating elements see reason.
- Constructive programs to offer occupancy to unemployed or the unoccupied.
- Wide usage of dharma or righteousness.
- Synthesis of conflicting views into one mainstream action.
- Concept of trusteeship—not ownership but shared usage.
- Clear and more effective usage of secularism and democratic energies.
- Cultivating relaxed plurality—unity in diversity.
- Ultimate unity of all religions, and amongst others.

- Employment of the 'soul force' in bringing around the deviants and conflict generators.

The Unique Capacity of Gandhian Philosophy

In one way, GP is a true exception: Its conflict resolution capacity (CRP) is not matched by any other approach known to the mankind.

> GP has the unique capacity to wage low intensity war on minds and hearts of people, including the terrorists.

In fact, GP can positively reorient the **mental thought process** (MTP) of all the key elements of terrorism such as:

- The unrighteous and selfish politicians who become partners with religious clergy in initiation and perpetuation of terrorism;
- The distracted clergy who misinterpret scriptures for the purpose of indoctrinating foot-soldiers of terror;
- The terrorists and their handlers who end up losing the power of logical thinking to the indoctrinating agents of evil designs; and
- The financiers of terrorism who play an equally important role—as this evil activity does not survive in absence of finance or even on dilution of its supply.

The GP has the capacity to sweep away the clouds of **'adharma'** and violence from the mental screen of the people of all the four categories engaged in terrorism, at its various layers and levels.

> It can soften the hardened minds of terrorists and their handlers—making the same receptive to ideas of conflict resolution.

A positively oriented MTP diminishes anti-people thought accumulation, in addition to shutting down its entry, neutralizing efforts of the evil seniors and mentors.

Thought of revenge is converted to the thought of futility of violence—and then repentance/regrets for wrongs done take root. From these germinates the desire to forgive and forget.

The GP, as per persisting logic of the author, is capable of giving terrorism a **decent and/or respectful burial** (despite its severity and spread) by:

- Cooling down the over-heated minds of jihadis, Islamic or otherwise, by allowing them an honourable exit or re-orientation;
- Softening the hardened minds of terrorists and their handlers—and making them receptive to dialogic conflict resolution;
- De-congesting or reverse indoctrination of the clogged minds of Jihadis—particularly the foot-soldiers;
- Letting them understand scriptures in a righteous manner;
- Prompting them learn to understand and appreciate others' point of view;
- Allowing them opportunities to re-assimilate into normal society;
- Encouraging them to introspect—and to finally forgive and forget;
- Letting them learn that Allah or the God did not want every-one in the world to be a Muslim or Christian, and amongst others,
- Making them learn that the multiplicity of faith or pluralism is capable of productive co-existence (secularism).

GP with its well-tested component tools, as briefed above, is not a weapon of the weak and incapable—or unprepared and undetermined. It is a weapon that can be wielded only by those who are strong, both at the thought as well as action level.

GP should also not be misunderstood as a bullet-proof jacket, which could be worn by anyone for jumping into the firing line of terrorism. It has to be applied as suitably modulated capsules—either as a preventive or as a terror regeneration antidote, after the active infrastructures of terror are effectively crushed through applications of the FCS. It can inactivate the roots, shoots and seeds of terrorism.

First, there has to be a steely determination to fight the evil—and than requisite toughness must emerge from every component action, at every moment.

In a way, GP can be a practice of '**multilateral jihad**' against evils of society and/or some of its groupings, employing the tools of **ahimsa, satayagraha, and dialogue**; it is a synthesis (a yoga) of the collective body, mind, and soul of the community, to fight the evil and unrighteousness through peaceful and/or non-violent means.

It is a technology of conflict resolution at the thought level—employing the energy of thought (the active mind)—because it is the seat of all actions, evil or non-evil. The GP, thus, attacks the very root of evil thought genesis—and its accumulation, by altering the very thought process.

GP can act on the mental screen of terrorists and their masters. It is capable of disarming even the most dreaded and heartless ones—because no one is truly heartless. Those posing so, only carry a mask of terror or heartlessness. It can do the job of de-masking the terrorists, allowing them to throw away the mask—like a caterpillar or pupa does through the act of metamorphosis, to finally emerge as a beautiful butterfly. **The only essential for its effective manifestation is that it should be home-grown and in adequate intensity.**

Mahatma Gandhi had conclusively demonstrated the above while facing the communal rioters in Naokhali and Calcutta, prior to and during the tension intense period of India's partition in 1947.

In fact, **it is terrorism that is the weapon of the weak people**—who have no capacity to confront issues and resolve problems in an overt manner, face to face with the opposing party, and by dialoguing intensely—either by moulding the other party to their point of view, or getting themselves moulded up as per demands of the time.

The **'foxy approach'** of terrorists does not bring any credit or respectability, either to the act, or the evil actors involved. Killing innocent and unarmed people, who are not even remotely associated with the issues that are over-heating clustered minds, is not an act of great bravery, or to be proud of, in any manner.

The methodology of GP, in reference to its applicability in this regard, is discussed in detail in Chapter 7.

The greatest USP of the Gandhian Philosophy is: It does not generate any negative response amongst targeted groups or people.

CHAPTER 1

TERRORISM AND ITS MANIFESTATIONS

What is Terrorism?

Terrorism is a misguided action, or series of evil actions, by a group of disgruntled persons, designed to create panic and terror through killing and maiming of innocent people, with the objective of influencing the apparatus of governance (and also the people supporting it) in favour of their unrighteous or righteous objectivity.

Terrorism, in its modern form, is never effected individually or in isolation; it is always directed or instigated by a group of disgruntled seniors or leaders who have their own axe to grind; they recruit, brainwash, and train its frontline operatives, without the latter often being fully aware of the actual objectivity.

India's former president, Dr. A.P.J. Abdul Kalam, while giving the L M Singhvi memorial lecture at New Delhi on 17th January, 2009, called terrorism a '**coming together of evil minds**'. He went on to say that good minds too should come together to fight it.

Attempted dominance and/or exploitation by one group of the others, in terms of ideology, religious faith, economic activities, and/or governance, is one of the main causatives of terrorism. And, the organized terrorism, as experienced presently, is essentially incapable of emergence without someone paying for or financing it. It is incapable of independent genesis and/or existence.

For the purpose of generally acceptable understanding, and for having appropriate laws for its control, precise and legally valid definition of terrorism was necessitated. The one developed by the US government is as under:

> The term "terrorism" means premeditated and politically motivated violence perpetrated against non-combatant targets, by sub-national groups or clandestine agents, usually intended to influence an audience.
>
> The term "international terrorism" means terrorism involving citizens of or the territory of more than one country.
>
> The term "terrorist group" means any group practicing, or that has significant subgroups that practice, international terrorism (22 U.S.C.2656f(d).

Violence being politically motivated and the target—as non-combatants, are the key formations of this definition.

Political analyst, security counsellor, and White House advisor, **Brian Jenkins[1]**, gave a somewhat different definition of terrorism, noting that:

> All terrorist acts are crimes. Many would also be violations of the rules of war, if a state of war existed. All involve violence or threat of violence, often coupled with specific demands. The targets are mainly civilians. The motives are political. The actions generally are designed to achieve maximum publicity. The perpetrators are usually members of an organized group, and unlike other criminals, they often claim credit for the act. (This is a true hall-mark of terrorism). And, finally, it is intrinsic to a terrorist act that it is unusually intended to produce psychological effects far beyond the immediate physical damage. One person's terrorist is everyone's terrorist.[1]

The problem with attempts to define terrorism is that they can never be complete from the stand point of encompassing all situations and varieties of terrorist acts—and hence, each country attempting to fight and/or control terrorism has to evolve its own definition and laws, specific to its situations and requirements. The definition of terrorism, among others, has to cover all varieties of violence related to political, religious, ethnic, linguistic, economic, and geographical causatives. There seems to be a need for a **'supra-national approach'** in this regard.

Terrorism is not a simple act of violence: It does not move without systematic planning and finance. There are, always, one or more sources of finance and a chain of command and enablers—amongst the latter, often one not knowing the other beyond a level—and each one being engaged into factual or designed camouflage activities or professions.

Accumulated anger, frustration, victim syndrome, envy and/or intolerance—or just plain misunderstanding on part of the evil mentor elements or terror leadership, normally act as the basic stimulants or causatives of these anti-people and anti-social actions of death and destruction. Political, religious, cultural, territorial, and economic causatives, in certain mixes, propel the evil brains that manage acts of terrorism from safe locations. Often state support, covert or overt, from within or outside, provides the sustaining fuel for the same.

Normally, terrorism practices '**illogical logic**' (IL)—and a majority of its followers, particularly the leaders suffer from a '**disturbed thought process** (DTP)'. They cannot think straight and righteously; the difference of what is right and what is wrong does not seem to bother them. At least, at the collective or public level they actively exhibit this lack of **righteous conscience** (RC). They develop strange logic and justifications for evil perpetrations. For them, their '**flawed objectivity**' becomes sacred—to be promoted at all costs.

Minds of terror masters seem, indeed, perplexingly wired—totally devoid of compassion and considerations of humanism and ethicality. As failures are encountered, fear accumulates to make them apparently (and increasingly) insensitive and wooden to pains and sufferings of others, particularly the innocent victims.

Some terrorists do suffer from **delusions of greatness** (DOG), without meriting or striving for it. Lives of foot-soldiers and innocent victims are a form of cannon fodder or compost material for them. They indoctrinate or coerce others, particularly the feeble-minded ones, to become suicide bombers: they never offer to do the dirty job themselves.

Terrorism: A Product of Struggle for or against Dominance?

Tariq Ali in his book **"Bush in Babylon: The Re-colonization of Iraq"** finds no fault with the Islamic world's predisposition towards violence in general, and the response of Palestinians and

Iraqis in particular, for the injustice done to them by the Western imperialistic forces. He goes to vigorously formulate that occupation leads to resistance, and ultimately to violence: He seems to be at a loss in understanding the West's inability to understand the same, as he wonders:

> "Why are otherwise intelligent people in Britain and the United States surprised on learning that the occupation is detested by a majority of Iraqi people?"

> "Empires sometimes forget who they are crusading against and why, but the occupied rarely suffer from such confusions. How could they when the regime being imposed on them is a mixture of Gaza and Guantanamo? The aim of resistance is to target occupation forces on a daily scale and in this they have been relatively successful."

There is no denying of the fact that occupation generates adverse reaction which could often take a violent turn, and grow ultimately into terrorism. It is a struggle against dominance, which whenever non-Gandhian in its nature and/or expression, is bound to generate violence. Similarly, struggle for dominance if it is not in acceptable or in adequately sweetened form too tends to generate resistance, with eventual possibilities of degenerating into violence.

Non-Gandhian struggle for and/or against dominance often easily spurts into violence, which in its terminal stage tends to assume the obnoxious form of terrorism. Often, inability and/or incapacity of rulers, democratic or otherwise, to understand this basic human reaction mechanism endangers the peaceful life of numerous communities.

Terrorism: War and/or Revolution

Are terrorism and war different? Yes, to a considerable extent; but, in both cases, there are innocent victims. In a war, the enemy is known and well-defined—while, in case of terrorism, it is not so clear. It is more of **an act of violence by deception**.

It is often argued that war kills far larger numbers than terrorism, but in certain situations this differentiation might lose significance. Normally, wars are fought by governments—and terrorism is perpetrated by certain ill-motivated, misguided or disgruntled elements, or their groupings. As per the international legal system, developed in the past century, wars are supposed to be fought as per certain rules, but terrorism knows or respects no rules of any type.

While war is an accepted means of conflict resolution, terrorism has gained no such acceptance.

Both, the army and terrorists, want to force their opponents to submit to certain demands. While the military accomplishes it by destroying the opponents and pushing them to a realization that the cost of continuing is more than giving up, the terrorist attempt to weaken people's support to their governments.

Most of the armed forces do not kill prisoners of war, as it does not weaken the enemy—but terrorists do not hesitate in killing, captives or otherwise, because these acts are designed to enhance the fear factor or terror, and also earn them unpaid publicity, which they always root for.

The difference between war and terrorism is not always one of effect, but of goals and purposes. In war, killing of civilians may be more an effect of accident or collateral but, for terrorists, it is often viewed as necessary.

Both, terrorists and revolutionaries have grievances and seek radical changes. Revolutionaries normally target governments, its forces and establishments—and damage to civilians, in that case, is only collateral. On the contrary, terrorism's priority is to cow down the people so that they reduce or stop supporting the targeted regime.

In India Maoists and Naxalites are active in several states; they primarily attack the states' apparatus of governance (or mis-governance as they perceive it), especially their security forces. Here again the objective is to demoralize people so that, at the grass root level, they start collecting funds and exert controls.

Revolutionary activities normally, by implication, are more focused, broad-based and systemic than those of the terrorism. A revolution necessitates some support base and some ability to replace the present system of governance by a more effective one (at least as per their subjective perception). Some terrorist campaigns too dream of initiating a revolution, but rarely succeed in so doing, due to deficiencies of thought and/or design on their part. Terrorists also lack the discipline of revolutionary outfits.

Terrorism: An Evil Ruthlessness

Despite being educated and intelligent, most terrorists fall victim to the loss of **righteous thinking (RT)** and disturbances in their **logical thought process (LTP)**. Coupled with evil accumulation, they assume the satanic character of **'Kamsa of Mathura'** who thought nothing while murdering thousands of innocent newborns in a futile effort to neutralize the forecast that the one destined to kill him had taken birth. Similar to the **'Kamsa methodology'**, their ruthlessness increases as time passes; they get deluded by their own evil activations.

Killing innocent people, who are not even remotely concerned with the issues that agitate or pollute terrorist minds, amounts to demonstration of their utter **'evil ruthlessness'**. They do not seem to follow any rationality of the civic society. Such ruthlessness is not encountered in any part of the animal world: thus, they qualify to be called as **'sub-normal animals,'** as in no other animal species large scale killing of its own members is ever attempted.

Ruthlessness of terrorism is visible not only in its victims' spectrum that often are unconnected and unconcerned to the issues central to the perpetrators of terror, it is also seen in their methods of usage of children and women as cannon fodder, fidayeens, and human shields.

Some terror outfits are known to have engaged into genocide of their own people or supporter population in order to spill blame on state agencies.

Terrorism; Where an Evil Minority Tends to Overtake?

In the process of terror genesis and spread, an evil minority overtakes the silent majority. A single misguided teacher, cleric or otherwise, in a madrasa or parivar school, or in a mosque and/ or temple, is able to implant superiority of one God (or philosophy) over the others, or create perception of non-existent or a wild discrimination.

A few terrorists, fidayeen or otherwise, terrorize and torment a large number of people; collect funds, grab lands, and raise armies of miscreants. They kill at will, trample human rights, hang non-confirmers on public squares, and justify their evil actions as a right response for some grievances, actual and/or imaginary.

Their self-celebrated but un-stated objective, invariably, is to dominate, imbalance and overpower people for their narrow selfish and obscure objectivity. Many fence-sitters start following them as power of arms, money, and authority helps people to grow blind to reality and righteousness—and in the process, terrorists gather an army of supporters, from general public as well as in the official apparatus of governance. This is what has happened in Pakistan, Afghanistan and Palestine.

It is primarily a failure of the majority in a society i.e. not being able to do a job which rightfully belongs to it—and then suffer the consequences. For misdeeds of few, everybody has to suffer: A whole society, or even a nation, pays the price of allowing dominance of a minuscule minority by a silent or inactive majority.

Terrorism: In Active Mode to Mislead Followers of Islam

Some masters of terrorism, in January, 2009, banned education of girls beyond 4th class in the Swat valley of Pakistan—and attempted to justify it as Islamic. It was, in addition to blasting to ground of over 150 girls' schools in the said area.

Most of the frontline leaders in Pakistan, religious and/or political, did not show active willingness to oppose this retrograde move. A strong condemnation of this backward move recently came from the highly unlikely quarters. Syed Ali Geelani, a hard-line separatist Muslim leader and Chairman of one of the factions of the Hurriyat Conference, based in Indian Kashmir, said that this move of the Taliban was far from being Islamic.

"Denying 74,000 young women the right to pursue education and burning and blasting of over 150 schools are unjustifiable acts," Geelani was reported to have said in a statement.

"It can be said without any hesitation that those imposing such ban and prohibition are ignorant of the Islamic values and principles. In Islam, the first revelation from Allah to the Holy Prophet Mohammad was 'Iqra' (to read). Prophet Mohammad himself has repeatedly stressed the value of education and made seeking knowledge an obligation on every individual. Preventing people—be they man or woman, from pursuing education is against Islamic teachings," said Mr Geelani, as per a report credited to *The Hindu* of 3rd January, 2009.

Terrorism, thus, seems to be capable of forcibly twisting 'unreal into real' or 'untruth into truth,' and its perpetrators, the half-baked clerics, do not hesitate in believing and/or attempting the same under the delusion—that force possessed this kind of magical capabilities.

The above is just one of the examples of this nature but, on a slightly analytical look a cascade of such lies and misdeeds shall tumble down from the dirty cupboards of the terror perpetrators.

Terrorism: Its Genesis and Spread

As per the author, terrorism is the response of the **weak and coward;** those who cannot directly take on their adversaries, factual or perceived, and resort to these foxy and nefarious acts of terror. Despite being weak and unequal, they want to damage their adversaries or perceived tormentors—and they, not being in a position or willing to face the consequences of such actions, resort to the hateful acts of terrorism. Foxiness or stealth is their armour of protection.

Accumulated misperceptions and/or **perception of unfairness**—and the resultant **load of anger,** and **grievancial muck accumulation** make them fall to evil machinations of their mentors or handlers. Often the lure of money, or the greed, too makes them ignore the consequences or not to actively think about the same.

Genesis and spread of the modern day terrorism gathered active steam after the humiliating defeat of Arab states in the six days war of 1967.It vividly demonstrated that the Arab states, individually and collectively, while looking tough, were indeed soft and weak. It created a severe ego hurt—and a crisis of confidence.

The fundamentalists, political Islamists, revivalists, Islamic activists, and the intelligentsia, and almost all those who prided the Arab Islamic culture—and its illustrious past, were hurt beyond easy repair. For them terrorism became a camouflage for their discomfiture—or simply a **failure management exercise**. The dismal failure of Arab states to deliver in the face of a small adversary (though supported by the West) infuriated them to a level of '**illogical thought warriorism (ITW)**'. They found solace in '**Jihad**' (or Jehad) and resultant terrorism, claiming it as Allah's way.

Seeds of active terrorism were deeply planted in the Arab world—particularly in Egypt, Saudi Arabia, Syria, Algeria etc, even much before the stunning defeat of 1967.

Historian **Ira Lapidus**[2] delved into the history of Islamic societies in relation to development of **militant Islam** with substantial precision. He also described the impact of interaction of European values on the Arab Islamic societies.

In this context, the failure of Arab states internally and externally, and a **"re-interpretation of Islamic tradition: in a way that it gives a revolutionary meaning,"** is stressed; it allowed ascendancy of fundamentalists. The process started with Hasan Al Banna in Egypt followed by other Egyptians thinkers like Abdul Qadir Awdah, Sayyid Qutb, Mohammad Al Ghazali, and Yusuf Waradawi. Elsewhere in the Arab world, Mustafa Al Sibai, and Said Hawwa of Syria, Hasan Turabi of Sudan, and Rashid Al-Ghannooushi of Tunisia made their contributions.

Abdul Hasan Ali Nadvi in India and Abdul Ala Maudoodi in Pakistan played their role in context of South Asia. In Iran, Ali Shariati and Khomeini generated current of thoughts, leading to the revolution of 1979.

In all the cases, '**Tokens of Islamicity**', advocating alternate political order based on Sharia, were promoted. As a co-product of these fundamentalist developments, a confusion of Islamic terminologies such as **Islamic resurgence, Islamic revival, Islamic fundamentalism, Islamism, political Islam, Islamic activism, militant Islam, and many more** crowded the Islam's religious and political space, leaving very little room for moderates to operate. And, in this confusion, terrorism grew unabated.

This Islamic radicalism did not occur in a vacuum; interaction of Muslim societies—particularly of the negative variety, with '**Western Imperialism**' fuelled and sustained it. The resultant situation was aptly summed up many years ago by **Wilfred Cantwell Smith**[3]:

> "The fundamental malaise of modern Islam is that something has gone wrong with Islamic history. The fundamental problem of modern Muslims is how to rehabilitate that history: to set it again in full vigour so that Islamic society may once again flourish as a divinely guided society should and must. The fundamental spiritual crisis of Islam in the

twentieth century stems from an awareness that something is awry between the religion which God has appointed, and the historical development of the world He controls."

The Egyptian hardliner Hasan Al Banna's vitriolic writings and ideological discourses compacted the mental thought space of fundamentalists, leaving no room for rapprochement between Islamists and the West—and elsewhere, they said or perceived **Islamic interests being in danger**. **Sayyid Qutub**[13,14] put more fuel to the fire of fundamentalism and its progeny, the **'Islamic Terrorism'**.

Continued failures of Islam to attain world leadership, and be decisive in conduct of world affairs, is a chronic pain in its body politic.

This spiritual crisis of the Arab and Muslim world was re-scratched into bleeding wounds by the six days 1967 Arab-Israel war.

This defeat dealt a deathblow to the carefully and passionately nourished pan-Arabism and Arab nationalism. And, the terrorism is the response of this weak and wounded tiger that decided to adopt a foxy methodology of incapables.

> Excessive dose of religion, particularly the fundamentalist, non-tolerant, and the non-inclusive variety, to a human society does leave side-effects, like an over-dosage of medication, allopathic or otherwise.

Petro-dollars, drug funds, particularly from international fundamentalist organizations, religious and otherwise, played active catalyzing role in this process. Political jealousies of failing neighbouring states, or their crab mentality, forced organizations like ISI of Pakistan, to play a nefarious role for and on behalf of their bosses and controllers, in creating situations of persistent mischief for a democratic and secular India.

Loss of dominance and delusion of grandeur too contributed towards fanning of fundamentalist and terrorist activities. It is essentially an expression of frustration for failure of Muslim states to grab lead roles in world affairs, an inability to adequately service Allah.

The statement made a few paragraph earlier, **"As per the author, terrorism is the response of the weak and coward,"** is not complete. In light of what terrorists from our neighbourhood did in Mumbai, 26th through 29th November, 2008, the thinking minds seem to add towards end of the statement, " —**and Jealous and incompetent."**

Jealousy generated in some, on seeing progress of neighbours, becomes a great destructive force, as was the case with the misguided youth and their mentors from across the Indian border. They felt terribly jealous of India's multilateral progress, and the lights, the wealth, and the pomp of Mumbai that dazzles the world, at least the South Asian one. It burnt them from inside! And their incompetence compounded the situation for them as they could not assemble resources—energies of thought and action to perform and compete. Frustrated, deluded, and burnt with envy, they killed innocents and burnt equally harmless properties.

In India, organizations like the Vishwa Hindu Parishad (VHP), RSS, and Bajrang Dal, just to name a few, too suffer in some measures, from this defective and non-performing mentality.

Terrorism: It can Grow to Force Parental Surrender

It is not rare in systems of human governance where a prince grows more powerful than his ruling father, and eventually overthrows him. Human history and mythology are full of such stories and instances. However, instances of deliberately created militia overtaking its creator are not easily visible in the modern history. In case of Pakistan, the Taliban created and nursed by its successive governments and the ISI so painstakingly, with the specific purpose to extending its strategic influence into its immediate neighbourhood, has indeed done the unthinkable.

Not only the Taliban consolidated its control over the Pakistan's picturesque Swat valley, it forced the NWFP provincial government to surrender its authority of governance —and, in the process, clamping the Shariat on its already socially and economically backward population. In the process, hundreds of girls schools in the backward valley were turned into rubble. And, the two secular parties of Pakistan—the Awami National Party governing the province, and the Pakistan Peoples Party heading the central government, have led the charge to this surrender.

In the view of some political commentators, it symbolizes total surrender of the Pakistan government and its mighty army to the militants—and that the latter, were viewed at one time as not far from overtaking the Pakistani national scene at Islamabad. And what compounded the already complex situation was the justification offered by the Pakistan's government for this onerous development to its American financiers and supporters.

Only American pressure in light of its Af-Pak policies forced the Pakistani army to take action against its own created Taliban in the Swat valley and South Waziristan. While the Pakistani reluctance to effectively cripple Taliban persists unabashedly its public's anti-Americanism has grown up multifold.

Terrorism: Exhibits Tendency to Negotiate from Position of Strengths

LTTE in Sri-Lanka tried hard to negotiate when its terror campaign was going strong but the government did not settle for the humiliating conditions that the militants were proposing. After a few years, towards end of the first decade of the current century, the situation turned totally unfavourable to it.

However, in Swat valley of Pakistan, the Taliban militants at one time had forced the provincial NWFP government as well as the central PPP administration into accepting totally humiliating conditions for an agreement that allowed the militants to force Shariat down the throat of a reluctant population which lost hundreds of its girls schools to the fire and explosives of the evil militancy.

Nepal was another example where Maoist militants, employing a narrow leaf of electoral process, forced its national government to surrender to the organized might of the militancy. Power tasted militancy normally does not show leniency of any type and, most likely, the PPP government in Pakistan too runs the risk to meet a fate very similar to that of Nepal, if it does not respond to American pressure on it to effectively act against terrorist outfits.

For a civilized and democratic society, such behaviour of militants and terrorists throw up situations of very uncomfortable and uncertain future.

Terrorism: It makes an Intelligent Geographical Selection

Any dispensation of lawless-ness, including terrorism, needs basic presence of illiteracy, poverty, ruggedness of terrain, history of violence and instability, scope for some illegal trade, and weak governance, to flourish on a long-term basis. Absence of one or more of these essentialities or facilitators is bound to reduce durability and/or intensity of terror violence, even if it is somehow initiated.

For instance, terrorism failed in India's Punjab because several of these essentials were absent. In case of Northern Ireland too some of the essential requirements were not available. It could not be ignited in Tibet again due to absence of some vital essentials.

Selection of Afghanistan and the north-west Pakistan, as a crucible of terror genesis, and export smells of some intelligent design or decision making, for locating this activity. The Saudi and Egyptian perpetrators of terror moved to this area, instead of attempting the same in their own countries, which enjoyed a much stronger base of religious fundamentalism and authority, in comparison to the selected locale. There, poverty and weak governance were absent for assigning it the requisite fertility.

This selection of this location by Al-Qaida and Taliban, the two most dangerous terror outfits of the modern world, is significant in view of the followings:

- This area has enjoyed a long history of violence and volatility;
- It is an excellent location for export of terror—located right on the old silk route;
- Rugged, infertile, and inhospitable terrain bestows on it multilateral advantages;
- People, here, have historically exhibited excellent poverty (and consequent misery) tolerance;
- This area is a centre for narcotics business and trade;
- Here, people are short on tolerance, rich in anger accumulation, and the tradition of revenge -and consequently high on violence;
- They are short on processes of thought but rich on unreasoned-action;
- It has an excellent supply of foot-soldiers;
- Being economically backward, it is fully free from the impediments that are often caused by economic progress, in direction of terror genesis and spread;
- Low literacy frees the population from possibilities of logic and/or wisdom dominance;

- They suffer from a high level of primary negativity, which comes in way of righteous thinking and wider cooperation; and
- Lack of governance, or weak governance, acts as a true hormone for this activity.

Employing the above yardsticks, it can be safely asserted that Pakistan's Punjab, despite its population being sympathetic to the causes serviced by terrorism, will never adopt any intensive form of such activity. Nor will the Pakistani origin Muslims of Britain, as being feared, shall pose a big danger to USA and/or to any other western country, except misguided individuals causing problems occasionally.

In both the cases, a large number of potential miscreants shall not elect to risk and/or lose their economic prosperity—and in the latter case strong and righteous governance shall discourage any large scale emergence of this evil.

Terrorism: Is it Dialogue Deficient?

On deep analysis of the mode of response of perpetrators of terrorism, it seems that they are deficient in the skills of dialogue; they prefer to use force over discussion. There seems to be little or no scope for them in creating mutual understanding and acceptance (U/A); they prefer to go directly to forcing acceptance while understanding may or may not follow.

> It is probably a reflection of the basic nature of the Abrahamic religions, as they are based on revelations rather than dialogue. When what is revealed becomes an unquestionable or gospel truth or a matter of faith, the scope for discussion and dialogue disappears. It causes intolerance of deviating views (in minds of leaders and/or dominants) or the virulent disease of intolerance—and those diseased with it prefer to strike rather than convince their opponents or even deviant co-workers and followers. Only appreciative interpretations and/or extensions are tolerated.

They prefer compliance over criticism—and elimination over co-existence of the deviants and opponents. It promotes mono-lithistic tendencies of thought as well as action, generating the need for issuance of fatwas and edicts. Such societies often get administered through dictatorships and/or monarchies.

Terrorism: Seems Infatuated with Destruction

Destruction is an extension of intolerance: It seems easier for terrorists and their handlers to blast, burn, shoot and kill without concern even for unconcerned and unconnected, rather than dialogue for conflict resolution. They seem to lack skills to build upon existing infrastructures, social, political and/or even physical: They prefer to destroy what exists—and build only from or upon ruins, physical and non-physical.

The recent-most such behaviour of Islamist Talibans reflected this in destruction of hundreds of girls schools in the Swat valley of Pakistan. Not long ago, even Afghanistan's ancient world famous Buddhist statues, cut laboriously into rock faces, were destroyed.

The 26/11 destruction in Mumbai was the recent one, though the author is sure it not the last one; their love for destruction is not yet over. Through destruction they see a way, though erroneously, to subdue all opposition and create monolithic societies of non-deviants and conformists, through fear genesis.

Basically, desire for dominance and control over physical as well as biological assets, including the human societies, without really meriting it rests at the base of this obnoxious ideology. False perceptions of greatness persist to propel their defective thought processes to such infertile delusions.

Terrorism: Spreading through Convenient Deals

Terrorism is a strange phenomenon: Nothing is simple about it. What is visible about it is normally not true—and what is true is normally not visible.

Was there a valid need for the Pakistan army to have an underhand deal with Taliban militants, as was alleged by Major General, Faisal Alavi, a former head of Pakistan's Special Forces, now assassinated for his attempts to expose the same?

Why should a creator army have an agreement with its own wayward product, a terror outfit? Taliban was created, nursed, and armed by the Pakistan army; first to ostentatiously fight the Russian forces in Afghanistan—and afterwards, to do its dirty job in Kashmir. Unexpectedly, both got bogged down in Afghanistan for their own efforts to control the Afghani apparatus of governance.

According to U K press, "The Times," as reported by "The Times of India", a New Delhi publication, on 15 December, 2008, Major General Faisal Alavi, brother-in-law of novelist V S Naipaul, the British Nobel Laureate, was unhappy about the Pakistan army's underhand dealings with a Taliban militant group headed by Baitullah Mehsud, now dead but once considered even deadlier than Osama Bin Laden.

Alavi in his letter to the present army chief had named some senior generals of the Pakistani army who were reported to have paid huge sums of money to Mehsud, just to refrain from attacking the army. Instead of getting a helpful reply, he was killed a few days after he dared to write the said letter. It must have been a very large sum capable of causing a huge embracement to the army, if it felt compelled to eliminate its own senior officer.

By the week ending 14th December, 2008, the demand for investigations into the death of the Major General grew loud, and on 18th November, his sister Lady Naipaul described her brother as **'a soldier to his toes'**. She said: "He was an honourable man and the world was a better place when he was in it."

Major General, Faisal Alavi was reported to have complained in his letter to the present Chief of Pakistan army, General A Kayani that he was unfairly forced out of service. It was his last ditch effort for getting his honour restored. He, however, had grown too inconvenient for the army to have him around. He paid a dear price for underestimating the evil ruthlessness of his own unprofessional army.

And, this is the same army that is said to be cooperating with USA and NATO powers in regards to **"war on terror"**. Then, is it not difficult for readers to comprehend why this war can not be won by Obama's Af-Pak surge?

Terrorism seems to possess superior grade expertise in deals cutting and benefiting from the same.

Terrorism: An Action-reaction Mechanism

Action-reaction principle that has applicability almost in all fields of science and technology, exhibits equally strongly in reference to the forces of human reaction, and terrorism in particular. All actions of terror do produce equal and opposite reactions, some overt and rest covert. The proportionality of overt and covert determines whether a community will respond violently to an act of terrorism, or will tend to tolerate it with the hope that the same won't be repeated. A community's basic tolerance limits, dictated by its culture and history, determine the extent of reaction.

Reaction to terrorism is always there—only the quantum and its expressions differ. The following instances, among others, brightly illustrate the point:

- Israeli-Palestinian long-duration conflict,
- Israeli-Syrian and rest of the pan-Islamic conflict,
- French—Algerian conflict,
- Northern Ireland and British forces,
- Basque separatists and Spanish forces,
- White and black elements in South Africa,
- Al-Qaida and US antagonism,
- US forces and pan-Islamic elements in Iraq,
- NATO forces—Taliban and Al-Qaida in Afghanistan,
- Russians and the pan-Islamic forces in Chechnya,
- Pakistan instigated militants and Indian forces in Kashmir,
- LTTE and Sri-Lanka conflict, and
- Taliban-Al-Qaida and Pakistan's conflict in its north-western areas.

All these are examples of '**action-reaction response**' of the forces of terrorism, irrespective of who initiated the same in the first places. Resources and indoctrination levels of the conflicting forces determine the intensity of conflict.

Communal riots, like terrorism, follow the same action-reaction mechanism. The riots that followed assassination of Prime Minister Indira Gandhi, demolition of the Babri Masjid, and Godhra train burning incident were all examples of action-reaction mechanism.

Terrorism: Hindutava—a Regenerative Response?

The numerous blasts and bombings, in crowded markets and places of worship in India, occurring with baffling regularity in the past few years—and the emerging association of Muslim youth and Pakistani ISI inspired elements with the same, seems to have generated a delayed reaction among some Hindu right-wing elements.

The Hindu community, despite its significant secular character, was never fully purged free of such reactionary elements: They were instrumental in elimination of Mahatma Gandhi, the '**Father of the Nation**', in 1948, as he was perceived to be positively partial towards Muslims during the upheaval caused by partition of the country.

The Hindu fundamentalist elements in organizations of the **Sangh Parivar** went into chronic ferment as per the **'action-reaction principle'** discussed earlier, some of which boiled over in the September-October period of 2008, and the Malegaon blasts in a masjid seemed essentially results of such a reaction. This boiling-over of some of these elements primarily resulted from an accumulation of frustrations caused by:

- Government's inaction or inability to find ways and means to slow down the frequency of bomb blasts in crowded markets (in festive seasons), hospitals, and places of worship;
- Some political parties' open support to (particularly by Mulayam Singh's Samajwadi and the Mayawati's BSP for narrow considerations of the vote-bank politics) the Muslim youth being caught by the police for such actions; and
- Failure of the Muslim intelligentsia, clergy, and politicians, to effectively raise their voice against the senseless acts of the misguided youth, which could always serve as a calming effect.

Some intellectuals in the majority community called it as the **"Vigilante Effect"** during the author's interactions with them on this crucial issue.

Widespread **'mis-nomerism'** too is complicating the already complex canvas of terrorism. Religious organizations, irrespective of their faith and spiritual allegiances, employ a variety of nomenclatures to mask their real intentions and functions, which in a way represents the devilish nature of some believers' minds. One instance that seemed truly outstanding in this context was that of a Mahant arrested as a co-conspirator in the Malegaon blasts case, who had named one of his trusts as **"Vedic Vishva**

Kalyan Trust", an excellent yet evil misnomerism. Thousands of such cases will emerge in the country if an actively investigative glance is thrown on the real purpose of the effectively camouflaged social, cultural, religious and philanthropic organizations and outfits.

Re-education and de-toxification of the clergy or the religious leaders, from all the major religions of the country, is an immediate essentiality for saving the country from the obnoxious evil of terrorism. Terrorism, in fact, is the pet being kept and cared for by the collective religious leadership of the suffering Indian community: None of its fostering constituents, except Jainism, is fully free from it.

How the Indian apparatus of governance and the silent majority of wise-ones, in the collective Indian community, should undertake this job, is a matter of crucial significance in the present times.

Terrorism: Fed upon Misconceived Ideologies

Seeds of terror are normally planted by religious ideologues and clerics—and afterwards or simultaneously, the same are irrigated by political elements. Righteous ideologies that aim at human good and progress can never support terror of any type. Misconceived ideologues or those who do not understand the true meaning of religion, scriptures and/or ideology, tend to divide the humanity for their own narrow interests—i.e. for acquiring and strengthening their hold of dominance on the people, and then exploiting them.

The ideologues of misconceived orientations abound the Hindu, Muslim, Christian and most other communities. Only the intensities of their evil orientation differ.

One interesting example, in this regard, that recently came to attention was that of Mr Indresh Kumar and RSS leader Mohan Bhagawat, the well-meaning operatives of the Sangh Parivar who wanted to attract Muslims to the Parivar outfits so that the ideology of Hindutava could be understood by the people who normally feared it the most. The hardliners of the Sangh Parivar got scared of these developments—and one Dayanand Pandey, a self-styled Swami and Sankaracharya, who viewed the move as an attempt towards dilution of the Parivar's ideology and objectivity , planned to eliminate the persons who had, with all the good intentions, initiated the righteous move. These developments came to light through the investigations of the Maharashtra ATS into the blasts of Malegaon which occurred in the last quarter of 2008.

If one looks a little closely, numerous such instances can be found scattered on the horizons of other religions' ideologues and clerics. These instances reflect the deficiencies of thought balance on a party of the people who assume or are given the responsibilities of leading the unsuspecting masses—and the result is genesis and spread of terror with accompanying loss of innocent lives and spoilage of human-living and working environments.

Terrorism—Neutral to Education and Background

For long, it has been argued by social and political analysts and Muslim intellectuals that the flow of youth to terrorism was a contribution of madrasa education, relative unemployment, and the overall backwardness of the community. These generalizations were thrown to pieces by the growing involvement of well-educated, IT savvy, and well-paid youth from corporate work environments, in the nefarious terrorist activities. The following head-line from **"The Indian Express"** of October 7, 2008, blows off the cover from the long held misconception in this regard.

> "Global Internet firm engineer among 15 caught in terror web."

Involvement of the Pune based, Yahoo employed, well-paid, and internationally travelled IT expert, Mohammed Mansoor Asgar Peerbhoy alias Munnawar/Mannu, along with a large gang of young well-educated Muslim youths, is not the first case of its type. It is one in the long growing surprises that are being exposed increasingly by the security apparatus, veracity of which is beyond reasonable doubt.

This terror operative came from a well to do family, educated in good schools and colleges, and was employed with a MNC, at a significantly high salary. He was married to a well-educated girl and had children. And on being caught, he showed no regret or remorse. Cases of several others, in the gang, were not very different.

What motivated him or his colleagues to be part of a terror cell? It is a challenge for the intellectuals of the community, who feel and often express that the Muslim community is being unfairly targeted, and also for the security agencies to find out—because if cause is not properly identified, cure can never be effective.

Such difficult to explain and/or understand situations lend credence to the perception that something was and is probably fundamentally wrong with the **'Muslim-mindset'**. This kind of coloration is not good to develop—as it is bound to trouble the vast majority of seculars, particularly intellectuals, in the subject community, and also its numerous well-wishers in rest of the Indian communities.

Interrogation of the members of this terror gang from Pune revealed that the objective of the gang leaders was to:

(a) To attract more attention of their mentors and handlers, and

(b) To secure additional funds from their financers.

So, what matters most is not only the mindset and the objectivity of terrorists involved, but also that of their sympathizers and handlers. The manipulators in the background, who finance and manage these operations, are of greater significance—as they are not interested in any normal affairs or progress of the community.

For them chaos, panic, confusion, and suffering of victims, among others, give maximum pleasure. They are the true manifestations of the evil forces.

Terrorism: An Organized-collective Evil

Terror outfits operate almost on the MNC design. Very much like MNC's foreign headquarters, they too are often guided and managed from outside. The local units do the dirty job but final profits accrue to their bosses only.

Local units, in any terror module, have numerous components like:

- Those who plant bombs,
- The ones who assess and photograph the damages,
- Those who arrange bomb manufacturing—including raw materials,

- The technically enabled ones arrange bomb assemblies,
- IT experts who send e-mails, SMSes or call up the media,
- The producers/distributors of indoctrination materials,
- The facilitators who provide/arrange housing/transport and comforts of the key cell members, and most importantly,
- Those who brainwash and indoctrinate the foot-soldiers and also the operatives at different levels, individually and/or collectively.

Principles of management, in addition to the technology, too seem to be being employed by these terror groups with amazing ease and efficiency. Communication within the group, as well as outside, is very selective and objectivity based. Structure of the terror capsules is their strength—but, in certain situations, the same becomes their weakness.

A Silver-lining: A Flicker of Righteousness

On 6th October, 2008, Mr Rakesh Maria, the Joint Commissioner of Police, Mumbai, while briefing the press on busting of the Pune based media cell of the terror group, the Indian Mujahideen (IM), which was responsible for bomb blasts in Ahmedabad, Hyderabad, Surat, and several other places, said:

> "Several Muslims have played a significant role in helping nab these people. They said they would not tolerate terrorism."

This is the most beautiful expression of the secular Muslim mind that rarely chooses to come out openly. Only they can help, through enhanced activity, cure the apparently ailing mindset of a section of the community. The non-Muslim people from the great Indian community, including the media, can only offer a helping hand.

The silver-lining representing the **'secular Muslim intelligentsia** should have shined itself more brightly than that it normally does It has not done its duty well enough; it is either not well-organized, or fights shy of speaking plain truth with requisite clarity and force.

> The forces that support and feed terrorism do not respect mildness or soft communication, as they mistake it as a weakness or of no consequence.

The secular intelligentsia of the victim community should get organized to make real hard and result producing persistent contributions towards this fight for righteousness. And no one but the secular Muslims, intellectuals and otherwise, have to make this effort. Some of them, in the process, might have to pay a price too as the forces of terrorism are often of evil **prakarti**; they do not hesitate in attacking whosoever crosses their path or is found on the wrong side from their angle.

Fight against the forces of evil and unrighteousness was never easy: Even **Lord Krishna**[4], despite being an incarnation, had to face substantial obstacles in his drive to set them right. Nor was the task of Prophet Mohammad any easien—and the story of Christ and his sufferings at hands of evil is so well-known.

Terrorism: Living in Denial—does it help?

A major section of the Muslim community in India (or even the world over) often attempts to live in denial that does neither help in solving its problems nor endears it to the secular elements in the national or international main-stream. Its unconvincing attempt to paint the September, 2008, Batla house, Jamia Nagar, New Delhi, shoot-out as a fake-encounter, and presenting the terrorists involved as innocent, did not show it in good colours. And, this was not the first instance of its self-defeating behaviour: Nor is it likely to be the last!

In a recent article, the University of Delaware's Director of Islamic Studies, **Muqtedar Khan**[5] lashed out at the **'intellectual dishonesty'** of representatives of the community who live or attempt to live in **'perpetual denial.'** They first deny that there is something as **"Jihadi Terrorism"** and then resort to conspiracy theories blaming every act of jihadi violence either on Israel, the USA, or India.

Then some of them argue that unjust wars by these three nations are the primary cause for the jihadi violence; a phenomenon whose very existence they had already denied. They are not true to themselves or to the cause that they pretend to service (including the alleged inspirations from the Holy book).

The limits of denial exercise were crossed by the Pakistan government in the post-Mumbai attacks scenario, when its own media dug out credible details about Ajmal Amir's (the sole alive/captured attacker out of the batch of ten terrorists) residence in a Faridkot village in Pakistan's Punjab. The fact that the local residents admitted, on live tapes and the assailant's father confirmed that Ajmal was his son, yet the Pak government was not ready to accept the facts that were hitting it so hard on the face.

The terrorist state had perfected the technology of perfect and permanent denial.

The Pakistani government and all apparatuses of terror perpetuation and spread should note, earlier the better, that living in denial does not help; one can not fool all the people all the time. Truth always tends to seep out, whatsoever hard one attempts to contain it behind false pretensions and smoke-screens.

Terrorism: Jihad and the 'Karma'

While participating in the deliberations of the **"Delhi Policy Group"**[6] held in February 2002, several speakers attempted to clarify what the term 'Jihad' or Jehad" really meant. All of them seemed unanimous that it did not relate to violence, which had no place in the Prophet's approach towards conflict management.

> Violence was permitted by the Prophet only in self-defence, when all reconciliation efforts brought no results.

The element of violence comes from the context—and it is said that the term 'Jihad' has not been used in the Quran even once in reference to violence. The word 'Jihad' only means to make **'effort or to strive'** towards selected objectivity. It came to be used as war, or in such context, much later—and not because of the Quran, but because of a certain historical context.

To the author, this vastly misunderstood, misused, and maligned term is akin to the term **'Karma'** employed by Lord Krishna,[4] which means action or righteous action, without concern for results. Like **'Karma'** has been interpreted in numerous ways, meaning several things over the ages, including results of one's past wrong doings, the term 'Jihad' too fell to its long-term misinterpretation and mis-use, and even abuse.

As **Lord Krishna** elaborated the need for action in **'Bhagavad-Gita'**, Islam too views human life as a struggle towards liberation—individually and collectively. For liberation from constraints of life, like anger, greed, fear, and expectation, etc **Lord Krishna** suggested four alternate routes namely **Dharma, Karma,**

Janana, and **Devotion,** but He insisted, while discoursing with Arjuna on the battlefield of Kurukchetra, that the path of '**Karma**' was the best approach. Quran too recommends peaceful struggle for liberation, individually or collectively; though, the use of force is permitted under certain circumstances.

It needs to be re-stressed here that **Mohammad,** like **Lord Krishna,** had shown exemplary patience and forbearance in dealing with the people who opposed him. Very much like **Lord Krishna** migrated from Mathura to Dwarka, **Mohammad** did from Macca to Medina; in both the cases safety of the leaders and their followers was involved.

Lord Krishna employed force to eliminate evil and unrighteous, when dialogue and persuasion did not work. Similarly, **Mohammad** permitted his followers use of force to defend themselves. From it emerged the validity of just war in Islam on grounds such as:

1. Persecution of a people to the extent that they have been forced to flee their homes, and
2. When denial of right to freely pursue religion occurs.

The idea of a defensive and offensive war gets blurred when one is asked to come to the rescue of an oppressed or exploited people who are not strong enough to stand up in their own defence.

There have been several instances in history of Hindus, Sikhs and other communities when this principle was upheld. That tyranny and oppression is inhuman and unworthy of toleration sprouts from the above principle. However, in all circumstances, the Islamic code forbids war for national or individual glory or aggrandizement. And, the present perpetrators of terrorism seem to be doing exactly what is forbidden.

Innumerable Muslim rulers and groups, including terrorists and jehadists, exercising or striving for dominance, have been violating this principle all through the history, which has given this religion not so flattering a reputation—being a war and/or conflict generating one.

It will be out of context of this work to go into fuller conditions where a just or unjust war is allowed in Islam.

However, there is no scope for any doubt in declaring that, as per Islamic concepts, the current terrorist practices of indiscriminate killing of innocent people, hostage taking, bombing and suicide bombing, using innocent public as shield, planting explosives and bombs in crowded areas, trains and buses, plane hijacking etc are all unlawful and anti-Islamic.

Still, they are being regularly justified by the mentors/handlers of terrorist groups, who so erroneously call themselves Muslims. Thus, there are no limits to which, perpetrators of evil, irrespective of religion or faith, can fall: Their deliberately cultivated misconceptions do not allow them to appreciate what is true or right even from scriptural angles.

As per views of the author, improvements in any community must start from within—and, hence, it is the primary responsibility of the Muslim intelligentsia, and its religious and political leadership, to deflate the Jihadi and terrotistic balloons currently clouding the Islamist skies. Muslim intelligentsia, particularly the scientifically literate, can no longer keep itself aloof as this vital job can not, and should not, be left to the theologians and/or the clergy, which is steeped in the 7th century perceptions of a desert culture.

The above cloud, however, occasionally flashes remains of a **bright silver-lining:** On 9th November, 2008, a large gathering of over 6,000 Muslim clerics gathered at the Indian city of Hyderabad, under the banner of **Jamiat Ulama-e-Hind,** to discuss various key issues being faced by the Muslim community. **Terrorism** and the so called jihadists involved, or perceived to be involved, in the currently growing incidents of explosions and bomb blasts in various parts of the country, which took so many innocent lives and strained the delicate communal fabric of the secular nation, were the central points of the discussions. There were resolutions on terror, communal riots, Afghanistan, Iran, and even Palestine, but the brightest sparks of the debates were reserved for terrorism and how to wash the Muslim community clean of this persistent stain.

In its resolution on terror, the Jamiat stated that the outfits linked to the right-wing Hindu organizations were found to have carried out explosions in Malegaon (Maharastra), but **"this house appeals to all government agencies to stop identifying terror with a particular community."**

A special representative of revered Hindu Sankaracharya, Swami Swaroopanand Saraswati of the Dwakapeeth read out the following message to the gathering:

> "Because of some countries, Muslim terrorism has become a hot topic. But it is wrong to associate any religion with terror: I know Muslims are wholly patriotic."

The developments, as well as, the resolutions emerging out of this large gathering of Muslim clerics underscored the realization on part of the community that the terror friendly labelling assigned to it, incidentally or otherwise, needed to be done away within its long-term interests.

In a secular democratic set-up no one single community can elect or be seen electing to destroy all those who do not subscribe to its philosophy and/or practices; the one-fifth of a vast composite humanity can not destroy the better equipped four-fifth, with or without the mask of jihad.

It is indeed comforting to note that the religious leadership of the Indian Muslim community read the situation rightly by responding to it in a righteous manner.

Terrorism: Muslim Rage Accumulation?

Prof. Mushirul Hasan while participating in the seminar on **"War and Peace in Islam"** held at New Delhi in February 2002, referred to the phenomenon of **'Muslim Rage' (MR)** and while so doing, he himself seemed to be suffering from the same. In Sept. 2008, in his post-Batla house incidence (Jamia Nagar, New Delhi) interactions with the press too, he exhibited symptoms of MR in a very conspicuous manner. In view of the author, he definitely was not the lone victim of this disease in the large Muslim community of India.

The manifestations of active MR are increasingly visible in the widely distributed Muslim community, almost all over the world, without exception of a country or continent. Anti-West MR in general, and anti-American in particular, is throwing a large percent of the international Muslim community to the ravages of this dangerous affliction.

Genesis of MR is normally a product of **defective thought process** i.e. the inability to think rationally or being able to act effectively under conditions of stress, in a short or long-term time frame. It is an expression of accumulating intolerance resulting from negativity interactions and/or inability to righteously understand and explain the challenging situations.

Many people, irrespective of religion or faith, lack effective mechanism for **'rage management'**—each one has to have his or her own. A community, interactive and conscious of its responsibilities, capabilities as well as limitations, could and should develop its own specific mechanism for release of accumulated rage, in a socially productive manner. Its collective intelligentsia is assigned or charged with the responsibility for doing so, without allowing the community suffer any loss or getting labelled. In case of the international Muslim community this deficiency seems to be reaching critical limits.

Some twenty years earlier, the Indian Sikh community, rightly or wrongly, too had landed itself with a massive accumulation of rage. And its inbuilt mechanism of economic engagement, religious tolerance, and reformative character helped it in getting rid of the major parts of the same. Similarly, the Muslim community, if it has any accumulation of rage, too, has to employ its own mechanisms of internal as well as external interactions, in getting rid of the same. Others can only help, if asked for, in a positive and reconciliatory manner.

Terrorism: Muslim Community in Ferment

The Jamia Nagar (Batla House, New Delhi) police and terrorists encounter that occurred in September, 2008, in which two alleged terrorists and a police officer were killed, put the Indian Muslim community in a **pot of fermentation**. It was difficult for it to accept that so many of its youth were being found involved in terrorist acts—or it was disturbed at the unexpected success of the police in nabbing the perpetrators of terror. Also, it seems that acceptance of the bitter truth had become excessively bitter for the community.

Mr. Salman Khursheed, a senior leader of the ruling Congress party at Delhi, admitted in his interview with the daily newspaper, *The Hindu* that appeared in its Delhi edition of 23rd October, 2008, that the Muslim community was in a ferment. In reply to the question, "Why is there so much ferment in the Muslim community over this incident?"—the veteran leader had said that:

"For the community the incident was the last straw that broke the camel's back. The ferment was simmering underneath. It is a social phenomenon that has grown to the level of a crisis. The community wants to blame somebody and the obvious target is the government. If the government ceases to be the target of disquiet and dissent, we will have a civil war. As a government, we should not be afraid to be targeted. It shows our democracy is working. It is a reassurance that there are legitimate channels for receiving complaints and grievances."

The ferment or anger accumulation, or the **directional confusion** about what approach to take (a) in dealing with its misguided sections or the youth engaged in acts of terror—and being caught by the police, and (b) how to defend itself from the allegation of criminality (even connivance) and terrorism sticking it so hard, has indeed left the community on dangerous cross-roads. It does not know what directions to take! A righteous and bold decision could be to admit the existence of the evil amongst it, and organise itself to actively encounter and diminish the same in due course, with the help of security forces and even with some help from rest of the Indian community.

The Muslim community needs to cool itself through internal as well as external mechanisms - and the burden of doing so lies on its clergy and intelligentsia. Does it possess the righteous energies to measure up to the challenges? It is to be seen in the future.

Terrorism: Contribution from South-Asia

Considering together the territories of pre-partition India, this area has become the world' greatest sufferer of terror acts and impacts—and, on impartial analysis, it comes to possess the credit or discredit for making the maximum contribution with causative inputs to the genesis and spread of terrorism.

The Taliban originated here and the remains of Al-Qaida, including its top leadership, are being sheltered in its north western mountain territories of the present Pakistan.

In fact, this crucible of terror and terrorism;

(a) has the largest number of madrasas, seminaries, and

training camps contributing to the philosophy and output of terror; and

(b) the human actors spearheading its spread to major parts of the world are being contributed to, from here.

We have achieved the distinction of developing, practicing, and exporting the '**inhuman technology of terrorism**'. Vast resources of people of this region, economic and non-economic, are being assigned towards this anti-growth and regressive activity i.e. for its promotion as well as containment.

This region, decidedly, has suffered more losses of men and material on the nefarious altar of terror. But, with all said and done, the South Asia has achieved a unique distinction of bleeding itself and, in a way, wounding the psyche of the whole humanity.

Terrorism: South Asia—Is Kashmir the Key Issue?

Almost all Pakistani politicians and intellectuals, a vast majority from other Islamic countries, and also a majority from the western world think that Kashmir is the central issue for the India-Pak tensions, and if it is solved to Pakistan's satisfaction, then magically everything would be smooth and pleasant. This perception is resulting from a shallow thinking; it is not a fact: It is only a mask for Pakistan's inborn anti-India thought and action concentrations, which seem to have clouded several other political and non-political mental screens.

The real cause or roots of the problem are buried deep in the centuries old history of Islam's relationship with India; for sometimes it emerged in form of the '**two nations theory**' or the TNT and the pre-partition antics of the Muslim League: It succeeded in befooling most of the leaders of the freedom movement, on both sides of the divide, in believing that TNT was the way to peace. It was only a well-crafted mask.

Brahma Chellanney, a political commentator of repute put the matter in the right perspective, in his '**Op-ed Page**' entitled **"Pak Terror a bribe ruse"** that appeared in *The Asian Age* of 17th December, 2008, a part of which is reproduced below:

"In recent years, India has worked with Pakistan to create a virtual borderless Kashmir to facilitate the free movement of people, goods, and services. New transportation links have been established as a first step. Given that Kashmir's division into Indian, Pakistani and Chinese parts can not be easily redone, what does a resolution of the Kashmir dispute entail beyond such steps?

The blunt truth is that Kashmir is not the cause but the symbol of India-Pakistan differences, which are rooted in history and politics of revenge, besides epitomising competing worldviews and a divide along civilizational fault-lines. As General Pervez Musharraf candidly put it in a 1999 speech, Pakistan's low intensity war with India would continue even if the Kashmir issue were magically resolved. The military for long has fancied India's Balkanization, as Pakistan's salvation."

That the situation now has moved even beyond—as Pakistan has been accepted by the whole world as the **'Crucible of Terror Genesis and its Spread'**. Further, it has pushed itself into a not so enviable position of a **'failed state'**—and additionally a basket one, while India progressed into an internationally acknowledged economic power-house. This is amounting to fuelling the already heightened Pakistan's jealousy beyond control, making its pot of hatred boil out of control.

Terrorism: Its Symbiotic Relationship with Failing States

Terrorism germinates and grows in a failing state

A failing state loves terrorism as a mother loves a son gone astray—and the trouble-some brat loves the indulgent mother's attention. The motherly rebukes uttered for public consumption, attention diversion, and/or as time-buying devices have only little and transitional impact on the devil.

Pakistan's relationship with terror and terrorism is exactly a symbiotic one. It created and nursed terrorism to serve its interests toward delivering what its disproportionately large army could not do for it.

Pakistan and its army consistently failed to humble and destroy India through their several attempts of overt war. And through the covert tool of terrorism, it desired and attempted to achieve what it had failed in its frontal attempts. Its intolerance of India's stability, development, democracy, and secularism was obvious and understandable. Pakistan elected to justify the reason for its existence in performances entirely reverse of what India did and achieved.

Instead of international cooperation and brotherhood that India promoted, Pakistan chose to embrace terror and bloodshed. It promoted Islamic brotherhood without realizing how the same could damage it; occasional gifts of petrodollars from oil rich Arab states and the reception that it got in the Organization of Islamic States (OIC) had blinded its leaders.

It wanted to be ahead of India at least in something. Technology export of terrorism, nuclear WMDs, running schools of terror, supply of terror foot-soldiers to the whole Islamist world, and lastly, the coveted leadership of the world in terror genesis, spread, and export was its, with no other country even remotely near to it to challenge in this sphere.

Pakistan helped fight America's war against the Soviet Union in Afghanistan; attempted to extend its depth towards the west by claiming exclusive interests in Afghanistan, and also championed Palestinian, Iraqi, Croatian, Kashmir, and Chechen causes with abandon of an irresponsible brat. The nuclear WMD technology, it presumed, made it a leader in the Islamic world.

It gained diplomatic expertise in negotiating favours with a gun to its own head: The prognosis of failed state gave it pleasure to extract some more favours from USA, Britain, China, and several other countries which either did not understand its game or so pretended.

Now, the trouble-some failed brat is engaged in its last ditch attempts to gather unearned gains and favours from most of the civilized world: And, the latter has to see and decide whether it wants to play the ball—and for how long?

Terrorism: Its International Roots

Terrorism does not recognize national or international borders, as its perpetrators tend to run from one location to another in search of safe and/or supportive sanctuaries when they come under pressure from law and order enforcing agencies.

Most of the Muslim majority countries in the world have either contributed to the genesis and spread of terrorism or have suffered its miserable consequences. And, the deepest roots of terrorism branched from countries such as Saudi Arabia, Egypt, Syria, Lebanon, Yemen, territories of Palestine, Iran, Iraq, Sudan, Afghanistan, and Pakistan, all of which are under Muslim influence and governance.

Much less uniformly, the Christian majority countries in Europe and elsewhere, such as Britain, Ireland, Spain, France, Italy, Russia, and USA too have suffered varied degrees of terrorist violence. Additionally, non-Muslim and non-Christian countries like Japan, India, and Sri-Lanka, too have had their share of it in varying dosages.

A wide analysis of the international arena compels one to arrive at the following two conclusions:

- **One—that the most significant contribution to the evil of terrorism has come from the Muslim countries, which number over fifty—and house about one-fifth of the total humanity; and**
- **Two—that the twentieth century, which slipped into history just recently, was probably the most terror filled period of the human history.**

Irrespective of the causes of the Muslim community's grievances and resultant anger accumulations—or motivations in favour of this evil, countries such as Saudi Arabia, Syria, Palestine (territory), Egypt, Algeria, Iran, Iraq, Afghanistan, Pakistan, and Sudan, just to name the major ones, have made maximum contribution toward the genesis and spread of the menace of terrorism.

> Some of these countries are operating (as per *National Geographic,* October 2008) their own **"Universities of Terrorism."**

Katherine Zoepf in a news input entitled: **"Reforming the young followers of jihad: Saudi centre tackles a complicated topic,"** that appeared in the Indian edition of the "*International Herald Tribune,*" dated 8-9 November, 2008, gave an in-depth analysis of what indeed motivated the Jihadists, and what most of them use as a mask to cover their failures and unviable/illogical justifications.

> As per this writer, "**The Saudi state was essentially built on the concept of jihad**, which King Abdul Aziz al-Saud used to knit disparate tribal groups into a single nation. The word means 'struggle' and in Islamic law usually refers to armed conflict with non-Muslims in defence of the global Islamic community. Saudi schools teach a version of world history that emphasizes repeated battles between Muslims and non-

believing enemies. Whether to Afghanistan in the 1980s or present day Iraq, Saudi Arabia has exported more jihadist volunteers than any other country; 15 of the 19 hijackers on Sept. 11, 2001 were Saudis."

Thus, **Saudi Arabia** has been the most consistent and persistent **"University of Terrorism,"** primarily enabled by its huge petro-wealth.

Now, under US pressure, Saudis are making amends but the effects of long and intense teaching to successive generations shall take a long time to dilute—and it might not ever fully evaporate.

Pakistan tried to compete in justifying the title of being an **Islamic republic,** and fuelled by its in-born anti-India orientation, as per author's assessment, it became, in recent years, a true **"Crucible of Terrorism."** And now, it is almost on the verge of being roasted by the fires of terrorism ignited by itself, in its misplaced enthusiasm to hurt India, on one hand, and assume the leadership of the Muslim world, on the other.

Pakistan President, Asif Ali Zardari, recently admitted to the press that the terrorists were trying to hijack Pakistan—but his government would not let them succeed in their nefarious design (*The Asian Age*, New Delhi, 22nd October, 2008). But, in view of the in-built reluctance of the Pakistani apparatus of governance to take on the terrorists, it might prove as a very difficult commitment to be kept, on part of the well-meaning President.

The vested interests of international terrorism and their mentors and well-wishers are so intense and deep-rooted that the governments of countries like Pakistan, Afghanistan, Iraq, and to an extent India, shall have to struggle long and hard to contain and/or minimize this evil. The flow of oil-dollars, narcotics money, and the misplaced zeal of a section of the Muslim clergy to convert the whole world into Allah's territory, will make the job extremely arduous and full of sufferings.

Export of terrorism, in terms of thought as well as action, has been a key factor in its spread and magnification. To a varying degree, countries such as Saudi Arabia, Egypt, Algeria, Syria, Palestine (territory) Iran, Iraq, Pakistan, Afghanistan, Sudan, Chechnya, Bangladesh, Sri Lanka, Russia, China, and Ireland, just to name the main ones, played a significant role in the spread/export of terrorism through material and/or non-material support.

The biggest contribution to the export of terrorism (apart from the initial contributions from Saudi Arabia), undoubtedly, has been made by Pakistan in terms of training, indoctrination, and material and manpower support. Through its madrasas, training camps, ISI, clergy, and narcotics funds, Pakistan became the most active "Crucible of Terrorism" brainwashing young boys in service of Allah's misconceived services.

Terrorists trained in Pakistan moved to India, Afghanistan, USA, Britain, Palestine, Iraq, Chechnya, Indonesia, Philippines, SriLanka, Bangladesh, and the Balkan countries in Europe, and even to the Zinziang region of China. For over two decades, export of terrorism became one of the most important businesses and foreign policy instruments of Pakistan. It did not hesitate even in exporting the WMDs based on nuclear technology. Today, it specializes in "Jihad Diplomacy."

Terrorism: Pakistan's Failure Syndrome Fuels the Crucible of Terror

Pakistan was a product of the "two nations' theory" (TNT). **Some historians have reported the origin of TNT was rooted in Islam's 1,000 years long failure to fully subdue Hinduism—and totally convert all of its adherents. Even the division of India in 1947 was viewed as loss of dominance for Islam over the long oppressed original or older inhabitants of India. The very fact that about 25 percent of undivided India consisted of followers of Islam was not a matter for consolation: The Islamists' dreamt of full conversion of India and the failure to do so was a great disappointment. In the concept of Pakistan, they had illusions of magical accumulation of Islamist energies for eventually subduing the Hindu dominated rest of India.**

Pakistan, soon after its bloody birth, longed to emerge as leader of the Islamist world, expand its depths into Afghanistan; but its three war attempts against India disappointed the Islamists, further concentrating their failure syndrome. Separation of the then East Pakistan, as Bangladesh in 1971, was a great loss of the elusive glue of religion.

Pakistan did not need atom bombs—but its desire to be a leader of Islamic world was too intense to permit it see and appreciate the realty. The need to do better than India, at least in some fields, completely blinded its illusionist leadership. Saudi Arabia helped with over a billion dollars of gifts and China with technology—while US and Europe kept their eyes shut to the emerging evil with the fond hope that they were not going to be hurt. But, that was an entirely misplaced hope.

Pakistan's attempts to export WMDs technology and earn recognition through it too backfired: Instead, it generated international community's suspicion and trust gaps for it. Al-Qaeda's internationalization of terrorism and carrying the evil to Western doors brought the latter out of a slumber. And 9/11 made them to kick and howl.

In creation of an infrastructure for genesis of terror, history tinkering, terror technology of madrasa education, and its energetic exports of terror, Pakistan again saw, though erroneously, an opportunity to dominate, bleed India white, snatch Kashmir, and finally grab the leadership of the Islamic world. It was not only a great failure—but the evil pet of terror so created, fed and trained by it, started tearing away the skin of its own creator.

The above failures, collectively over a period of over 60 years, have led Pakistan to suffer a great accumulation of **'syndrome of inabilities'** that fully disables it for thinking in any righteous and constructive direction.

In the process of losing the very justification of its creation—and becoming a failed state, it has metamorphosed into a rogue—that now poses danger to its own friends, as well as, supporters. It has been done in by its love for the nefarious activity of terrorism.

The dreadful animal of terrorism that Pakistan cloned in a precise and well-planned strategy, is now grown too big for it to control—and it seems that Pakistan shall have to pay, through its nose, for all its evil misdeeds in this connection. Now it wants American money and arms (and also drones) in order to subdue its own created devil, in most of its northern and western territories.

Terrorism: Intolerance to the very 'Idea of India'?

India is multi-ethnic and multi-lingual, with more religions here than any other country of the world; it is crowded and chaotic, and it works with its not so perfect democracy. There is tolerance for inefficiencies of every type; there is scope for dialogue on any and every issue, and its system of governance, though slow and not very sensitive, attempts to correct social injustices that are centuries old.

In India, we share each others' festivals and don't allow anyone feel alone and unwanted. Though substantially imperfect, there is an inherent tendency here for inclusiveness. We tend to forget and forgive, even the unforgettable incidents such as the Mumbai carnage. Welcome and assimilation has been in India's blood. Though we differentiate and discriminate for colour of skin and wealth accumulation, but the same tends to evaporate with economic progress of the so discriminated individuals and/or classes.

Our fields are green and we produce enough for every one. We have swanky cars for some and many happily pull their own bicycles. Some of our homes are better than five stars hotels, and many of us still enjoy the simplicity of over five millennia old thatched huts, with no furniture and nil amenities.

We export a lot; and our technologies today help resolve technical challenges encountered by many. We produce world's largest number of films—and many in the world think that we live by dance and songs alone.

The juggar of India moves on—faster and better balanced than those of many countries, in an uninterrupted and unstoppable manner. That is the "**Idea of India**" which the terrorists, their mentors, supporters, and financers do not like.

They would like to damage, or preferably destroy us and our juggar—and see us as a failure. But, shall we allow it?

Terrorism: Where a Product can get Bigger than its Producer

Terrorism is a strange phenomenon where a product becomes bigger or stronger than its producer or creator. In other words, here a pet becomes mightier than its master and dictates terms, follows no commands, and finally its lawlessness puts the master into trouble. This is exactly what has happened to terror organizations in Pakistan: They are assuming the form of a mighty **Frankenstein.**

LeT's masking front, the Jamaat-ud-Dawa, did exactly the same to the Pakistani apparatus of mis-governance, as evident from the following report carried by the Express News Service, datelined 22nd December, 2008:

> "Thumbing its nose at the UN ban and slamming the Zardari government, the Jamaat-ud-Dawa rallied virtually every religious party in Pakistan at a meeting in Lahore yesterday to issue a ten point charter of demands. These include an immediate end to military operations along the Afghan border so that tribals can defend (Pakistan) against an Indian invasion, closure of supply lines to NATO troops, and amongst others, an end to the support to US-led coalition forces."

The said meeting was especially called to discuss the UN ban on the J-u-D, and the India-Pak tensions: The conference was attended by J-u-D's central leaders, Moulana Shamshad Ahmad Salfi and Moulana Saifullah Khalid; its public relations heads for Frontier province and Punjab, Ateeq Chouhan and Khalid Bashir; and its deputy spokesman Abdullah Muntazir.

Conclusion of the meeting, as announced on the website of the J-u-D, announced an all parties defence of Pakistan—and threatened to launch a nation wide agitation against the ban and for release of Lashkar founder Hafiz Mohammad Sayeed. It also called for recall of Pakistan's UN representative for his failure to stop slapping of the said ban. And, all those gathered promised that they were with the J-u-D.

Amongst those present in the meeting were leaders from:

> Jamaat-e-Islami, Jamaat-e-Ahle Hadees, Jamaat-e-Ulema-e-Islam, Jamaat-e-Ahle Sunnat, Majilis-e-Ahrar-e-Islam, Jamia Manjoor al-Islamia, Al-Kidmat Foundation, Tehreek-e-Khaksar, Tehreek-e-Istiqlal, and Imran Khan's Tehreek-e-Insaf. Besides, the Chief of Pakistan's ex-servicemen's society too participated in the deliberations which to any discerning mind represented thumbing a nose at the Zardari

government, with keeping silence on their feeding agents—namely the Pak army and the ISI.

With such a display of arrogance and unmanageability, there is little hope that the Pak trained and fed terrorists shall listen to any call for logical behaviour. They need to be treated with a most potent combination of fortified anti-terror strategies.

Terrorism: Is it a Striving for a New Caliphate?

As the first decade of the 21st century coming near to closure, Western political analysts are seen getting increasingly confused with the failure of the American and NATO forces in Afghanistan and on the lawless Pakistan-Afghanistan border areas, in regard to their well publicized mission, including the recent Obama surge. Over 70 percent of Afghanistan is reported to have come again under the re-invigorated Taliban and Al-Qaida forces.

Pakistan's non-operative government under Asif Ali Zardari, its all-powerful military and mischievous ISI have finally become a recurrent migraine for the US administration—as they are, in all covert manners, undermining and frustrating the US-NATO efforts against terrorism.

In fact, presently the USA is paying dearly for its wrong diagnosis, and consequent inappropriate prescriptions on terror management. Instead of dismantling the **"Crucibles of Terror-genesis"** and **"Universities of Terror-education,"** operated in Pakistan by all implied consent and cooperation of its mischievous administration, army and the ISI, it has been barking up the wrong tree in Afghanistan. While the real culprit was being rewarded, in form of billions of dollars, for services not rendered or for the impediments created, the **"War Against Terror"** efforts seem to taste the Taliban dust, in an inglorious manner.

While the emergence of the wrong diagnosis on part of USA (by design or default) awaits analysis by future historians, the Juggar of Islamist terrorism inches ahead, as per assessment of Western political analysts, towards establishment of a **'Caliphate'** in Central Asia. With Afghanistan and Pakistan as its initial centre, it is to extend into India, central Asian republics, and finally encompassing and absorbing the old Caliphate boundaries in the Arab world and beyond. This grand design, as per plans of Taliban and Al-Qaida leadership will be propelled by energies of the Islamic nuclear WMDs of Pakistan.

In progress of this grand design, the real challenge for the Islamist campaigners is the democratic and performing secularism of India in the East, and the little troublesome dot that is called Israel, in the West. The Shia Iran will either fall in line or will be dealt with later on.

The **"Idea of Successful India"** is the real pain in the neck of the scheming Islamists: The utter failure of the **'two nations' theory'** that gave birth to Pakistan, is their greatest disappointment. The Pakistan backed terror attacks on India, from Jaipur, Hyderabad, Ahmedabad, Varanasi, Delhi, Rampur, Gauhati and many others, to the recent most on its financial, entertainment and tourism capital that is Mumbai, are seen in line of this evil intolerance.

Robert D Kaplan in his editorial, **"The other Middle East"** that appeared in the Indian edition of the *"International Herald Tribune"* just recently, viewed India as a delicate inter-communal interface of long standing between the two major communities, which got activated to an extent by India's successful dealings with the forces of globalization. In this regard, among others, he said the following:

> "The terrorist attack in Mumbai had a number of aims, one of which was to set a fuse to this tense inter-communal standoff. The jihadists not only want to destroy Pakistan, they want to destroy India as well. India is everything that they hate: Hindu, vibrantly free, and democratic, increasingly pro-American, and militarily cosy with Israel. For Washington, this is no simple matter of defending Pakistan against chaos by moving troops from Iraq to Afghanistan. It is a whole region we are dealing with. Thus for Jihadists, the concept of 9/11-scale attack on India was brilliant."

How the Caliphate dream of Islamists unfolds will have to be carefully watched. Even if it fails to flower and/or bear fruit, it is bound to create a lot of crises, chaos and sufferings in the process of its unfolding and failure.

The author sincerely hopes, in interests of the humanity, that the above apprehensions of the Western analysts do not progress beyond their formative stages.

Terrorism: Its non-Material Impetuses

Spread of terrorism is catalyzed substantially by the **factors of thought and perception (FTAP)** or the psychology of its perpetrators and victims, more than the physical and material inputs. Motivation of the perpetrators of terrorism and/or their mentors and supporters undoubtedly works as the fuel for its genesis and spread.

However, more important than the above is the **psychological determination** of those mounting the resistance efforts to fight this evil i.e. not to entertain the thought of submitting to the assaults of terrorists. Even a minor **indication of fickleness (IOF)** in this regard, factual or otherwise, can undo the decades of anti-terrorism efforts and investments. In a war against terrorism, the **'weapon of thought (WOT)'** is more decisive than any collection of weapons and/or manpower.

> Show a little weakness of determination, intentional or otherwise, and the evil animal of terror will catch it quickly and use it against you.

Americans, in the past just over two decades, produced two most decisive thought (**terrorism stimulating contributions or TSCs)** inputs; one that encouraged a decisive spurt of terrorism against their interests—and the other that caused decisive dampening against the campaigns of counter-terrorism. The twin effects resulted from the hasty and not well-thought out decision of the US government to withdraw the American Marines, soon after a terrorist attack (masterminded by the Iran trained Hezbollah terrorist group) on their barracks located at the Beirut airport, that killed 281 (plus 58 French soldiers, part of the same multinational peace keeping force, were killed at a military base located nearby) of the elite soldiers.

This inference emerged loud and clear from reminisces of Robert C. McFarlane, the then national security advisor to President Reagan (a report from Mr. McFarlane in the Indian edition of the "*International Herald Tribune*", on the eve of the 25th anniversary of the decisive incident). He recalls that after detailed investigations it was established that the dastardly attack was planned over several months at Hezbollah's training camp in the Bekka Valley, in central Lebanon.

Within a few months of the attack, a joint American and French counter-terrorism plan was ready to suitably punish the evil Hezbollah through an air attack on the said camp. But the mission was aborted, just before its launch, by the US secretary of defence, Caspar Weinberger, arguing that in view of American interests in the oil resources of the region; no action detrimental to the **'Muslim Goodwill'** should be taken. This amounted to singing the enemy's song or supporting their objectivity.

Four months later, all the marines were withdrawn: It capped the most tragic US policy failures that led to a God-sent active motivation to the Islamic terrorists of the region; it emboldened them to a point that, for the next over two decades, USA had to pay for it very dearly—and by implication, several other countries perceived anti-Islamic by the terror outfits, too paid a price for the blunder committed by a superpower in pursuance of utterly selfish interests.

> As per assessment from experts in the field, it came to be known as the **most crucial policy defeat of US counter-terrorism** from which the Islamic terrorists concluded that the United States neither had the will nor the means to respond effectively to a terror attack.

US fickleness towards terrorist attacks continued in the 1990s: In 1993 on the World Trade Centre; on its air force troops at Khobar Towers in Saudi Arabia in 1996; on US embassies in Tanzania and Kenya in 1998, and on the destroyer Cole in the year 2000, established this contention beyond all doubts. There was no effective response from the United States to any of these absurdities of the Islamic terrorists. They concluded that the US was weak and hesitant to face them—and that it could be pushed the way they liked.

> And, as terrorists do not respect display of any weakness, intentional or otherwise, the US had to pay still more dearly for the said policy failure, in form of the 9/11 attack.

India too made the same type of mistakes in not responding with adequate toughness to the Pakistan inspired and controlled terrorism in J&K and several other parts of the country. Its **greatest folly of mismanagement of anti-terrorist policy** was exhibited in relation to the hijacking of Indian Airlines flight IC-814, while on way from Kathmandu on 24th December 1999, carrying 190 passengers and a full contingent of crew members. Despite opportunities, it could not decide to intercept the flight within Indian space, letting it to go and land in Khandhar, via Lahore and Dubai. The weak-kneed policy was capped by its decision of not only freeing the following three dreaded terrorists from its jails—but also in its foreign minister Mr. Jashwant Singh[17] accompanying them, honourably or dishonourably, in a state aircraft to Khandhar, where the hijacked India Airlines plane was parked with its contingent of captive passengers and crew.

(1) Maulana Masood Azhar of Laskar-e-Taiba,
(2) Ahmed Umar allias Sayed Sheikh—a British national who turned Islamic terrorist, and
(3) Mushtaq Ahmed Zargar—a Kashmiri turned into Pakistani based terrorist responsible for over forty murders.

From all angles of policy and perception, it was a shameful capitulation—and, as a consequence, it sent signals to the effect that India was a weak and a soft state. The so emboldened terrorists attacked Red Fort, Delhi's very symbol of strength, and the J&K Legislative Assembly during the opening year of the 21st century. Their boldness and audacity climaxed when a batch of five Pak-based terrorists of Laskar-e-Taiba and Jais-e-Mohammad attacked the Indian Parliament on 13 December 2001.

Even this daring attack on the very seat of India's democracy did not move its NDA government into any equal and effective punitive action. And as a consequence, the country continues to suffer frequent attacks from terrorists, who by appearance look home-grown but are controlled by their mentors and financers from across the border.

> As was decisively displayed, not long ago, by Mr. K P S Gill's tough handling of terrorism in Indian Punjab, terrorists respect only a strongly punishing force.

The above conclusion is also born out of the impact of the post 9/11 handling of terrorists by the United States and its allies. But, it is yet to be seen whether they shall carry the above conclusion by effectively completing the job of finishing the terrorists, or at least weakening them conclusively, in Afghanistan and north-west Pakistan, through the logical progression of the multinational war against terror, currently being waged there.

Terrorism: Is Religion a Mask for Jihadists?

Several writers and psychologists seem to believe that more often than not, religion is not the true motivator for jihadists. Questioning of former jihadists, under detention and/or reformation, seems to confirm this conclusion.

Katherine Zoepf in her article referred to earlier cited responses from such persons under reformation programs in Saudi Arabia, which after 9/11 took to intensive de-indoctrination of captured and under detection jihadists, in order to clear its deeply sullied image. The article, in this reference, added:

> "Though the exact nature of the role that religious belief plays in the recruitment of jihadists is the subject of much debate among scholars of terrorism, a growing number contend that ideology is far less important than family and group dynamics, and psychological and emotional needs."

"We are finding that they don't generally join for religious reasons," said John Horgan, a political psychologist at the **International Centre for the Study of Terrorism** at Penn State. Horgan has interviewed dozens of former terrorists and concluded:

> **"Terrorist movements seem to provide a sense of adventure, excitement, vision, purpose ,camaraderie," and went on, " and involvement with them has an allure that can be difficult to resist. But the ideology is something you acquire once you are involved."**

In Saudi Arabia, psychological disorders are primarily thought to emerge from a person's falling out of traditional family and community orbits of accepted interactions. A consulting psychiatrist from the King Faisal hospital at Riyadh was reported by Katherine Zoeph, saying that the global jihad is still a socially acceptable path for a young Saudi man with few options.

> "You have a young man who is depressed, frustrated with life, may be he fails an exam. He can go from being a loser, a failure, to being a jihadi, someone with status."

The main idea of jihad continues to be good with a large number of Muslim youth, the primary responsibility for which rests what they are taught in schools and madrasas, and how their families and society reacts to acts and concept of terrorism.

When a society actively discourages a type of behaviour, youngsters invariably tend to fall in line. And teachings in early age, particularly the unrighteous ones, formal and/or otherwise, take a very long time to dilute and moderate: They are never fully erased from the mental screen.

One Abu Sulayman, an ex-terrorist under reformation in Saudi Arabia, was reported to have reminisced:

> "Now our government is saying, "Don't go to Iraq: It is not in our interest'," he continued, "Now I think, I did something with my life. I went out and fought for my beliefs, and I found things were not as I had planned. But, at least, I fought for my beliefs. God knows my heart."

Even though Saudi public opinion has largely turned against Al-Qaida, many Saudis remain concerned that American-led efforts to fight terrorism are anti-Muslim and are infuriated by just a mention of Guantanamo.

On further analysis, the author gravitates to the view that the factors that motivate youth to go in for terrorism extend far beyond religion.

Though religion might act as the initial spark for thought expansion or thought concentration in this direction, it often is **misused as a camouflage or mask** for real causatives, which might differ from case to case. Some of there are:

- Early life's failure masking (the need for an individual's self-image management),
- Desire for prominence and acceptance in society,
- Lure of arms—and fulfilling the desire for power and dominance through the same,
- Easy money coming through petro-dollars, drug funds, extortions, contributions and collections from public, and several other sources including simple loot,
- Escape from social conformity and earning an honest livelihood,
- Opportunity for ego-servicing, and among others,
- Expectations of prominence or leadership in post-terrorist period.

Lure of arms, ability to kill through rapid-fire, real or imagined enemies—and the perception of power, without resorting to workouts and sweating, is a great feeling that services '**human**

male thought requirement' (HMTR). Arms tend to turn one powerful without really having to work for it—and evil human minds often mistake the same as their own accomplishment.

Return of ex-terrorists to society, their subsequent style of living, stories of their exploits (mostly unverified and deliberately exaggerated and planted) and how they are treated by the community, including their entry into politics and/or community organizations, leave decisive impressions on growing minds.

How such cases are talked about and treated in close family environments determines, more often than not, the response of young minds towards the obnoxious activity of terrorism.

Terrorism: Is Islam a Failing Ancestry?

Children follow the faith, culture, and behaviour of their parents (and that of the society a little later). They eat, live, dress, and speak the way their parents do. Most of their thought processes, faiths, beliefs, and interactions are cemented under the influence of their parents. And when a child misbehaves, the blame gets apportioned invariably on to the parents, at least in part, in all cultures and religions of the world.

> If Muslim youth are going happy with guns and explosives, Islamic governments continue to disregard democracy, and religion and faith continue to be mixed with politics for selfish interests of those involved in governance; when masters in madrasas continue to teach what had relevance to the 7th century, where tolerance is in short supply, when the faiths and practices of other religions/communities do not seem to matter, where jihad continues to be misunderstood and misinterpreted, and when science and technology gets only a secondary attention, then the ancestry of such a society is definitely failing in its duty, in terms of its responsibilities towards its progenies in particular—and the humanity in general.

In fact, no religion, least the Islam, operates by itself—it works through its people only, primarily the families, leaders, and the clergy.

Only grown-ups and elders interpret and/or misinterpret a religion. So, the blame squarely rests on the seniors—the elders, the educated or literate; and particularly when they claim to be strong believers in their faith and its practices. Rest is only contextual and circumstantial.

In this context, impartial assessment leads one to conclude that Islam (comparatively more than other religions—in context of terrorism), on account of the laxity or deficiency on part of its seniors, leaders, intelligentsia, and the clergy, is not measuring up to its responsibilities towards younger generations—in terms of keeping them on the right track—and help them grow competitively in the scientifically and technologically progressing world.

A doubt also germinated here that goes to suggest, though without supportive verification, that in case of Islam, a section of its seniors and clergy deliberately exploits its young generations to do and achieve what they failed to do by themselves.

Terrorism: Playing Politics through Fatwas

Islamic clergy is known for playing politics (real as well as religion) through the use and misuse of fatwas. For anything that does not suit them, religious or otherwise, they jump to issuing a fatwa or get one issued.

The Iranian fatwa against Salman Rushdie is well known. While the international intelligentsia perceived it as an act of terrorism, the famous writer was condemned to living a constantly security restricted life.

Even against a progressive act, as establishment of an institution of modern learning by Sir Sayed Ahmed at Aligarh (presently known as the Aligarh Muslim University), about a century ago, a fatwa was got issued from some cleric located in Saudi Arabia. This mindless misuse of fatwas has given a bad name to the Muslim community, to the effect of creating a strong impression that this community does not respect civil laws and rules of the country where it lives, as a minority or majority.

A recent report entitled **"Cleric issues fatwa against U.S.-Iraq pact,"** carried by the global edition of *"The New York Times"* dated 23rd October, 2008, highlighted the point with relevant emphasis:

> "An influential Iranian cleric living in Iran issued a fatwa on Wednesday condemning a U.S.-Iraq security pact that would

> keep American troops in Iraq for three more years and warned Iraqi leaders not to back the deal.
>
> Ayatolla Kazim al-Hosseini al-Haeri, an Iraqi citizen born in Iran, called the proposed agreement "haram"—which in Arabic means 'forbidden by Islam'—and said that approving the deal shall be "a sin God will not approve." Haeri is believed to be a mentor of Moktada al-Sadr, an anti-U.S. Shiaite cleric whose followers oppose the deal.
>
> Tens of thousands of Sadr's followers protested in Baghdad against the proposal last Saturday."

Even a truly harmless act, as the practice of **"Yoga"** does not meet tolerance standards of some clerics. This age-old art of physical and mental health exercise was developed by Maharishi Patangeli, when Hinduism had not even taken its first breath: It is surprising to note how Muslim clerics in Malaysia and Indonesia feared it as possessing active potential for diluting and damaging the faith of Muslims who tend to eagerly benefit from this proven health rewarding activity.

In pursuance of the said apprehension, Malaysia's top Islamic body on 22nd November, 2008, banned Muslims from practicing Yoga, saying that the Indian physical exercise contained elements of Hinduism and could corrupt its Muslim practitioners. The National Fatwa Council of Malaysia, which holds authority to rule on how Muslims must conduct their faith, issued a fatwa or edict saying that yoga involved not just physical exercise but included Hindu spiritual elements.

The Council Chairman, Abdul Shukor Husin told the reporters that many Muslims who practiced the globally popular yoga failed to understand that its ultimate aim was to be one with the God of another religion. He had added:

> "We are of the view that yoga, which originated from Hinduism, combines physical exercise, religious elements, chanting and worshiping for the purpose of achieving inner peace and ultimately to be one with God."
>
> "It is inappropriate. It can destroy the faith of a Muslim," he continued to elaborate (as per a report in New Delhi edition of *The Asian Age* of 23rd November, 2008).

The actions and reactions of the Islamic clergy, as the one that emerged from the multicultural democratic state like Malaysia, are indicative of the community's unease towards anything that is not of Islamic origin: It shows its **intolerance** even for totally harmless activities picked up from its tolerant and cooperative neighbours.

Does the Islamic community suffer from insecurity on account of totally imaginative possibilities of losing its hold on the believers of Islam?

Such actions and reactions on part of Islamic clergy do not lead to signals to say and confirm that the international Islamic community was ready for a constructive cooperation in the current environment of economic globalization.

The recent most unacceptable preference for 'Fatwa' came from Abdullah Hussain Haroon, Pakistan's permanent representative at the UN, when the post Mumbai carnage pressure became too much for him to handle. In a debate in the Security Council, he drew a thread between Pakistan's evil terrorists and the clerics of Deoband (an Indian seminary). He had argued:

> "It is for the clerics of Deoband, who wield great influence in the north-west frontier ... and the FATA, to come to Pakistan, get together and embed, offer a fatwa in Pakistan against suicide bombing and killings of Muslims in Pakistan and also in India."

In his active self-interest, he had completely forgotten the fatwa issued by over 6,000 clerics of this genre, who had gathered on 6th November at Hyderabad, for this purpose. It had forbidden terrorist violence of all varieties. But, Pakistan's representatives are known for their selective memories, as they suit them.

Almost immediately afterwards, a senior representative of the Darul Uloom from the Deoband seminary, told the press that the Pakistani representative was not telling the truth—and that they did not wield any such influence in the said areas of Pakistan.

The blatant practices of issuing fatwas for things, small and big, and/or happenings, only gives a bad name to an otherwise good Islam; they interfere with constructive cooperation by the followers of Islam with other communities. They raise tensions—and indirectly plant and irrigate the seeds of terrorism.

Terrorism: Its Causative Elements:

Irrespective of religion or community, the intellectual elements or the '**thought warriors**' of evil orientations who read and interpret scriptures (or twist the same as per their selfish interests) and seek to influence and dominate the less-endowed masses, are responsible for the destructive directions which their community meekly picks up or submits to.

If they have acquired or accumulated grievances, real or imagined, or possess designs of grandeur, attempt to manipulate lesser or weaker minds—washing and colouring them in line of their evil thinking or selfish purposiveness, then the responsibilities for mishaps that a community might eventually meet (or the muddy splash of blame that it attracts) are to rest solely and wholly on them.

Since they have the controlling levers, the blame for the mishaps too has to land at their doors. Politicians, maulavis, pundits, preachers, and the so-called teachers, who develop expertise for exploitation and enticements based on misinterpretations of truth, spreading of untruths and myths, and unrighteous perceptions, are the greatest culprits for development of the disease of terrorism in the society.

The less logical, undiscerning, and impressionable minds fall prey to such '**designer miscreants**' who suffer from '**conflict of self**'—they see and perceive their own-self different than the other-self—while, as a scientific fact, the two are same and identical.

> **Lord Krishna**[4] had discoursed the humanity in this regard over 5,000 years ago. He had emphasized the unity and uniformity of all living and non-living beings, a balance for good of every one.

A **Muslim-self** is made from non-Muslim inputs (elemental and material ones) and so is a **Hindu or Christian-self,** as per Buddhism's basic tenets of non-self. The problem arises, as per Thich Nhat Hanh, the Vietnamese peace advocate, when one's-self is set against another's-self. Conflict at the self level grows into conflict at society level. He visited India in September 2008, and put across his philosophy in several gatherings of intellectuals.

The religious, community, and political leaders, particularly the **mis-managers** in these essential domains, must learn and/or be taught the basic elements of the **Gandhian and Buddhist Philosophy,** in order to correct their defective thought processes—and the resultant **"Mind-sets."**

Terrorism: Maoist and Naxal Violence

Maoism and Naxalism have undoubtedly taken recourse to active violence—often brutal: They have used terror for:

- Weakening and/or near destroying the apparatus of governance with the express objective of taking over reins of state management,
- Softening local apparatus of governance through fear and punishment and thus becoming a de-facto system of governance,
- Extortion, funds collection, and controlling economic life of people,
- Weakening public support to the apparatus of governance and finally shifting it in their favour,
- Establishing territorial controls and change of governance, and
- Finally effecting multilateral changes in people's life.

Here, in other words, terror has some design.

Regime change is their prime objective: Normally, they do not treat people differently on grounds of caste and/or religion: They are basically class warriors—**they do not fight and kill in service of God. In fact, they do not believe in existence or primacy of any God.**

Normally, the rich and landed upper class is their target. They believe in making everybody poor and then controlling with the dreams of eventual development and well-being.

The recent-most governance change enforced by such forces was in Nepal, though countless instances of similar nature occurred in the past century. Despite their violent methodology of imposing change, they do mot damage communal harmony of people.

They are not soldiers of God but soldiers of a system in disguise of being the soldiers of society. Such communistic movements have never emerged and/or survived in Muslim dominated countries. Afghanistan, under Russian influence in the 1980s failed to sustain its short-lived socialistic zeal, because Allah was not assigned a right place of significance.

It did not grow beyond a level in Indonesia. In central Asian countries, despite predominance of Soviet influence, communism could not make permanent inroads. **The softer or less closely controlled religions like Christianity, Buddhism, Confucianism, and Hinduism have not been able to resist spread of communism that stoutly.**

Very much like the Islamic terrorism, Maoist/Naxal terror too initially grows and spreads in limited areas with outside support in terms of ideology, mentors, arms, and finance. Both take pride, when comfortably established, in extending/exporting their influences beyond their own existing geographical boundaries, or to neighbouring countries.

In recent years, these communist forces have shown substantial flexibilities for participating in electoral process for expanding and/or stabilizing their influence. They are also not averse to modernism and/or equality of sexes.

India's large population and poverty intensive areas of Bihar, Orissa, Chatishgarh, Jharkhand, and Andhra Pradesh are deeply affected by the Maoist/Naxalist influence but, neither the government nor the people of the country, see it as obnoxious an evil as the Islamic and/or Hidutava terrorism.

State Terrorism and its Objectivity

In the past century, several governments have been found to employ organized terror and mass killings against the very people that they were supposed to protect and work for. The Nazi apparatus of governance in Germany, before and during the Second World War, inflicted organised terror of immeasurable proportions on Jews who were legal and peaceful citizens of the territories under German control.

The Chinese Cultural Revolution under Mao Zedong, beginning in mid 1960s, and the regime of Cambodian dictator Pol Pot starting in mid 1970s, represented brutal radical efforts to reshape the society, which led to millions of people losing their lives and means of life sustenance. Attempts to re-educate people to work and adopt life-systems entirely different to what they were used to, also amounted to a type of state terrorism.

Ultimately, such misguided movements fail to sustain in the long-term, as people's traditional living fabric is broken, and they either lose tolerance or dictators disappear by force of providence, as happened in the case of Pol Pot, after the Vietnamese invasion of Cambodia in 1979.

A significant fraction of the international intelligentsia, particularly those of Islamic origin, views the USA's war against terror (though several other countries are involved in it under a UN mandate) in Iraq, Afghanistan and the north-west Pakistan, as an act of state terrorism—and this point has been argued very passionately, for as well as against, and opinions don't have a chance to exhibit any uniformity.

In other situations, state terrorism can be more subtle when it becomes part of an ongoing struggle between a regime and the insurgent forces. Any attempt to discuss and/or explain situations such as Palestine-Israel conflict or terrorism in Jammu and Kashmir, tends to become a chicken and egg story—as it is nearly impossible to decide (and make people accept) who initiated or accelerated the problem.

The instances of state terrorism, actual or perceived—or just and/or unjust, do not justify or condone organised efforts of a religion or community to become a **crucible or university of terrorism** and, as a consequence hinder the economic development of people.

Terrorism: Playing Politics through it

Inefficient politicians, who are not able to attain their political aims through normal political means and methodologies, take recourse to terrorism for meeting their objectivities. Those intolerant of progress of their neighbours too often take recourse to this **scores-settling methodology**.

This evil dance of politics is enacted at the international, national, and sub-national levels with amazing diversity: Some instances of countries promoting terror in their neighbourhood are listed below:

Initiator of terror	Target country	Nature of terror activities
Ireland	Northern Ireland	Separatist activities of permanent nature.
Arab nations: Syria, Egypt, and Lebanon.	Israel.	De-stabilization and eventual annihilation
Pakistan	India and Indian state of Jammu and Kashmir.	De-stabilization of India and eventual separation of Kashmir from the Indian union.
Pakistan	Afghanistan	Initially to free it from Soviet influence—and afterwards to help establish a Taliban regime.
Pakistan	Jingiang province of China	Spread of Islamic terrorism.
Pakistan	Sri-Lanka	Assistance to LTTE for separation of territories into an independent nation.
Iran	Iraq and Lebanon	Promotion of Shia terrorism and opposing American presence there.
Bangladesh	N E-states of India	Helping ULFA and other militant groups with the objective of weakening India.
USA	Cuba	Helping anti-communist forces.
USA	Iraq	To help anti-Saddam forces and eventual regime change.
Russia	Chechnya	To crush anti-Russian terror forces.
China	NE-states of India.	Helping separatist groups.

To establish and expand the area of influence and dominance is the prime reason that stimulates such **anti-neighbourhood activities**. Personal incompatibilities of some politicians do come into play in some such situations.

There have been numerous other instances of such terror promotion listing of all of which is beyond the scope of this work.

Terrorism: A Conflict of Cousins?

Roots of the modern day terrorism extend to **Jerusalem**, the **crucible of origin** of the world's three great religions. First Christianity, and than Islam, rose there from imperfections of Judaism. Followers of all the three religions have 'Abraham' as the oldest known ancestor—and, in a genealogical sense, all of them are **'cousins'.**

Their differences are scriptural, which from all practical considerations are more deadly than the territorial or economic ones.

The **Indian mythology**[4] is fully alive to the great conflict of cousins that took the shape of **Mahabharata**, a great battle fought over five millennia ago between the Kauravas and their supporters on one side, and the Pandavas and their allies on the other, on the battlefields of Kuruckchetra. While the Kauravas represented accumulation of the forces of evil and wicked, the latter serviced those representing the good and virtue.

Lord Krishna, the greatest known supporter of virtue and merit, supported the Pandavas. The great battle led to loss of several million human lives in addition to the immeasurable losses in terms of war materials, horses, and elephants. The good part of this mythological conflict was that it ended with the total elimination of the evil and wicked, and led to the establishment of the rule of good law and peace.

In the present day **'conflict of cousins'** or the **'Clash of Civilizations,'** as some western intellectuals prefer to call it, we do not have:

(a) The so well-defined lines of differentiation, and

(b) The benefit of the presence of a prophet like Lord Krishna to support and guide the righteous and the virtuous side.

'The Tony Blair Faith Foundation' is reported to have established an **"Abraham Hall"** where young intellectuals and religious leaders from all the three faiths can discuss their differences and attempt to find common grounds for resolution of the same or, at least, for minimizing the misunderstandings. Additionally, in partnership with the Yale University, it is exploring how they could help show that religious faith could be a constructive force for progress rather than a reactionary and destructive one.

Saudi Arabia, the most prominent leader of Muslims in the world, called as the **'University of Terrorism'** by some western intellectuals and also known for religious intolerance of the Wahahbist variety at home, sponsored a discussion at the United Nations on religious tolerance, in middle of November, 2008.

More than a dozen world leaders gathered, including President George W. Bush, of the United States of America, Prime Minister Gordon Brown of Britain, and the Saudi monarch, King Abdullah, making a rare appearance for the purpose at the UN headquarters.

Since the UN officially does not sponsor religious discussions, the two days conference was billed as a meeting on the **"Cultures of Peace"** and most of those attending it were governments—not religious leaders.

In a way, it is an admittance of unease of the situation of the spread of the evil of terrorism in major part of the Muslims inhabited world.

Terrorism: An Unholy Nexus between Politicians and Clerics

Religious leaders, irrespective of religion and geography, are the main culprits for initiation and perpetuation of terrorism. In religious gatherings, in secluded interiors or in open expanses—Churches, Masjids, and Satsaghs, they grab exclusive attention of lay people and twist their mental apparatus against followers of other religions, for factual and non-factual reasons.

Slogans such as, **"Islam is in danger"** always originate in such gatherings of Islamists, later to be taken to select locations with evil intentions of inciting communal violence. Clerics from Hinduism, Christianity, Judaism, and several other religions follow the same tactics, except that their slogans and the tone of the same vary as per context. The main objectives of the clergy, in all such cases, are as under:

- To strengthen their hold over their followers or believers;
- To establish, covertly and/overtly, their leadership with eyes on future events: It is an exercise in establishment and perpetuation of dominance; and
- To collect funds in larger volumes and regularity.

Clerics are normally better educated than the masses that they guide and/or misguide as per their objectivities. They use language, terminologies, and quotations which are not easily understood by their gatherings. Their objectives, always, are not to educate or inform, but to motivate the audiences in a particular thought line and action direction.

They are **"thought warriors"** who ignite fires and let their followers face the music—kill and/or get killed. They like situations of uncertainties, confusion and chaos: They are a type of politicians for whom people are a raw material to work upon—or to play with.

Only a few of them know their scriptures deeply and righteously—and still fewer employ the same for the good of people.

They are primarily deeply selfish and narrow minded people—not men of God but agents of evil or Satan. The initial recruitment and indoctrination of people for the purpose of inciting violence, riots, blasts, and even suicide bombing is done by them.

They coordinate the anti-social activities with the second level of terror generators i.e. the managers of terrorism, who handle and direct the foot-soldiers of terrorism for actual placement of bombs and blast devices, send e-mails, and claiming credit for the chaos so created.

If terrorism has to be handled effectively, through conventional methodology and/or with the applications of the Gandhian Philosophy, the first line of evil perpetrators namely the clerics, have to be re-educated and de-toxificated.

Often politicians and clergy are found in '**unholy nexus**'—they collaborate with each other in sowing seeds of terror and irrigating the same in a manner that their evil interests are served irrespective to the costs to a nation and/or its people.

Politicians, in view of the author, have their prime interests in securing dominance over the **thought as well as action processes** of people. They flourish through chaos and confusion: Misery of people offers them the best opportunity to meddle in and extract greatest benefits.

Interests of clerics too coincide with those of politicians, though the latter never relish the formers growing too big for their shoes. Despite being perpetually suspicious and wary of each other (being mutually conflicting and competing species living and targeting the same victim populace), they tend to cooperate excellently in reference to terror and terrorism, as both stand to gain from the resultant misery of people.

Clerics, often, easily transform into politicians – and instances of them having taken over governance are not too few. On the other hand, politicians are not capable of such transformations as they lack skills in the field of religion. Hence, they take help of clergy in mismanaging interests and actions of the public.

In India, Muslim politicians and clerics had developed a strong association in the pre-partition times which resulted in division of the country. This association weakened in the post-independence period for a variety of reasons. But on the other hand, due to failure of the Sangh Parivar to grab political power from the Indian National Congress led them to employ more closely this unholy nexus – threads of which came bare and clean in the last quarter of 2008, with the Malegaon blasts for which activists of Abhinav Bharat and its associated saints were arrested. Investigations of the Maharashtra ATS seemed to link these elements to several earlier incidents of bomb blasts, which had killed several innocent people.

Exposure of the linkages of Parivar's political and religious elements unsettled the BJP (the political wing of the Sangh Parivar) politicians at the time of elections for five state assemblies including that of Delhi NCR (November/December, 2008). In an attempt to escape the adverse impact of this nexus on these elections, the BJP tried its best to blame the Congress party for deliberately implicating its saints and sanyasis for acts of terror.

Terrorism: Politician's Incapacity for Righteous Stand

With the arrests of Sadhvi Pragya SinghThakur, Lt Col Shrikant Prohit, and their mentor Swami Dayanand Pandey, a self-styled Shankaracharya, in connection with the Malegaon blasts of 29 September 2008, for BJP, the India's leading opposition party, terror became a commodity or product interchangeable with the others identical to it. For years, it was crying about the **"Islamic Terrorism."** Now, there was an increasing talk of a countervailing **"Hindu Terrorism,"** so far represented by these three accused persons connected with the Sangh Parivar.

Prior to the general elections scheduled for middle of the year 2009, in addition to the five states election round in a few months earlier, the other political parties like RJD and BSP, in addition to the Congress party, and also the Muslim organizations like Jamiat Ulema-e-Hind, raised alarms regarding the emerging **"Saffron Terror,"** which the BJP was unable to handle in a forthright or righteous manner. It was unable to accept that Islam did not have exclusive right to terrorism, and that other organizations could fall in its trap as revenge responce.

The BJP and the associated Sangh Parivar elements were first chary of being associated with the terror elements but soon they did a rethinking, ran a re-analysis of the political fallout; took an about-turn and soon came out openly in support of these elements accused of having been involved in the evil activities. The then BJP national President, Rajnath Singh, talked of a conspiracy to defame the Hindu saints and malign army officers, which did not cut any ice with the public.

The Sangh Parivar, including its projected Prime ministerial candidate (at that time), L.K. Advani, showed no strength of character, to admit the facts and face the problem in a politically more matured and acceptable way, for the well-matured and fair-minded Indian electorate. He found it easier to blame the UPA led Central Government for a conspiracy and attempt to appease the minority vote-bank, and accuse it of practicing pseudo-secularism.

The Sangh Parivar's own weakness of **'cloudy thoughts'** became visible in its desire, on one hand, for the Hinduism to cast away its traditional image of response inadequacy or traditional softness, and to protect it from attracting the label of terror perpetrator, on the other. In a subdued voice, it tried to say that the **'Hindu Radicalization'** was the right response to the **'Islamic Terrorism.'**

It was indeed a matter of shame for the Sangh Parivar not being able to take a righteous stand, while the 6,000 strong gathering of Islamic clergy, primarily those aligned to the Deoband seminary, unequivocally and categorically condemned all forms of terrorism as fundamentally un-ethical and agaist the basic spirit of Islam. The way this religious gathering at Hyderabad, did a bright honour to itself was a slap on the saffron face of the Sangh Parivar, which often prided itself as the sole well-wisher of the Indian nation.

Luckily, the India's majority community has the secular maturity for not falling to these manipulations and inconsistencies of the Sangh Pariwar. But, the politics of semantic cynicism that is allowing the investigations by a state investigating agency called the ATS, being blamed as an anti-Hindu plot by the UPA led Central Government, is the true ally of the terror. Such unrighteous political motivations are grossly dangerous for peaceful and progressive future of the country. **The capacity of politicians to apportion blame where it does not belong is truly phenomenal.**

> **Truth becomes the first innocent victim of this kind of unrighteous politics**.

That the descedents of Lord Krishna and Lord Rama, the two great ancient adherents of righteousness and dharma, are today unable to observe even a little semblance of these values, is a matter of great disappointment to the well-wishers of India.

For the good of India, let us hope that the maturing Indian secularism eventually defangs this evil tendency.

Terrorism: Misplaced Defence of Terror under cover of Human Rights

Should the terrorists who kill and maim innocent, unarmed, and unconnected people, have any human rights?

This question has recently engaged the attention of the senior Indian judiciary and the intelligentsia—and the dominant view emerging is that the terrorists who kill indiscriminately—and without remorse, innocent and unconnected people—are more of an animal breed than being humans and, by implication, cannot be entitled for any rights under the garb of human rights, as the same are invariably misused by friends of terror and their fronts camouflaged under the covers of NGOs.

Judicially sound views that meet demands of the nation's defence in these difficult times, on one hand, and are also acceptable in a elections dependent democracy, on the other, shall take some time to crystallize.

This question needs to be thought over and argued upon in great depth as India is a dialogue-friendly nation. The currently prevalent concepts of human rights, as prescribed and advocated by the Western world, do not fully meet the challenges posed by the evil activities and designs of terrorists.

The moment a terrorist or a group of them is apprehended, human rights advocates and NGOs jump in their defence, while none of these elements is ever seen advocating and defending the human rights of the innocent victims of terror attacks. It is a uniform situation all over the terror affected world, irrespective of the fact whether governed through democracies or otherwise.

No terror perpetrator, irrespective of his/her religious orientation, can be called or considered **'spiritual,'** as a truly spiritual or religious person can never get involved in acts of terror. The so called people of religion, saffron or otherwise, who engage themselves in mentoring or indoctrination of people to undertake acts of terror, are, in fact, manifestations of evil under the masks of religion. They should be de-masked through collective efforts of neutral and righteous people. Let the energies and resources of such a righteous concept as human rights, should not be wasted upon perpetrators of terror.

Particularly, the people of religion and spirituality should not morally insult themselves by standing up in defence of terror advocates and its perpetrators.

Terrorism: Encouraged by the Soft Indian State?

Mr G. Parthasarathy, the renowned ex-diplomat with Pakistani exposure, re-raised the often asked question, **"Is India a soft state?"** in his editorial of 29th November, 2008, in the New Delhi edition of the *Business Line*. He stressed that India had created a number of instances, through its own actions of commissions and omissions, for people to conclude in this manner. He elaborated that:

"Terrorist attacks are not new to Mumbai and its law and order machinery, starting with the bombings of 1993, masterminded by Dawood Ibrahim and his ISI sponsors. Yet the trial process of those accused of this heinous crime still drags on and the mastermind lives in comfort in a spacious villa in Karachi, travelling around the world on Pakistani passports.

"With three of the Pakistani perpetrators of recent terrorist attacks under custody, there is going to be no difficulty in establishing the involvement of the Lashker-e-Taiba, now functioning under the name of Jamat-ud-Duwa, in the terrorist attacks. Its leader Hafiz Mohammed Saeed had openly boasted of how he organized the attack on the Red Fort in January 2001.

Yet, instead of taking note of his actions, the NDA Government chose to invite Pakistan's then "Chief Executive", Gen.Pervez Musaharraf for a Summit at Agra, just a few months later—an event that preceded attack on our Parliament by yet another Pakistani group, the Jaish-e-Mohammed, in December 2001."

The renowned diplomat and writer cited numerous examples when India dithered from taking actions with requisite toughness, and added that:

> "New Delhi now has opportunity to expose Pakistan as being the epicentre of global terrorism to the international community."

Though international support has its value but one has to fight one's battle oneself and in light of this truth, Mr Parthasarathy added:

> "In these circumstances, India has to use its own resources to make it clear to Pakistan that supporting jihadi terrorist outfits on its soil will have its consequences."

He proceeded to say that India's intelligence network was made ineffective through interference by successive governments—as is evident from his assertions given below:

> "The R&AW, responsible for external intelligence, has been effectively de-fanged by successive Prime Ministers having illusions that they will go down in history and get a **Nobel Prize** for making friends with Pakistan."

He continued to say:

> "The net result of entertaining such illusions and delusions of grandeur is that New Delhi's covert capacity to inflict costs on errant neighbours, through overt actions, is virtually non-existent."

In these situations, development of the impression that India is a soft state and that people with evil designs could always take advantages, cannot be avoided. Until and unless we are able to create evidence to the contrary, the interests of the nation shall continue to suffer because terrorists love to deal with a soft state.

Terrorism: Non-justifiability of Violence

Some people take pleasure in justifying violence. It is most intolerable when people in authority, political or otherwise, indulge into such in-defensibles.

The New York violence of 9/11 was justified by a number people forming the leadership of **Al-Qaida and Taliban,** and also by significantly large sections of the misguided Muslim clergy. While some were shamefully vocal, others rejoiced silently.

In India, we have for long paid the price for not condemning terror in toughest possible terms. An inadvertent (though not untrue) comment from Rajiv Gandhi, after the assassination of the Indian Prime Minister Indira Gandhi in 1984, was widely misinterpreted. Ordinary people were seen justifying revenge killing of innocent Sikhs as a **natural display of anger**. Sikh militants, in turn, justified murder of innocent people across Punjab and in adjoining areas, for almost over a decade afterwards.

In the late 1980s, killings of Kashmiri pundits were justified as expression of anger eruption from the long but self-perceived sufferings of the Muslims of the Kashmir valley.

In 1993, a number of **Mumbaikars** argued that the **Shiv-Sena** engineered violence was a justified expression in response to the organized bomb blasts there. Similarly, violence in many parts of the world has always been justified by its perpetrators and/or their supporters, as response to some wrong doings.

Why do justifications for violence or attempts in this direction emerge in the first place? There seems to be an urgent need for understanding this unrighteous eruption of human reactivity.

Human beings, very early in their history, found merit in collective action: Hunting was one activity that, along with collective action, involved violence. Collective violence gets easily justified or it sits easy on the doer's conscience because:

- It avoids individual responsibility—and guilt accumulation or evil perception for wrong doings; and
- Provides intra-group bonding in collective action.

Collectiveness, whether in violence, welfare activity, resistance to aggression or any other event of this nature, generates a **feel good factor** (FGF): In the process, individuals are afforded opportunities to excel and service their self-ego and also attempt to gain leadership.

Such justifications have never solved any problem or issues—except complicating the same. Conversely, they have acted as an incentive to perpetrators of violence—and also towards creation of a feeling that they can always gather some support , even appreciation, through acts of terror.

Justification of pre-meditated violence or terror should never be attempted—it should, by itself, become a crime against humanity (a significant cognizable offence meriting immediate state attention), through some effective national/ international legal arrangements. And NGOs should not continue to ignore this vital area as it prompts more violence and rights violation.

Terrorism: A Product of International Mis-governance

No one single country, or even a religion, can be convincingly blamed, on exclusivity basis, for emergence and spread of terrorism, as presently threatening the world peace. Several dozen countries in the Arab and Islamic world, in the dominantly Christian west, and some in Asia and Africa, have contributed to the genesis and spread of this most dominant evil of human creation. And, an equally large number of countries seem to have contributed to its spread through needless tolerance. India, decidedly, falls in the second category, while Pakistan has a prominent place in the first group.

Same is the situation about the various religions of the world. While Islam corners the maximum credit and/or discredit for the genesis and spread of this great evil, Christianity and Judaism too contributed significantly, while Hinduism and Buddhism could largely be blamed for its needless tolerance, though exceptions to this generalization are not difficult to locate.

Efforts towards unrighteous dominance, economic exploitation, intolerance of dissenting views, faiths, and philosophies, and attempts to convert people (through misguidance, allurements and coercion), amongst others, led to the generation of conflicting ideologies and positions, the cumulative impact of which is being witnessed in form of the present day vicious terrorism.

Blaming one or the other, country and/or religion, shall serve only a limited purpose—as the demon of terrorism is today grown beyond the controlling capacity of any single country, superpower or otherwise, and essentially has to be tackled through a collective international effort (please refer to FCS discussed elsewhere). And, its seeds, roots and shoots have to be treated with the elements of the GP, as discussed under a latter chapter, for the purpose of preventing regeneration of the evil.

Terrorism: An International Challenge

After the incident of 9/11 and Al-Qaida's open advocacy of action against USA and its international interests, the international community assumed terrorism as a serious challenge to the established order. Though under strong US pressure, the UN mandate for action against Iraq by a multinational force was refection of this perception, which is showing no signs of any diffusion or alteration as yet.

The large international Christian community, particularly the European and American, has not discarded the possibilities (or fears) of **"Clash of Civilization."** The Jewish community of Israel lives in perpetual apprehension of its future in the Islam dominated neighbourhood. Small minorities in countries like Syria, Lebanon, Afghanistan, Pakistan, Bangladesh, Malaysia, Indonesia and other Islam dominant states too live in perpetual fear and uncertainties.

India sees significant challenge developing to its basic secular democratic fibre and also to its current demographic balance from persistent terrorist actions, on one hand, and the inadequate integration of its dominant minority into the national main-stream, on the other.

Internationally, in the non-Muslim world (more prominently in Europe), a perception of **"Islamophobia"** of varying intensities seems to be taking strong roots—and as a result, in several cases, innocent Muslims are inconviened while on genuine work at airports, in malls, and even in collective work and living environments.

Press comments during the 2008 campaign for the 44th

President for USA too were not free from the perception of **"Islamophobia."** Nicholas D. Kristof's piece in the *International Harold Tribune's* Indian edition of 27th October, 2008, among others, had to present that:

> "The transcendent challenge of our time (is) the threat of radical Islamic terrorism," McCain, the Republican presidential candidate for 2008 election, had said in a major foreign policy speech in heat of election, adding, "Any president who does not regard this threat as transcending all others does not deserve to sit in the White House." The article proceeded to further add:
>
> "That is a widespread conservative belief. Mitt Romney compared the threat of militant Islam to that from Nazi Germany or the Soviet Union. Some conservative groups marked **"Islamo-fascism Awareness Week"** earlier this month."

A Washington based report from columnist Kimberly Kindy that appeared in New Delhi edition of *The Indian Express*, dated 28th October, 2008, reported a truly scare-mongering story about the **"Islamophobia"** of the West. It added that a New York based organization had sent copies of a movie about the **"Islamist Extremism"** to 28 million homes and religious institutions in the last presidential election battleground states, over the past several weeks.

It is said to be a 60 minutes documentary type movie entitled, **"Obsession: Radical Islam's War against the West,"** which includes images of terrorist attacks world over, historic footage of Nazi rallies, and the modern day scenes of Muslim madrasas, children reciting poetry in praise of suicide bombers.

A non-profit organization, which spent approx. US$50 million on this effort, was reported to have stated that it attempted to educate voters on the key issues of the US national security.

Another US election related report from Boston, by a columnist named Knneth J. Cooper, entitled **"Terror pattern worries America,"** that appeared in *The Asian Age* dated 28th October, 2008, published from New Delhi, highlighted the active infestation of American minds about **"Islamophobia."** The report added:

> "The last two times the United States elected a new President, Islamic Terrorists launched attacks inside the country.
>
> First Joe Biden and then Barack Obama have come close to saying what anyone familiar with that historical pattern might surmise, but US officials are wary of saying it out loud for fear of alarming Americans or encouraging Al-Qaida and its allies."

If past trend is any guide, the new US President, should expect that a terrorist attack on the US could be a possibility, after he takes office in January, 2009, said the commentator.

There could be no clearer confirmation of the presence and manifestation of the undercurrents of **"Islamophobia,"** in western minds.

Despite the fact that some of these reports or symptoms represent an active political effort, the concerns of West's **"Islamophobia"** get automatically under-scored by their circulation in the western/international media. Subsequent events, such as killing of 13 of his innocent colleagues by Major Hasan— and arrest of five young Muslim youths in Pakistan during their efforts to join Al-Qaida or Taliban, among others, have succeeded in further cementing such fears in western minds.

Such fears about Islam, which is widely asserted by its followers as a peace-loving faith, are not good for its future— particularly for its younger generations, which have to work and move in close interaction with the technologically and economically dominant West.

Evaporating the **"Islamophobia"** is primarily the job of Islamic intelligentsia, Islamic clergy, and the governments of Islamic states, as its fruits will primarily benefit them. Shouting from roof-tops that Islam is a peace-loving religion is of no consequence. Muslims, individually and collectively, shall have to generate solid and visible evidence through their actions, in long as well as short-term, that it is factually so.

When there is an awful stain on robe of a man, only he is supposed to wash it off; one can't expect the job to be done by his neighbour, until and unless the latter is a washer-man.

Terrorism: A wide-spread and Intricate Economy

The economy of terrorism is very large—multilayered and multifaceted; its tentacles are spread all over the world like roots of a banyan tree, very few of which are visible to a non-discerning eye. Its vast network is underground and no part of human activity, economic or otherwise, is free from its direct and/or indirect involvement and impact. In the complex economic process of terror organization and implementation, funds flow through multiple channels in a covert as well as overt manner.

Terrorism primarily operates through the parallel economy, hawala being the main conduit for the flow of its funds. The open or normal economic channels come to service its interests through numerous cover organizations that are run by terror outfits, as an instrument of camouflage. Some critical equipment and services suppliers are paid through such cover organizations. International arms dealers and drug lords are its customers as well as benefactors.

Some religious organizations, NGOs, non-secular republics or governments, and even banks such as Islamic ones, are known to make open contributions to the front organizations of terrorism. Amongst all the religions of the world, Islam decidedly suffers the highest misuse of its philanthropies for anti-social and/or terror supportive activities.

Some Muslim agencies are known to reward the Muslim males who entice and marry girls from other religions. Funds for conversions, for running and maintenance, as well as, for new additions of places of worship and madrasas follow the covert as well as the overt routes.

Terror is always sponsored by rich and resourceful—and the apparatus of terror does not move an inch without its wheels being well-greased. And funds so collected from rich and resourceful are partly used and hugely misused by the managers and perpetrators of terror: They are never audited. The funds for terror flow, among others, come from the following sources:

- Religion based states/republics—including democracies and dictatorships;
- Intelligence outfits such as CIA, ISI, M-16 etc;
- Diversions of defence funds and supplies;
- Diversions from diplomatic channels;

- Misappropriation and diversions of relief funds and supplies;
- Religious institutions and/or places of worship: Churches, Masjids, Temples, Gurudwaras, etc;
- Philanthropies with misguided orientations;
- Traditionally rich individuals and businessmen;
- Drug lords, smugglers, and international arms dealers;
- Money laundering activities of the under-world;
- Extortions and bank-lootings;
- Front organizations profits from investments in capital and commodity markets (including foreign investments), transactions in real estates and alike;
- Printing and supply of counterfeit currencies, and among others;
- Local collections and protection lovies.

Funds collected through the above and associated channels are spent for procurement of weapons, arms and ammunition, and for maintenance and movement of members of terror cells and outfits, in addition to payments to foot-soldiers. A considerable part of such funds are misappropriated by the managers of terror, as there are hardly any checking and/or verifications of expenses.

It is difficult to estimate the true size of the terrorism's economy but rough estimates by the author indicate that about 15-20 percent of world's total defence budgets get diverted to terrorism—its genesis and spread on one side and control on the other.

Several countries, especially the victims of terrorism, are deeply worried about the ever-increasing spread of the tentacles of the terror economy and its impact on the stability their economy. India is particularly vulnerable in this respect and signs of unease in its economic apparatus are distinctly visible.

In India, its **'Administrative Reforms Commission'** or ARC in its eighth report highlighted the need for greater coordination in this regard. It added:

> "For concerted action on the financial leads provided by information gathered by various sources, a specialized cell may be created in the proposed **'National Counter-terrorism Centre'** drawing upon expertise from Union Ministries of Finance and Home Affairs and the Cabinet Secretariat. Further, different investigation agencies dealing with

financial transactions may set up anti-terrorist finance cells within their organizations to augment the efforts of intelligence agencies involved in counter-terrorism activities and facilitate coordination among agencies."

The ARC also noted that while the normal channels of financing terrorism continued to be active, methods such as online payments, trade based money laundering, abuse of charities, false claims, etc. have assumed centre-stage in the recent years; their magnitude is reaching truly worrying scale. Since probe/ investigations into these and related matters requires specific expertise, the ARC prescribed multi-faceted teams in the agencies charged with the responsibilities of conducting investigations under the anti-terrorist law.

The report went to prescribe various ways of gathering the requisite manpower and expertise. While it is not an easy job, governments like that of India have no real alternative except to incur scarce manpower resources on this indispensable responsibility.

Since finance is the fuel of all terrorist activities, international financial institutions (IMF and others) under the UN should become more proactive in blocking the terror funding channels, and by restraining and punishing the countries and their agencies engaged in generation and transfer of terror supporting funds.

Terrorism: Mumbai Carnage—India's 9/11

Mumbai, India's financial capital was attacked by over two dozen Pakistan based terrorists who came from Karachi in boats and seemed so well organized that they looked like gorilla soldiers hell bent upon destroying an emerging India.

Meghnad Desai, a respected member of the British House of Lords called it as India's 9/11, which in his views must change India's soft behaviour towards such acts of terror originating from its neighbourhoods. A few paragraphs reproduced from his article in *The Indian Express*, New Delhi edition of 28th November, 2008, justly underscored the point.

"This time it is different. Forget Batla House, forget Malegaon, or Godhra or Ayodhya. Set aside the normal activities about minority community or Hindu terrorism.

This is war. This is not a problem of the government or of a political party. It is an attack on the Indian state. It is an attack on all political parties, secular and communal, left and right, on fundamentals of all faiths and no faith.

It is an attack on Mumbai and Maharashtra and on every city and state of the Union of India. It is an attack on all Indians as much as all those who are our guests. *Vasudhaiva Kutumbakam.* All our guests are our family.

This is India's 9/11

The world and India will never be the same again. India has stood alone for 60 years in South Asia and indeed South-east Asia as the one nation state which has not broken up. It has never had a national civil war. It has contained all the enemies within—whether we mean Khalistan, Nagaland, Kashmir separatists, communalists or Naxalites. The lives of our soldiers and our police, our citizens and even our leaders have been sacrificed to achieve that. But when it comes to the enemy without, the Indian state has been notoriously soft. It was unprepared against China in 1962 and against Pakistan in Kargil. It was held at ransom in Kandahar. This has happened once again."

What the Lord Meghnad meant is that India must stop behaving as a soft state. It must stand and fight to safeguard its interests. He further added:

"Right now we are all Jews.

The time for partisanship will come again. But right now we need a national dialogue on commonalities which unite us, to fight forces which threaten to destroy the nation state. We need a truce amongst us to fight those who war against us.

In other times and other countries, during emergencies such as war, political parties have sunk their differences and forged a government of national unity. Has the time come to do so in India?"

He has raised the most vital question; India's political system has to respond. And the author would like to wait, see and evaluate the emergence of such a response, if and when it comes.

Some intelligence experts termed the Mumbai terror attack as a **'complete strategic failure'** on part of the Indian state, and said that terrorists in India are now following the lines of Al-Qaida and

Taliban. New methods of countering terror are now necessary and the security apparatus of India has to start thinking beyond law and order.

On the other side, there is widespread view amongst security experts that India needs tougher anti-terror laws in order to thwart terrorist strikes. Legal experts feel that under the present laws it is nearly impossible to effect convictions of terror culprits—and they seem to know that. Laws of the land must keep pace with the kind of terror encountered. Terrorists should fear the law of the land if they are to be deterred -and for that the anti-terror laws have to be truly tough.

The widely perceived view that India is a soft target for terrorists and that Mumbai type of attacks could reoccur here, has been re-stressed by components of the new Barack Obama administration, which now faces the most un-enviable task of countering the international terrorism, particularly the variety cultivated in Afghanistan and Pakistan, and exported there-from.

India has to get rid of its own softness in the realm of counter-terrorism.

Terrorism: Exhibits Masterly Diversion Tendencies

Perpetrators of terrorism, whether by state or non-state operators, have acquired extreme expertise in diverting attention of its national or international victims and confusing all forms of media, diplomats, and international organizations responsible for limiting its spread and impact, and ultimately combating it.

This came into sharp focus in the aftermath of the 26/11 Mumbai terror carnage that left a large number of Indians and foreigners dead and wounded. The Indian government's and international community's clear identification of Pakistan based evil forces, propelled the managers of this unholy terror into frenzied action to cover its tracks and deflect everything that got pointed towards them.

- First, the Pakistani apparatus of terror asserted that India was in a habit of blaming it every-time anything happened in its territory.
- When evidence accumulated about the involvement of ISI and the terror groups nourished by it—and consequent to build-up of the international pressure, Pakistan

President Asif Ali Zardari dented his already questionable credibility by saying that the Pakistan based organisations accused for effecting the Mumbai terror were "**Non-State Actors,**" meaning that his government was not involved.

- This less than intelligent argument (invalid from all angles) did not bring any relief to the entangled Pakistani government, as the international community said that a state was responsible for actions of even the non-state operatives emerging from its territories.
- Being nervous at the emergence of strong international pressures, the Pakistani government persuaded the already not so credible Zardari for inventing the so called '**phone threat from India's foreign ministry**'—and said that in view of India's threat it was moving its forces from its western borders with Afghanistan where they were supposed to have been involved in a farce of joint anti-terrorism activities. Some forces were actually moved to pressure US and NATO, so as to dissuade them from supporting India's allegations.
- In the meantime, Pakistan came up with the very cunning proposal for a "**Joint Investigation Mechanism,**" which indeed was laughable in the sense that a thief could never investigate a theft committed by him, in association of a victim.
- Despite having been provided with all the proofs of involvement of Pakistan's ISI and its front organizations in the carnage, Pakistan continued to shamelessly want more proof to be handed over to it. Confirmation of its involvement by USA, UK and several other countries did not cool its appetite for such a demand.
- Writings in the Pakistani media by its own reputed nationals such as Ahmed Rashid, Amir Mir, and Suja Nawaj, which gave graphic details of the ISI's total involvement, did not suffice.
- On March 6, 2006, Lt Gen Javed Ashraf Qazi, a former Director General of ISI, and then Pakistan's Minister for Railways, had told its Parliament: **"We must not be afraid to admit that the Jaish-e-Mohammed was involved in the death of thousands of innocent Kashmiris, the bombing of Indian Parliament (American journalist)**

Daniel Paul's murder, and an attempt to assassinate President Musharraf." Yet, Pakistan wanted more proof in a shameless and terrorist-typical manner.

- The process of attention diversion continued unabated: ISI and Taliban forces torched a large collection of over 200 combat vehicles and trucks, meant for US-NATO forces in Afghanistan, at a Peshawar depot in an attempt to scare away the Western powers from righteous support to India.
- Pakistan's injured innocence protestations are nothing new: Interpol investigations had established that ISI gave a pistol at Lahore airport to the hijackers of the Indian Airlines flight IC-814. These facts don't shame Pakistan in any manner when it demands proof of involvement of its criminals in killing of innocent people in India.
- Pakistan's own permanent ambassador in Washington, Hussain Haqqani had written and acknowledged that the LeT is "Backed by Saudi money and protected by Pakistani intelligence services." The distinguished diplomat confirmed what the Lashkar proclaims: "Muslims ruled Spain for 800 years but were finished to the last man. Christians now rule Spain and we must wrest it back from them. Whole of India including Kashmir, Hydersbad, Assam, Nepal Burma, Bihar, and Junahgarh, were part of Muslim empire that were lost because Muslims gave up Jihad
- Hafiz Mohammed Saeed once boasted to the Pakistani leaders that he had unfurled the Pakistani flag on the Indian Red Fort; yet they needed further proof of his involvement.
- **Terrorists are slippery characters, and their managers and handlers are fully like mucilaginous leaks, capable of saying one-thing and doing another. They are expert in raising attention diversion issues, as chaos and confusion are their favoured directions. They need to be handled with a toughness that does not allow them this kind of escapism.**

Terrorism: An Army's Wicked Strategy for Continued Dominance

In several countries armed forces have gained perpetual control over the apparatus of governance. Once they taste total power, it becomes difficult for armed forces to give it up. Pakistan and Bangladesh are two shining examples in our neighbourhood and a lot more such situations of governance are spread all over the world.

Just a few months after the death of Benazir Bhutto at hands of terrorists, a civilian government came into place in Pakistan—and the friendly noise that the new President of Pakistan made towards India was not to the liking of the army.

Further, the Pak army was not relishing the job of having to fight its own people in the NWFP and FATA areas, which had virtually gone under control of terrorists of the Taliban and Al-Qaida variety. Yet, it was being forced to do the unpleasant job under US and NATO pressure—and, in the process, was losing support of people, on one hand, and earning doubts of intention from the Western powers, on the other. It wanted to get out of both of these sticky situations. And, like Musharraf had planned and executed **'Kargil,'** a few years ago with the express purpose of discrediting the then civilian government of Pakistan, the present army setup planned and executed the '**Mumbai Carnage of 26/11**', for the covert purpose of activating its old but convenient enemy, namely India.

This episode forced the present Pakistani President to stop his India friendly campaign, on one hand, and find a convenient excuse for the troubled state's military masters to pull or at least threaten to pull forces out of its unpleasant duty in the west, for deployment on to its eastern borders with India.

As India restrained from moving its forces to battle formations, the Pak army lost the opportunity for fulfilment of its second objective of again endearing itself to the Pakistani public.

Yet, it was able to let the civil government know its secondary place in the unstable apparatus of Pakistan. Its evil strategy for maintenance of undisputed dominance succeeded, at least in part—and for the time being.

Terrorism: Is it in Process of Assuming Nuclear Dimensions?

These days, the above question is increasingly occupying the 'mental thought space' of many intellectuals. Such thought genesis and reappearances are not without foundations. We have nuclear WMDs now in hands of an irresponsible state. And the WMD technology is being hawked like peanuts on a winter evening. The finances of Saudis, designs of Al-Qaida, and complicity of a failing Pakistan state might act as the 'right crucible' for this horrific development.

A Washington based draft report submitted to the US Congress confirmed this possibility (Joby Warrik's report from Washington, as appeared in *The Indian Express*, New Delhi edition of 3rd December, 2008).

> **"Without greater urgency and decisive action by world community, it is more likely than not that a weapon of mass destruction will be used in a terrorist attack somewhere in the world by the end of 2013,"** says the draft report, a copy of which was reported to have been obtained by *The Washington Post*.

The subject draft report is said to have been prepared by the **"Commission on Prevention of Weapons of Mass Destruction Proliferation and Terrorism,"** which was instituted in the US as a post 9/11 follow-up, and for developing an assessment for the US Congress. The commission spent six month working on the subject and the report afterwards went in hands of the new setup of President Obama.

The said report has singled out Pakistan as the likely source of nuclear WMDs. Most likely, if the assessment comes true one day, the victim city would somewhere be in India, USA, or Israel.

Terrorism: A Manifestation where Professional Army Runs Jihad Complexes

Terrorism is no more an act of small isolated groups, angry for some specific reasons. It has progressed and matured to a level where a large professional army and its spy apparatus run ultra-modern jihadists training centres, in collaboration with its unofficial offshoots or off-springs, sometimes conveniently touted as non-state actors.

As per a terrorism investigation expert from **Columbia University,** USA, (editorial in the New Delhi edition of *The Indian Express*, dated 16th December, 2008) there have existed in Pakistan, for some time now, **"Army-ISI-Jihadi Complexes,"** wherein retired army officials/generals routinely participated in terrorist training camps run by jihadi outfits such as LeT and JeM. In turn, these outfits actively assist the ISI in its nefarious activities.

Based on the above, the erudite political commentator asserted that even if there is no direct contact between the government of Pakistan and the LeT, specifically in relation to the Mumbai attacks, the Pak army and its ISI bear full responsibility, in an essential way.

This variety of terrorism is **a patented exclusivity of Pakistan,** which allows its elected President, though most un-convincingly, to assert that the Mumbai terror perpetrators were **"non-state actors."**

Terrorism: Are its Perpetrators Acquiring Toxic Afflictions?

As per a story in Indian mythology, one negativity afflicted devotee of God prayed hard and undertook almost impossible penances in his efforts to please the almighty. Finally, when his prayers were heard, the great Lord appeared and asked what he wanted—and the unscrupulous devotee blurted his well-thought-out demand:

"I must get on demand all types of riches and comforts without striving for them; give me a boon for the same."

Since the great Lord had promised to give him whatsoever he wanted, the wise one was at a loss to see how this, not so scrupulous devotee of him, could misuse the boon of such wider capabilities? The wise Lord quickly retorted:

> "OK, you have the boon to ask for and get anything of material or non-material richness or beauty, but the condition is that whatsoever you get, your neighbour would get double of it. You just hold this small boon in your hand, close your palms and ask for what you desire."

The Lord disappeared after issuing the boon—and the devotee, who was in a hurry to try the boon, did not see through the conditionality very thoroughly: He went home very happily.

Reaching home, he immediately handled the boon in the way suggested by the Lord and wished, "Give me a wife who is extremely beautiful and docile."

Immediately, a beautiful apsara appeared and said, "I am your new wife." But before he could rejoice and proceed to enjoy the beauty of his new wife, he saw his neighbour jumping with pleasure and shouting that he got two beautiful apsaras. The jealous devotee was almost burnt of a burst of negative feelings. Whatsoever the cost, he could not see his neighbour so happy!

He thought through quickly and said to the boon, "Make me lame in one leg." Immediately, the neighbour became crippled in both legs; it gave some cool pleasure to the holder of the boon. He wanted to teach a bigger lesson to the neighbour, and hence demanded from the boon, "Make me blind in one eye." His evil wish was granted and despite being lame and blind in one eye, he was beaming with happiness, because his neighbour had lost both of his legs, as well as, both the eyes.

Pakistan's army, ISI and heads of the terrorist outfits created by them are behaving very much like the unscrupulous devotee; they are not worried at all if they suffer large damages at hands of terrorism, as long as India suffers much larger ones and is fully crippled. Their negativity concentration is compelling them to see even the damages coming to their direction as gifts from the divine because India goes through terrible sufferings.

In Indian mythology, during the Mahabharata times' Duryodhana had exhibited exactly the same tendency. He had put on stake his whole kingdom of Hastinapura, his family and friends, simply because he wanted to see the Pandava brothers suffer tremendous hardships, and have no material possession and emotional happiness of any type. Despite **Lord Krishna's** wise and sustained dialogue, the devil-minded Duryodhana did not agree to give the Pandavas even five villages to settle and survive.

Where will the evil concentration of the Pakistani apparatus of governance finally lead it to…will have to be answered only by the passage of time?

Mahir Ali, a journalist working for *Dawn*, saw a very similar terminal disease developing within the apparatus of Pakistani governance. In regards to the responses emerging in Pakistan to the pressures being applied by the international community, in wake of the Mumbai carnage, for it to dismantle its highly dangerous terror infrastructure (as reported in *The Asian Age*, New Delhi edition of 19th December, 2008), he said, among others:

> "It is not particularly helpful, meanwhile, to pretend that Pakistan is being scape-goated or miscast as the epicentre of Islamist terrorism.
>
> A host of factors, external as well as internal, have contributed to the spread of **toxic fanaticism in Pakistani society**. The primary sources responsible for spreading the poison need to be curbed not so much to please the US or India, but chiefly because they carry the germs of a **potentially terminal affliction**."

Terrorism: A Four-tier Apparatus

Terrorism, to the author, resembles a boiling pot where:

- **The fire represents the terror finance coming from Islamic philanthropies/philanthropists, governments, underworld, and funds collectors' from world over.**
- **The liquid inside the pot are the foot soldiers and their handlers and managers.**
- **The stick that stirs these contents of the pot is the religion.**
- **And the movers of the stick and handlers of fire are the clerics and the politicians.**

In this boiling apparatus of terrorism, the first and the most important constituent or input of terrorism is finance: No pot ever boils if the energies of fire do not heat the container (the apparatus) and also the contents within.

So, if terrorism is to be controlled or contained with any success, the fire or fires heating up the system have to be withdrawn, which by implication means that local as well as all international sources of terror support finance, covert and overt, have to be blocked, either through persuasion and/or coercion.

The liquid inside the pot is a passive input: It (the foot soldiers and their enablers) is put there by some interested or selfish elements. It will get cooled the moment fire is withdrawn.

The stick that stirs the liquid of terror is again a passive input—the religion: It does not act by itself—it is manipulated, and interpreted erroneously by the selfish clerics. They have to be separated from political activity and forcefully confined to their area of action. A strict separation of religion and politics will do the trick.

As per the suggested strategy for elimination of terrorism, i.e. the combination of FCS and the GP, when implemented properly, would work as under:

Strong dosage of punitive inputs should crush the apparatus of terror—the boiling pot. In the process, the infrastructure of terror is broken to non-reassembleable pieces, and the liquid inside is spilled to non-collectable splashes.

The stick that stirred the content is separated from the system and its handlers are thrown out of balance wide apart.

The channels of terror finance are blocked, as its handlers too are crushed in the massive inputs of anti-terror punishments.

Simultaneously, the Brahmastras of GP must be applied at all levels to douse the remains of fire and cool down all separated and crushed constituents, so as to disallow their reassembling and re-activation.

The forces of GP act on hearts and minds by activating thought of righteousness, compassion—and finally help in forgetting and forgiving.

Terrorism: A Mutual Love-affair with Media?

The greatest objective of a terror outfit is to get publicity; get noticed and create fear amongst the exposed public with the objective that the apparatus of governance loses credibility and support—or ends up being viewed as ineffective. It is part of the process of terror attaining dominance and then grabbing control over target areas and the people living there. It has happened in Palestine, Afghanistan, North-West Pakistan, Somalia, and Sri-Lanka. Sometime earlier, this process climaxed in Northern Ireland, and presently several parts of India, Indonesia, Philippines, North-West China, along with numerous areas in Africa and elsewhere continue to experience it at somewhat lower scale.

Publicity is the prime nutrition of terrorism without which it can not sustain itself for a day, excluding all possibilities of its growth to any threatening proportions. In all types of terrains and societies, local media—whatsoever rudimentary, backward or modern loves to report acts of terror, for selling itself and earning TRP—and, in the process, do or help to do the job for which the terror outfits strived in the first place. Terror outfits feed the media with stories of their exploits through handbills, wall-writings, letters, phone call, e-mails and whatsoever else is available to them as the means of communication.

All elements of media tend to go haywire in reporting and magnifying the acts of terror, whatsoever gory and or nauseating in nature. And it happens in all countries and continents, except in dictatorships and closed societies. Indian and Pakistani media, particularly the TV, went fully berserk in intensity and insensitivity of reporting as well as in choice of words and terminologies during and after the Mumbai carnage.. The self-restraint or the self-regulation that it was expected to exercise was nowhere visible—the TV channels went out of control on 24/7 basis and terrorists and their handlers back in Pakistan took full advantage in advising and instructing, on real time basis, for maximising loss of human-life—including that of the Indian security forces, and also the properties involved.

The media and the elements of terror talked to each other on real time basis using all modern tools and facilities—and both were seen being very happy about it—as if a great job was done. All of them possibly looked for rewards from their bosses for a good job done (from their angle of unrighteousness, with or without realization to this effect).

There was no remorse on part of either the media players or the terror perpetrators for over 170 lives lost unnecessarily. If this nature of obnoxious collaboration was not there between the terrorists and the media, the author feels sure that some of the people killed could have survived the ordeal.

Several TV channels attempted to get ahead of each other in claiming exclusiveness to certain shoots and stories, howsoever small or irrelevant the same happened to be; and these attempts lasted well over two months after the cruel incident.

Moreover, the evil perpetrating and magnifying elements of the media were not comfortable with the criticism that they received at hands of the well meaning public, always attempting to take shelter under the freedom for or right to information provisions that they excessively enjoyed at the cost of a suffering democracy.

The terror apparatus of LeT (and also the ISI and other evil agencies in Pakistan) extracted worldwide publicity for their evil acts and capabilities: It had such elements of overdoing that the principle of diminishing returns started to be visible in terms of the international condemnation that they received.

Terrorism: Tends to Block Righteousness?

Agreed, terrorism blocks capacity of those involved in it to face truth because, otherwise, they would not be able to fall as low as killing (or getting killed) unconnected and innocent people, just to score some points against the people or regimes that they have come to hate.

But, what surprises most is that normally uninvolved high-ups in politics, religion, and public life so easily lose capacity to speak out, or say what is right. Whether it happens by default or design is a mute point but its very happening in a civic society is a very dangerous situation. Terrorism, indeed, is an abhorable act but closing one's eyes towards it is no less criminal, particularly when one is in a position of responsibility.

Asif Ali Zardari, initially, had shown some sparks of righteousness after taking over as President of Pakistan, but soon after the Mumbai episode, the spurts of his righteousness were stifled, and soon he went full speed backward. Most other political leaders and clerics kept quite as if they did not exist. Nawaz Sharif , the former Prime Minister of Pakistan showed some courage to admit that Ajmal Amir Kasab, the lone surviving terrorist of Mumbai carnage identity was from Pakistan—and that Mr. Zardari and his government should not need any further evidence—as they had themselves collected enough of the same from Kasab's village in Faridkot, located in Pakistan's Punjab.

Why Musharraf, comfortably sitting in London, kept quite—as he had always prided him-self for being forth-right? Why did not some clerics of Pakistan and Saudi Arabia issue some fatwas? Even the Indian Islamic intelligentsia did not do the needful.

Does not it go to confirm that terrorism blocks righteous

actions, if not the thinking of this nature? And this happening on part of the followers of Quran, which is full of righteousness, is indeed perplexing.

This kind of reaction amongst the high-ups, politicians and non-politicians, is nothing new. It often happened in the past. In the court of Hastinapura, the terror act of disrobing of Draupadi was not adequately challenged by glitterati of the Kaurava clan and their gurus. And, the result of tolerating this kind of unrighteousness was indeed catastrophic—a great war in Kurukchetra occurred resulting into loss of several millions of precious lives.

Terrorism: Giving it a Decent Burial

The prime objective of the present work is not to analyze and discuss the monstrous problem of terrorism, and leave it at that: A viable design or way out, to give this evil human behaviour a decent burial, should emerge from this effort. A conceptual blueprint of such a design, with preventive as well as curative measures, both short and long-term, on all relevant planes, is discussed in the subsequent Chapters of this work. On reading this work, managers of security apparatus of a nation shall be able to collect a lot of input directions for developing an effective strategy for defeating the wicked animal of terrorism at its own game.

Chapter 2

Secularism and Terrorism

What is Secularism?

The term, **"Secularism"** was first used by the British writer **George Holyoake**[6] in 1846. Although it was a new term, the concept of secularism was emerging, with little clarity, all through the known history of mankind. The early secular ideas related to separation of philosophy from religion—and the same could be traced way back to Ibn Rushd (Averroes) and the Averroism School of Philosophy[7].

Holyoake invented the term the "**Secularism**" for describing his views with the purpose of promoting a social order free from the limitations of religion, without actively criticizing or dismissing the religious beliefs of his time.

He argued that: "Secularism is not an argument against Christianity, it is independent of it. It does not question the pretensions of Christianity; it advances others. Secularism does not say there is no light or guidance elsewhere, but maintains that there is light and guidance in secular truth, whose conditions and sanctions exist independently, and act forever. Secular knowledge is manifestly that kind of knowledge which is founded in this life, conducive to the welfare of this life, and is capable of being tested by the experience of this life."

In Holyoake's days, Christianity was very powerful in that part of the world and, in certain ways, it was stifling the human thought processes, and development of new ideas of social and cultural interactions.

Kosmin Barry[8] from the "**Institute for the Study of**

Secularism in Society and Culture" broke modern secularism into two types: Hard secularism and soft secularism.

According to Kosmin, "The hard secularism considers religious propositions to be epistemologically illegitimate, warranted by neither religion nor experience." However, in view of the soft secularism, "the attainment of absolute truth was impossible and therefore scepticism and tolerance should be the principle overriding values in the discussion of science and religion."

State Secularism and Secular Society

From political standpoint, secularism is a movement towards the separation of religion from the state i.e. the government and its functioning (in the West often termed as separation of church from state). In other words, it amounts to reduction of ties between a government and a state religion, replacing laws based on scriptures (such as the Torah and Sharia laws) with civil laws, and eliminating discrimination based on religion. In democracy, it adds to protecting the rights of minorities.

Secularism is often associated with the **'Age of Enlightenment'** in Europe, and plays a major role in Western societies. The principles, not necessarily the practices, of separation of church and state in the United States and in France draw heavily on secularism.

As in the West, the idea of separation of religion and government has also existed in India since ancient times. The modern Indian society is based on these values and, to a certain extent this attempt has been successful as well. But, in recent years, fragmentation and mushrooming of political parties and the total loss of value-based political operations on their part have substantially spoiled the **'party of secularism'** in India.

As per **Lapidus**[9] secular states were reported to have existed in the Islamic world too during the late middle ages. During the 20th century, most of the Islamic world was flooded with Islamic regimes, mostly undemocratic in nature as well as in practice, except Turkey which had absorbed substantial western influence during this period.

Despite the separation of religion from the apparatus of governance, religious organizations in West too continue to poke their nose in matters such as marriages, divorces, marriages of same sex, abortions, family planning, sex education, stem cell research, etc and also teaching of science and religion in primary schools. Opposition from the Catholics to abortion and divorce is a classic example.

In India, the situation due to multiplicity of religions is much more complex in this regard. For Muslims, their personal law becomes very dear and sacred as it suits their injudicious clergy, which is worried about retaining its hold on masses, even at the cost of keeping them backward.

Most of the major religions (except Islam in a number of countries) accept the primacy of the rules of secular and democratic society but still attempt to seek to influence political decisions or strive to achieve specific privileges or influence agreements with states, like the church-state agreement-known as **'concordat.'** Many Christians support secularism because they find support in the Bible in this regard. However, some Christian fundamentalists, particularly in USA, oppose secularism, often claiming that there is a **"radical secularism"** ideology being adopted in current days and they see secularism as a threat to Christian rights and national security. They also continue to be unsure about the validity of creationism and evolution.

The most stringent forces of religious fundamentalism in the world are currently limited to the "Fundamentalist Christianity" and Fundamentalist Islam."

Some of the well-known constitutionally secular states are India (as per preamble to the Constitution of India), France, USA, Turkey, and South Korea, although none of these states have identical forms of governance.

In general, modern Western societies are recognized secular, primarily due to their **near-complete freedom of religion (NCFR)**; one might believe in one religion or more—or none at all, with little legal or social sanction. Also, they enjoy a general belief that religion does not (and should not) ultimately dictate political decisions.

Nevertheless, the moral views originating from religious traditions remain politically important in many states such as France, Canada, Turkey, United States of America, and some others. In some of these states, religious references are considered out of place in mainstream politics. As per one Western expert, a secular society is characterised as one:

- That does not have a restricted view of the universe and role of man in it.
- That is pluralistic—not homogenous or restrictive.
- That is tolerant to views of others.
- That widens the scope for individual/private decision-making.
- That promotes a common framework of laws, agrees on common aims, and mutually acceptable methods of problem solving.
- That practices rational problem solving, through logic, dialogue, and examination of facts.
- And that does not inculcate any official image that favours a particular section of society.

Some positive ideals behind a secular society are:

- Deep respect for an individual.
- Equality of all men or the human beings.
- Each one encouraged to realize his/her potential.
- Breaking down the barrier of caste, class, and religion.[10]

Secularism can also be viewed as a social ideology wherein religious and supernatural beliefs are not seen as key to understanding the world and/or the universe and are instead segregated from matters of governance and reasoning. Secularism, in this sense, is involved in the promotion of reasoning, science, and the scientific temper.

In practice, an advocate of socialism does not have to be secular as per its complete spectrum of specificities. It does not necessarily equate to atheism, as many secularists are religious. Atheists too often accept the influence of religion on politics. Secularism is seen as an essential component of **secular humanist social and political ideology**.

In 1896, **George Holyoake** further refined his concept of secularism as under:

> "Secularism is a code of duty pertaining to this life, founded on considerations purely human, and intended mainly for those who find theology indefinite or inadequate, unreliable or unbelievable.

Its essential principles are three:

(1) Improvement of this life by material means,
(2) That science is the available providence of man, and

(3) That it is good to do good.[6]

Whether there is other good or not, the good of the present life is good, and it is good to seek that good."

In view of the author, Holyoake's perception and presentation of secularism seems resulting from his interaction with the common approach of the Christian clergy to make people often look at life beyond the present one, which decidedly is uncertain, un-provable and not worthy to depend upon for basing human actions on the same, in priority to the present one which is real, definite—and beyond uncertainties of ifs and buts.

Holyoake held that secularism and secular ethics should take no interest at all in religious matters (as they are irrelevant) —and thus, it was distinguished from strong free thought and atheism. Subsequently, followers of secularism of that time got split into two groups:

One—those who argued that anti-religious movements and activism were not necessary—and Two—the ones who argued that it was.

Desirability and Undesirability of Secularism

During the period of development of the concept of secularism and even after, it has been argued that due to arrival of the **'age of enlightenment'**, spread and popularity of this concept was desirable and indeed unstoppable. Orientation of people towards science was bound to shift attention of humanity in favour of secularism. Something provable and verifiable is always better than that is vague, illusionary and that based on uncertainties of next life.

Opponents of secularism have been saying that secular government created more problems than the religious ones.

Pope Benedict XVI recently declared that the on-going secularization was the fundamental problem of the modern society: He has made it as a goal of his papacy to oppose spread of secularism as it reduces his areas of influence. He conveyed his thoughts and behaved as he was expected to.

Some political philosophies like Marxism generally hold that the religious influence in a state or society is negative.

There have been numerous arguments in favour and against secularism and to deal with the same in detail is beyond the context of present work.

Is Secularism—a Pain in the Neck?

Under malpractices of vote-bank politics, active interest of clergy in politics, multiplicity of parties, and the widespread ethics deficiency of politicians, secularism in India has not taken as strong and righteous roots as it should have otherwise done in the past six decades of the post-independence period.

Our minority communities, in terms of their educational and socio-cultural stringencies, have not moved adequately in support of secularism. Yet, it continues to survive in some disabled manner or form. And, we seem to have (not even actively thought of) no really viable alternatives, available at the moment.

Many well-meaning Indians, who are pained by the persistent non-integration of minorities in the national main-stream, and emergence of the recurrent bomb-blasts culture and communal strife, feel that on the eve of independence/partition of the country in 1947, India should have declared itself as a **'Hindu Nation'**, giving the Muslims and Christians a clear picture of their future status, making them clearly aware of the limitations or parameters through which they could work and progress.

Additionally, it could have put a little soothing balm on the wounds that Hindus, emotional and otherwise, suffered due to the division of the country. Minorities too could have been saved from build-up of excessive expectations in the newly defined country. But secular idealism of the Indian National Congress came in the way, as even after the departure of Mahatma Gandhi in 1948, such an opportunity was not explored.

Consequences of such an action, the author is sure, would have been less damaging and painful than those manifesting from the currently failing management of secularism, amid the minoritism afflicted politico-cultural mess into which we seem to be landing ourselves.

Has Secularism become a Problem?

If a national opinion poll is conducted today, a large percent of respondents, irrespective of their community background, age and occupation might agree with the question because:

- It is come in the way of national integration as minorities are striving hard to stick to their personal laws, distinct identities of education, dress, and festivities.
- It is allowing uncontrolled and unrighteous/questionable conversions, flow of foreign funds for the purpose, and an active conflict genesis which by implication stimulates terrorism.
- Implementation of family planning and population management (even disease prevention, like polio campaign) has become substantially controversial and ineffective.
- While certain sections of minorities are claiming accumulation of anger and frustration on their part, the majority community is seeing an attempt on part of the state establishment towards harmful appeasement.
- And last, but not the least, recurring bomb blasts and violence are hindering with the economic growth of the whole nation.

In fact, secularism and the Indian state seems to have become a **'snake and frog story'** as it is neither being swallowed for eventual assimilation, nor being left to flee...

Vote-bank Politics—Bane of Secularism

When originally selected for India, the **multi-party democratic system (MPDS)** had had no opportunity to fully exhibit its deficiencies and unsuitability for a multi-cultural and multi-religious society. UK and USA constitutions, which the major part of the Indian Constitution was primarily based upon, did not have India—similar peculiarities. None of these countries had been divided on religions grounds—and had no similar variety of religious multiplicities and peculiarities.

Those involved in its selection and framing had seen some of its emerging colours 10-15 years before independence—but idealism prevented judiciousness from exerting itself, well in time.

As long as the Indian National Congress dominated the national political scene, **management of minoritism** (MOM) was not much of a problem, despite attempts of appeasement being visible to keep its Muslim vote-bank intact. But at end of the first decade of the 21st century, when parties of Mulayam and Maya in UP, CPM (and Mamata) in West Bengal and Kerala, and the very similar ones, almost everywhere, competed with each other for the minority votes; the Indian National Congress finds itself at a total loss as how to retain even a small fraction of the minority vote-bank.

As a result, when Congress struggles to find a balanced way of dealing with the Muslim terror perpetrators/suspects, as evident from the Batla house episode of Sept. 2008, Mulayam's party goes full speed in support of the Muslim youths killed/arrested for the bomb blasts in several cities. It labelled the Batla house (Jamia Nagar, New Delhi) shoot-out, as a **'fake encounter'** staged by the police. How, and how much, such irresponsible statements damage our democratic interests, does not seem to bother it in the least.

In almost all the states, small or big, political parties—particularly the regional ones, are not hesitating at all in creating state/region specific problems which persistently challenge our secular and democratic multicultural fabric. It is, in deed, amazing to see that our **socio-political structure** is able to withstand all these attacks, on almost every day basis.

The present situation is throwing up very hard challenges to political managers and bureaucracy as how to efficiently handle the fully entangled net of secularism. In absence of a code of conduct for politicians, for what to say and how to behave, the interests of whole the society are being damaged beyond repairs.

Dangerous Majority-minority Partnership Against Secularism

"Majority-minority communalism feeds off each other" said Prof. Harbans Singh (formerly professor of history at JNU, New Delhi) in his article entitled **"Two Sides of The Same Coin,"** that appeared in *The Times of India's*, New Delhi edition of October 10, 2008.

On the communalism front in India, he saw two divergent yet complementary forces at work—one that of the **Sangh Parivar** and its myriad organizations which desire to respond to each and every act of violence and terrorism in the same coin—and two, the minority Muslim community that is not able to give a constructive direction to its disgruntled youth, on one hand, and a clergy that is steeped in the 7th century myths and assertions, on the other.

The law of the land seems to be of no concern to the former in perpetrating its dubious political policies and practices in states under its direct control. The minority communalism, on the other hand responds to situations inconvenient to it, factual or perceived, by resorting to acts of terror on temples and in markets, with the help and guidance of some mischievous elements located across the border. And when its members are caught being involved in acts of terror, the community finds itself at wits ends in responding to media explorations. The massive demonstration by the youth and clerics from Ajamgarh (UP), at Jantar Mantar in New Delhi, on 29th January, 2009, and the causes elaborated by the same, was an appropriate representative of what is said herein.

The minority communalism and the resultant tendency of youth being misguided towards acts of terror is not entirely in response to acts of commission and omission on part of the Sangh Pariwar: It has had a long history and a persisting background of unrealistic perceptions—and even illusions. The **'siege mentality'** that it displayed actively in the pre-partition days has not fully evaporated from its body-politic. Since independence, residues of this siege mentality got fuel contributions from the Sangh Pariwar-BJP combine, and the vote-bank compulsions of the Congress and numerous unprincipled regional parties: And the minority community's own multiple deficiencies have not helped it in shedding the old baggage—and taking new routes to development and integration in the national main-stream.

The Left, ideologically well-equipped to handle communalism and its interactions, too has not shown any suitable agility either in West Bengal or down South in Kerala, primarily due to its own inconsistencies of thought as well as action. It has, by consequence, overlooked the nefarious linkage between the majority and minority communalisms.

Today, our secularism is not able to help us in effectively solving the complex problems that the nation is faced with--and a feeling of helplessness of the state as well as that of its thinking section of citizens, seems to pervade unhindered. Since, it is state's responsibility to fight the divisive forces including terrorism, a more concerted and tough her action is becoming overdue with the passage of each day. The state has to shed its hesitancy for tough action thinking that it would annoy a particular community —since it is a misplaced perception: It is in every one's interest that the evil of terrorism is done away, once and for all.

Does Indian Secularism Promote Conflict?

"Defective Indian secularism is not serving our secular interests," is felt by lot of active intellectuals: Instead of uniting different communities into a great nation, it is putting them against each other. Some of the key defects that are conflicting with growth of secularism and nation building are:

- It allows interplay of vote-bank politics—and consequently the appeasement of minorities and/or majority, depending upon the situation;
- Allows personal laws of a community to over-ride national laws;
- Freedom to promote religion—and inflow of foreign funds and manpower) for the purpose and creation of active conflict situations;
- Conversions, voluntary or otherwise (as they are never fully voluntary), as permitted in India, are a serious act of violence—not much against the converted but his/her extended family and the community. It tears away the old social fabric and disturbs the communal harmony;
- And seeds of violence and eventually terrorism are its consequence.

Thus, the Indian secularism is acting against the very purpose—for which it was incorporated in the Indian constitution.

Appeasement—The Greatest Danger to Secularism

In a heterogeneous society (like India) characterized by a multiplicity of castes, religions, and ethnic groupings, practice of secularism in governance is a hard act to balance. It requires a high degree of training in righteous governance (politicians, bureaucracy, and security forces) so as discrimination is neither done nor allowed to occur even by default, beyond a minimal tolerance level, otherwise disaffection is bound to set in.

When perception of imbalance and inequality sets in, demands for correcting the same are unavoidable. Setting reservations and protections, in education, jobs, or in any other types of benefit distribution creates more problems than it solves—as there is, always, demand for more from those who have tasted such benefits.

In a multiparty political system, where with the progress of development, levers of governance are bound to shift to people who were undeveloped or underdeveloped at one or the other time, competitive politics is bound to take serious roots. Parties in power or those attempting to gain power, and when there is no code of behaviour for them, are bound to attract maximum support from the groups that have grievances, perceived or factual. Such attempts allow politicians to behave in a manner that is not conducive to national or secularist interests. Small and regional parties in India have given ample evidence of such behaviour on their part, in the past 4-5 decades.

The sections of society which act as coordinated groupings or vote-banks, particularly the minorities and/or the OBCs, tends to get or are promised maximum benefits at the cost of depriving and/or annoying others, particularly the deserving ones.

It activates **latent tensions** in the society, and such practices of vote-banks over a period, are bound to encourage tensions leading to **'discrimination perception'** and/or **'anger accumulation'**, and even to genesis and emergence of acts of **terrorism.**

In fact, all acts of appeasement—economic or otherwise, irrespective of community, caste or creed are dangerous in a secularist system of governance, and must be resisted.

If practiced for too long, as visible in case of India, Pakistan, and to an extent in UK and France, appeasement can sow seeds of terrorism—as it interferes with judicious decision making, including misadventures of some troublesome groups not being countered with a decisive response.

Secularism and Terrorism

Secular states namely USA, UK and India are amongst the greatest suffers of terrorism in the modern times. Similarly, non-secular countries like Israel, Afghanistan, Pakistan, Iraq, and Indonesia, etc. too have suffered at hands of terrorism—and as such, one cannot say that terror elements are active only in secular or non-secular regimes.

But, one thing is more than sure—the origin and spread of terrorism has been primarily from non-secular environments—as particularly from Saudi Arabia, Pakistan, Afghanistan, Iran, Palestine, Lebanon, Syria, Algeria, Sudan, Yemen and Egypt have served as the '**nurseries of terrorism**'.

Greatest contribution in the genesis and spread of terrorism is decidedly made by Pakistan in its unwise quest to assume the leadership of Muslim nations, on one hand, and its in-born **anti-Indianism**, on the other.

Saudi Arabia, in addition to originating the world's most deadly terrorist, has fuelled the flames of terror due to its fundamentalist Wahhabist culture of non-inclusion and intolerance and the surplus petro-dollars. The latter is being aggressively employed, through its state as well as non-state pro-terror actors, for spread of **madrasa education** and building of mosques in numerous countries where training in fundamentalist Islam is the main occupation.

Egypt made its contribution in terms of the fundamentalist clergy and its preaching. Bangladesh, on the other hand, made its contribution in escalation of terrorism by providing foot-soldiers and staging grounds to the activities of bomb planting etc, on behalf or as per guidance of their Pakistani mentors.

Amongst the secular nations, the greatest contribution, though indirectly, was made by USA in its quest and pleasure to see the Soviet forces being defeated in Afghanistan. Emergence of Al-Quaida as well as the Taliban got promoted in pursuance of these injudicious objectivities, which looked great in the short-time.

Additionally, its injudicious and hasty action of withdrawing the Marines from Beirut, a few months after it had lost a large number of its soldiers in a nasty attack by the Iran trained Hezbollah terrorists in 1983, served as a strong incentive to terror elements. This act of withdrawal was considered as a **symptom of incapacity** of US in encountering the forces of terror.

And USA got paid for it, in right currency, and to a very right extent through the numerous terror attacks that its interests and installations faced in the next over two decades, with the final peaking of it in form of the events of 9/11. Now, Pakistan too is paying a very high price for its consistent inconsistencies in the field of terror genesis and dispersal.

Secularism also makes an indirect contribution towards spread of terrorism: Its democratic character creates difficulties in taking timely decisions of requisite toughness, which makes fighting terrorism difficult for such governments.

Freedom of speech, free press, lax-laws, politics of vote-bank, and often its undisciplined politicians complicate situations for democracy, particularly the secularist and developing type.

Western democracies too have had their share of terrorism. The leftist movements of 1960s planted seeds of terrorism (though of a different variety and intensity than the one being encountered in large parts of the world in the first decade of the 21st century) in countries such as Italy, Germany, Spain, North Ireland (UK), and France.

The focus of terrorism in western democracies, from mid 1980s through 1990s, shifted from leftist to rightist inclinations. In 1970s, the leftist ideology was distinctly visible in agitations and actions of groups such as IRA, ETA (the Basque separatist group), and the Palestinian terrorists.

In the 1980s, the leftist influence on terrorist groups diminished, and the trend continued all through the decline and collapse of the Soviet Union, the communist mammoth. Theories of progressive character of terrorism stopped making any sense, and lost their noise levels. In the meantime, the old wisdom about one person's terrorist being another person's freedom fighter, no longer had much validity.

In current times, terrorism across the world, has lost its leftist or rightist directions and has assumed religious colorations, particularly the Islamic ones.

Since tolerance of terrorism is as bad as committing acts of violence, secularism in collusion with democracy, though unintentionally, ends up supporting its spread and magnification. States limited by these characteristics are slow and hesitant in countering this evil monster with requisite force.

CHAPTER 3

CLASH OF CIVILIZATIONS

The **crescent of Islamic world** extends from the Straits of Gibraltar to the east along the length of Mediterranean, up through the Balkans, the Black sea, across the Caucasus and southern Russia down through western China, across India (as a minority population), along the Burmese border with Bangladesh, through southern Thailand, Malaysia, and down into Indonesia and parts of the Philippines. Southern borders of Islam dive deep into Africa, particularly along the east African coast.

Except in South and East Asia and Africa, Islam mainly borders and interacts with Christian states.

Despite their own history not being very peaceful and non-violent, the Christian Europe and its West-ward extensions into Americas view Islam with a lot of concern and apprehensions. The Europe has had a long violent past in dealing with the Islamic regimes in its immediate neighbourhood.

Not long ago, **Samuel Huntington**[11] frankly exhibited possibilities of **'bloody borders'** and **"clash of civilizations'** and his apprehensions have been strengthened by the events of 9/11, Iraq, Afghanistan, and the north-western Pakistan.

A large section of political and/or non-political intelligentsia in Europe and USA seems to actively apprehend development of more bloody interactions/clashes with the Islamic world, which is being driven, as per their assessment, towards such possibilities, by the accumulated strengths of black gold and narcotics money in the Muslim world.

They view **religious and cultural incompatibilities (RACI)** of Islam with other leading cultures as the main causative of such eventualities. They find the religious leadership of Islam unreliable and the rulers of Muslim states, a curios mix of monarchies, controlled democracies and dictatorships, as incapable of any effective correctives or preventives. The recent experiences of NATO members and USA in Iraq, Afghanistan, and north-west Pakistan are only cementing their apprehensions in an undeniable manner.

Islam and Terrorism

In the international as well as Indian public space, terrorism is being increasingly associated with Islam and its followers. There is a common talk of Islamic terrorism, Islamic jihad, and jihadists. The actions of a few misguided extremist elements, particularly the Taliban and Al-Qaida, are tarnishing the whole canvas of Islam and its followers. A section of Muslim clergy and its intelligentsia too are active in generating such an impression.

In public communications, especially in India, there is an active effort to avoid and minimise the association of Islam and terrorists—but in private, this association quickly springs out without hesitation. As there is no smoke without fire—this linkage, perceived or factual, tends to stick in a persistent manner—and it causes discomfort to the secularist elements amongst Muslims as well as non-Muslims.

Subsequent to the terrorist attack on Mumbai 26th through 29th November, 2008, the situation of perception and/or fact in this regard became much more clouded and disturbing even for discerning secular minds.

Meghnad Desai, the renowned member of the British House of Lords, in his article on, **"The end of divisive politics,"** that appeared in a New Delhi edition of a daily date-lined 30thNovemver, 2008, seemed to comment on the demise of V P Singh, a former short-term Prime Minister of India who initiated the politics of caste-based divisions, which subsequently grew to a level that the divided political apparatus of the country was not able to decide as how to effectively respond to the Pakistan based terrorists who attempted to destroy all what for stands the great city of Mumbai and its accommodative culture. He expected the divisive politics of NDA, UPA, BSP, SP and the Maxists to diminish to allow a unified response to the growing evils of terrorism. He concluded by adding:

"The biggest danger is the slide back into politics as usual. Don't be fooled by the knee-jerk game of Pakistan. The danger is from Global Islam. They mean to attack India as a nation state and not just sections of it. They are against India's democracy and its prosperity. India needs defending not because it is a jumble of seven thousand vote banks or its minorities. India is unique and it needs a politics to value it. Those who died over the sixty bloody hours deserve no less."

A few weeks earlier, the then NDA Prime Ministerial candidate L K Advani, (as per *The Indian Express*, 5th Sept. 2008) made a strong pitch for not communalizing the war on terror. In a politically correct tone, he had said:

> "Terrorists have no religion and no religious community can and should be blamed for the criminal acts of some individuals belonging to that community. Stigmatizing any community in the fight against terror is wrong, counterproductive, and must be condemned. Even if the Quran is quoted in threatening emails by terrorists, we should not malign a religion. It is the particular interpretation of the Al-Qaida type of groups," said Advani.

For political or diplomatic reasons it was desirable what the NDA's lead politician had to say but the assumption of linkage, a fact or non-fact, does not disappear. It adds a great responsibility to the shoulders of the Muslim intelligentsia, political, religious, and non-religious to work together and eliminate the conditions that impose such a linkage.

And let the community that feels victimized by such linkages, not complain for unfairness but work diligently to erase the same.

Political statements as those of Mr L.K. Advani are no longer effective enough to ward off serious discussions/perceptions in reference to terrorism as innocent people are being killed—and the police, a specific section of the apparatus of governance has to face the music for every blast and each single life lost.

Consequently, the **'Perception of Islamic Terrorism'** or **POIT,** in brief, is no longer limited to private or drawing room discussions: The genie of **POIT** is getting out on wider screen. In middle of October, 2008, a workshop on **"Islamic Terrorism"** was organized at Jaipur by the **Rajasthan Police Academy** (as reported by *The Hindu*, dated 21st October, 2008).

The three days workshop was attended by 88 senior police officers from all the key districts of the state and was addressed by the Director General of the state police force. It dwelt on subjects such as:

- International and national Islamic terrorism organizations,
- Concept and genesis of Islamic fundamentalism,
- Development and philosophy of Wahhabism,
- Concept of Jihad, bombs and anatomy of blasts, and
- The present Islamic terrorism scenario in India.

Senior experts from the intelligence bureau and police trainers from various states of India addressed the workshop.

Though the People's Union for Civil Liberties criticised the tone and tenure of the workshop, but the truth could no longer be kept hidden behind polite considerations. One can't live in denial for too long without inviting dangerous consequences.

The **"Cancer of Terrorism,"** in general and the **"Islamic Terrorism"** in particular, have to be handled in all seriousness. The argument that being frank about it hurts sensitivities of a particular religion can no longer be taken as an excuse for pushing facts under the carpet. In fact, no carpet of any type is now capable to keep this menace beyond critical eyes any longer.

Prof. Mushirul Hasan, the Vice Chancellor of the Jamia Millia Islamia University, New Delhi, while answering the media, as reported by *The Indian Express*) in context of the September, 2008, Batla house police encounter with the terrorists, felt visibly agitated on the question of association of terrorism with Islam, and its followers. He seemed to complain that over half a dozen conferences and seminars that the JMI university had organized on Islamic terrorism did not get the kind of media attention that the same deserved.

> His outpourings seemed devoid of righteous approach, as when young boys from a specific community are caught repeatedly after each blast, and when some of them and/or their handlers boast of their creativity and efficacy in

destructive actions, the alignment of blame in their direction can not be stopped.

With all said and done, the community that is getting associated, rightly or wrongly, with these acts of terrorism (not only in India but all over the world), shall have to work hard by itself towards the target of looking cleaner or free from such blames. Others could only extend a helping hand, if such a hand is invited or welcomed.

If an intense review of the acts of terrorism in the world during the last half of the 20th century and afterwards is conducted by impartial agencies, a majority of such acts shall end up having been caused by members of the Muslim community. There are bound to be substantial justifications on part of the perpetrators of these acts of terrorism, but the same do not seem to be an effective and/or acceptable way of conflict resolution. It has not helped the community or the causes that the terrorists attempted to service.

The Muslim community should look for some peaceful means for addressing or getting addressed the problems, actual or perceived, faced by it. Instead of being traditionally biased in favour of violence, it should look for some out of box approach that could draw international appreciation and acceptability. Possibly, GP is the only effective way available for the said community to wash itself clean of the terror colourations.

The Muslim Mindset

Many experts believe that a substantial percent of the Muslim population in the country, or rather world over, suffers from a typical mindset, often called the, '**Muslim Mindset.**' And its presence in the non-Indian Muslim communities too is more or less a confirmed expectation.

The said **Muslim mindset** seems to emerge, largely from the factors enumerated below:

- Muslims enjoyed the fruits of governance in India for over half a dozen centuries. After the Mughal power deteriorated, Britishers took them under their fold without letting them feel any substantial power vacuum. The colonial rulers benefited from the continuation of the Muslim bureaucracy—and the Muslim nawabs, zahagirdars and tallukedars continued to rule the masses to a substantial extent on behalf of their British masters.

- Urdu, the official language of the Mughal times continued to be the language of the colonial administration and judiciary (at least at the district level and below) during the two centuries long British rule over India.
- In the 4th and 5th decades of the 20th century, the very likelihood of Britishers moving out of India made a substantial section of the Muslim community nervous—particularly its creamy layers felt uncomfortable at the thought of having to be governed by a Hindu majority, which among others, became the main cause of the genesis of the demand for Pakistan.
- Some of them even succeeded in evolving the **'two nation's theory'** and sticking to it.
- For certain reasons the Muslim world had accepted the dominance of European colonial powers: Probably the technical superiority, discipline, and industry of the white Europeans had subdued the Muslims with a certain dose of comfort. But it was unthinkable for them to fall under governance of a Hindu majority, which they had ruled and exploited for several centuries.
- Even after partition and formation of Pakistan, a sizeable fraction of the Muslim community that stayed back continued to allign its sympathies with Pakistan. Even today raising of pro-Pakistan slogans at end of India-Pak cricket matches, and furling of alien flags in some locations are seen and reported occasionally. Pakistan President Asif Ali Zardari recently exhibited the **strength of conviction (SOC)** and truth by admitting that terrorists were operating in Kashmir. How many Indian Muslims would be willing and ready to match this appreciation of the truth? Conversely, several Indian Muslim leaders whose politics is dependent on continuation of terrorist violence openly disagreed with Mr. Zardari.
- All human relations and interactions are governed essentially by the principle of **'righteous give and take' (RGAT)**. If one's own conscience is cloudy, then one can not and should not expect the other side to be totally impartial and forgiving for all times to come.

- Disappearance of Urdu from day to day official usage in independent India too is an uncomfortable thought for some people, though most of the community has taken well to the new national and provincial languages.
- The Muslim community's inability to integrate with rest of the population in terms of personal laws and education too is a strong indicator of its residual unease.
- The relatively greater involvement of the community with the activities of terrorism (irrespective of reasons) is decidedly visible to impartial eyes—and the same can not be denied or ignored with absolute certainty.
- The tendency of some select Muslims, particularly the conservatives and fundamentalists, to look upon the 7th century vintage book, which was designed for the then nomadic society of Arabia, for solution and guidance in matter of modern day problems and challenges, does not endears the community to the rest of the fast progressing masses in India and/or elsewhere.

Muslims as Poor Losers?

Rightly or wrongly, Muslims nurtured a '**perception of superiority**' (POS) for their religion and faith: Some continued to carry the residues of Arab nationalism and the fact that once they ruled a substantial part of Asia, Europe and Africa, into the modern times.

They lost the strings of governance to western colonial powers—for which they never seemed to have reconciled with. Subsequently, after partition of India, the idea of minority existence in a secular democracy did not appeal to a lot of them. Additionally, failure of numerous Muslim majority countries to perform well in field of governance, as well as, development did not suit their psyche either.

Collective defeat of several Arab Muslim countries at hands of a tiny Israel in 1967 did the final damage to their mental apparatus. And successive defeats of Pakistan at hands of India too did not help their thought process.

Has this repetitive **failures accumulation (FA)** made them poor losers? They seem to have lost the capacity, as well as, the desire to look deep into their hearts and do an impartial appraisal.

A large number of Hindu and Buddhist temples/places of

worship were destroyed in India, during over 700years of Muslim rule. It is not that secular Muslims too enjoyed this destruction—what is significant is that destruction of the Babri Masjid, a non-functional derelict structure, in 1992 was reacted to in a substantially violent manner. Had the subject community shown magnanimity and cooperative understanding, in view of the fact that Ayodhya is the accepted place of birth and rule of **Lord Rama**, their accommodation could have been vastly appreciated, leading to a much greater and smoother integration of the community with the Indian secular main-stream!

Subdued dislike of a section of the Muslim community to the Indian secularism, lack of active participation in the family planning programs, keeping Muslim personal law as distinctly separate, non-integration of madrasas into the main-stream of Indian education system, and falling back in female education, among others, are some of the symptoms the community's somewhat deviant behaviour and time related insufficiencies.

The above, coupled with some other indicators, do confirm the existence of a typical '**Muslim Mindset' (MM)** that attempts to hold back this highly potential and competent community from fuller integration into the national main-stream of India. To sum up, the community exhibits a **'victim syndrome,'** which is neither good for its own health nor for the whole Indian nation.

The onus for correction of the said mindset or the syndrome lies primarily, or rather squarely, with the upper classes and ulemas of the victim community. The other part of the great Indian society, the Hindus, Christians and the Sikhs, can only respond with a willing and understanding hand, when there is a strong and persisting self-effort.

Violence and Peace in Islam

In February 2002, an association of intellectuals known as the **'Delhi Policy Group'**[5] organized a comprehensive dialogue in regards to **"War and Peace in Islam."** Despite the designed tone of most of the participants, a number of interesting highlights emerged on this topic of national importance—and the ones relevant to the present work are summarized below.

- It took notice of the declaration of a **'Global War on**

Terrorism (GWT)' as per the resolution No.-1373 of the United Nations, which committed all member nations of the world body to fight terrorism and root out sources and perpetrators of this menace.

- It also acknowledged the wide-spread accusation of Islam, as contributor to terrorism, and the resultant perception that Islam is hostile to the followers of other religions and political systems.
- They actively strove to assert that the **war against terrorism** should not be contrived as war against Islam. Also they brought forth the questions on the relationship between Islamic tenets, terrorism, and the growing conflict—and they took the discourse beyond defending Islam.
- The relationship between **religion and statecraft**, and its implications and undesirability was discussed.
- The failure of the Western assessment that the role of religion was likely to diminish in the third world with economic growth and spread of education, as evidenced by events in West-Asia, Bangladesh, Pakistan and Malaysia, was taken note of.
- The central issue of whether religion should encompass politics or be separate was discussed in view of its growing importance, particularly in the Islamic world.
- Off and on, several ideological movements have been directed towards cleansing of Islam and declaration of jihad, as those of Saiyad Ahmad Bareilvi, followers of Shah Wali Allah school, and the Wahhabis; did these really do any good to Islam, in terms of relationship-image vis-à-vis other religions.
- It was noted that the puritanical approach of most of the Muslim theologists who took uncompromising positions to state that true love and friendship between the faithfuls and the non-believers was not possible—and that attempts be made to establish in India a **'daral-Islam'** where the non-Muslims would only be given status of **zimmis** (protected people), were expressive of the non-compatibility of Islam with other faiths.
- Even Sir Saiyed Ahmad's efforts for promoting enlightenment and modern education were firmly

opposed—and that the Islamic theologists seem to have vested interests in keeping the masses attached to the centuries old unpractical concepts and practices, came out clearly through the said discussions.

- That Quran is an ideological book—and it does not advocate violence too came out fairly clearly—but this impression has not travelled far as it has not been communicated well and widely enough.
- That Islam values peace a great deal—even when countering persecution by opponents and that the ways of peace must be adopted, at all costs. It is, however, no where perceptible to a majority of non-Muslims all over the world.
- According to the teachings of Islam, waging war is the prerogative of an established state alone, and does not fall within the province of non-governmental groups or organizations. All non-governmental actions have to stay totally peaceful. Then why the making and hurling of bombs on innocent/unconnected people? Whose responsibility is it to restrain youngsters on the right path?
- An undeclared war is totally illegal in Islam—and so is the guerilla one. Then how come the Muslim clergy does not actively condemn the terrorist violence in J&K and elsewhere?
- In regards to conflict management, Quran calls for patience. and avoidance—and reconciliation is strongly recommended—but, in practice, it is not visible. There is a verse in Quran that says:

  "Whenever they kindle the fire of war, Allah puts it out."

  This verse shows us clearly what the actual spirit of Islam is, regarding war and peace. But unfortunately, a good number of the believers do not seem to listen to the Prophet in this context.
- A study of the Quran tells us that it differentiates between the **enemy and the aggressor**. It is recommended not to nurture hatred for the enemy, but rather, with the help of good behaviour and wise strategy, try and turn the enemy into a friend. Is it **Mahatma Gandhi** speaking in Quran or did he study it and imbibed its true spirit?

- The great book adds further: "**And fight in the way of Allah with those who fight you, but do not be aggressive (2:192).**" Islamic aggressors, however, did not adhere to it—nor do they do so in the present circumstances. Thus, there is no logic in calling oneself a believer without really being one.
- Despite being cousins in terms of their origin and growth, Islam and Christianity are not comfortable with each other owing to the over thirteen century long conflict of varying intensities. The more recent history of Christian/Western imperialism has not helped in dispelling mutual fears.
- The situation of Islam's conflict with the Judaism (another cousin) is equally complex and uncomfortable. Hinduism too can not claim to have received a better treatment from the followers of Islam. In such a situation, Islam can not and should not expect not to be a candidate for active suspicion as promoter of terrorism.
- On the other hand, after the demise of the Ottoman Empire, almost the whole Islamic world had fallen victim to Western imperialism—and it has not forgotten or forgiven even a bit for the treatment that it received at hands of the colonial powers. Hence, the reasons for mutual distrust seem genuine—and it will need the true spirit of Quran and Bible to minimise it to a comfortable level. Let the two communities compete to prove who is more compassionate or more forgiving?
- **Is Islam particularly prone to terrorism?** Apparently, this kind of impression has gone fairly deep—but an in depth analysis does not seem to support it. Notwithstanding, by implication it is the responsibility of the followers of Islam to work hard and dispel this formation.
- A considerable part of the blame, for this sticker or label of violence lies with various radical Islamic groups which compete with each other to show their capacity for terror and violence. They, by design, attract extra negative publicity. Many groups in middle east have proudly used the phrase of **"Islamic Jihad"** or its deviations while naming their organisation or their activities. Then, blaming others for comprehending that Islam harbours or promotes violence is futile.

- USA, through its CIA and other related agencies, among all the countries of the world, has played most vital role in creating and nurturing terrorist organizations—and terrorism, their main work output. They were very proud when it was directed against the Soviets in Afghanistan.
- And USA is not free from blame in converting Pakistan into a nursery of terrorism. All protestations of India were not paid any attention, as it did not hurt them decisively before the incidence of 9/11.
- The deliberations came to stress clearly that the world of Islam has to seriously review its failures and shortcomings, the inflexibility and ambiguity of the Islamic clergy, the inferior status of women, low employable literacy, and political will of its leaders, religious and otherwise, towards promotion of secularism and democracy. Its antiquated approach is no more conducive in the modern living and work environment.
- Misconceptions and mistrust between the West and Islam have to be minimised to a working level. The **clash of perspectives** between the two worlds is fairly strong in the Western mind—and the Islamic mind too can not be free from it. While the West sees **Islam as fundamentalist, feudalistic and rigid; kingdoms with 'lusty kings', 'flowing breaks' and suppressed women,** the other side paints the West as hedonistic, permissive, materialistic, and exploitative. The two must minimise the difference of perception in the present globalized times.
- The West's assessment of Islam as a **static phenomenon**, doctrinally as well as culturally and hence, anti-modern and retrogressive, non-creative, anti-reformist, steeped in the 10th century, is generally accepted by a great majority of traditional as well as modern Muslims, particularly while talking in private.
- Being closed to reason and reasoning or to the faculty of reason, so evident with a large section of the followers of Islam, is totally contrary to what Quran said about the value and utility of reasoning (8.22 and 29.69). It contributes to a lot of the problems that this community faces today.
- Evaluation of Islam in the present environment was

attempted in a non-apologetic, non-justificatory, and frank manner. That the 7th century book is an **imperfect scripture** was highlighted. **The tradition now had to be looked at through the eyes of reason.**

- That no religion (including Islam) has monopoly to truth must be accepted and promoted actively. The tendency of Muslim intelligentsia and clergy to fall back on Quran for guidance or interpretations of present day situations is defective; **logic and the current situation must be given due consideration.**
- That the Islamic history is full of blood-shed and that people who wrote it took considerable pride in presenting it in that manner, was taken note of. It needs to be corrected and put in right perspective from requirements of future generations.
- There are over fifty countries in the world who officially call themselves Islamic. What do they get extra out of it? Don't they contribute towards development of the concept of **"Clash of Civilizations"** by so doing" What is the use of putting the rest of the world against yourself, even in a sub-conscious manner? It needs to be reflected upon calmly.
- As per one participant in these deliberations, **Quran teaches re-thinking on issues**. The Prophet did not want his followers to live in the 6th or 7th century, so much behind the rest of the world. Misinterpretation has stifled the growth of Islamic thoughts and its people for wrong doings on part its theologists and the clergy.
- The active association of state with religion is not very desirable—as powers of state are often misused by the agents of religion. For keeping a balance, a separation of the two is essential. But, Islam and/or its followers do not seem to appreciate such a separation.
- In the Muslim world, the contemporary scenario of state and religion association is not progressive or healthy approach from requirements of the time. There are all forms of government in the Islamic world, varying from monarchies to military dictatorships, to controlled democracies. **The fact that there is not even a single free democracy in the Muslim world does not diminish its**

unease of association with other communities of the world.

- It is also true that in traditional Muslim countries, orthodox ulema wield a lot of non-progressive powers. They strongly resist modern legislation and scientific temper – perpetuating stagnation and practices that smell of energies of clash and conflict.
- The Shariah law has become totally stagnant in hands of the obstructive ulema in most of the Islamic world.
- What is the possibility of a positive change if **democratization of Islamic regime**s is not attempted? This question was posed in the said seminar but effective proposals did not seem to emerge.
- The need for rethinking in Islam for the propose of facing today's and future's challenges was repeatedly stressed in these deliberations. Separation of religion from state and democratization is necessary if any positive movement is to be made for rest of the world's better understanding of the situation in the Islamic society.
- Perpetuation of the concept of Islamic states evolves from the traditional conspiracy of politicians and the orthodox ulema, for protecting their dominance and exploitation of people, under the influence of the opium of the religious confusion.
- **Creation of modern Islamic mind, tolerant and progressive, is the need of the present times** – and finding the ways and means for the same is the express responsibility of the Muslim intelligentsia. It should not continue to fail in doing its duty.
- Muslim ulema see truly Islamic social order incomplete without an Islamic political order. In secular India, they must find a way of peacefully reconciling with this mental limitation of theirs. Some intellectuals like Sayyed Abdul Hasan Nadwi[12] (1913–99) attempted to balance this challenge but the community is yet to respond in a meaningful way. He considered the **two nation theory** that led to creation of Pakistan, an absolute folly.
- Nadwi had recommended that Muslims should adopt a pragmatic approach that enables them to reconcile on one hand with the need for living as a cooperative minority –

balancing their religious needs, and on the other, the responsibilities as citizens of a secular democracy.

- An effective and persistent inter-religion dialogue, as per Nadwi, was a necessity. It should operate at different strata of the multi-community society.
- It was felt that Muslims have played an important role in building modern India and they should be able even to better their contribution in the future.
- The Muslim scholars—intelligentsia as well as the ulema, have a challenging task of re-aligning the classic Islamic law, wherein a Muslim minority effectively and happily operates in a political environment that is conditioned and managed by a mixed non-Islamic majority. They must discharge their duty and provide new compatible directions in this context.
- The Muslim community has to learn how to look ahead and engage with the larger issues that the humanity faces today rather than on every little provocation jump fourteen centuries behind to seek guidance from scriptures which were developed/written for a different society and its specific needs. We are living in the information age where people are striving to reach Mars, on one hand, and the difference between matter and God is likely to be bridged by international scientific effort, on the other.

  The Prophet did not come here to make a state for the Muslims. He gave them a state of mind—keeping which clean and balanced is their own job.
- As per Mushirul Hasan, the then Vice Chancellor of the Jamia Milia, who responded through the press to the Batla house episode (September 2008), the Western intelligentsia views Muslims as **a monolithic community**, acting in unison at all times, leading their lives as per the Islamic law, and guided by Muslim divines. Such perceptions, whether right or wrong, are not entirely a product of Western mind—Muslims themselves have made a large contribution towards their development. Now, they must work hard to clear them off since these do not hurt any body else.
- Some scholars talked of **"Scholarly Inertia"** and inability

of low level Muslim madarsas to change their curriculum as per the altered needs of the time, which has blocked the opportunity to interpret Islam, analyze Muslim societies, and explain the dilemma and predicaments of their co-religionists. The few Muslim intellectuals surviving uneasily on the fringes of India's vibrant intellectual life, as per some of the seminar participants, seem to be lazy and lackadaisical in breaking free from inherited mental frames. The principal cause for it is said to be the lack of vigorous **secularized intellectual discourse (SID)**.

- The Muslim community collectively can not escape the blame for keeping the curriculum of its madarsas remaining un-secularized and steeped in the 7th century. The blame can not be left to the state apparatus. The role of makatib and madaris must be secularized and modernized with great speed.
- It emerged in the discussions that the traditional presentations of Islam are not adequate for active cooperation of its followers with rest of the world. Similarly, West too, despite its diversity of concepts and practices, is not adequately forthcoming. Still, in the aftermath of 9/11, Iraq and Afghanistan, a lot of bridges need to be built between the West and Islam—and the greater responsibility in this regard rests with the latter because it is vastly misunderstood by rest of the world.
- Religious leaders like Imams of great masjids should limit to their assigned duties and refrain from making political announcements or siding with one or the other political party. **Mixing of religion with politics** has to end—or at least minimize itself, in interest of the Muslim community. In legal situations like the Shah Banu case, they should either be neutral or support the progressive/modern trends, in order to help the community grow in tandem with rest of the communities.
- Anti-national calls (like boycotting the Republic Day function) or separatist statements should not be allowed to go unpunished. Usage of offensive expressions like 'kafir' has to be done away and deleted from all vocabularies.

- The Muslim intelligentsia should move beyond the simplistic approach of deploring and denouncing the West. In today's global environment, it should be **vigilantly self-critical**—and work relentlessly for removal/minimization of the numerous social and economic ills of the Muslim community—so that it could be seen progressing, hand in hand with rest of the citizens. When they shirk responsibility, the blame will locate them where-ever they hide.
- Radical Islamic leaders have interpreted traditional Islamic concepts to either suit their political designs or feed their internal compulsions. Similarly, radical ideologists and scholars across the Muslim world have quoted/interpreted certain passages from Quran to justify aggression, violence and terrorism. The contextual applicability of such verses is grossly misused. The radicals deliberately leave out the verses that emphasize on peace and compassion towards all human beings.
- Clerics, kings and warlords, throughout the Islamic history have used or, more precisely, misused religion to misguide public and clamp strict control on it for their utterly selfish reasons.
- The radical Islamic groups consider confrontation between Muslims and non-Muslims, between moderate Muslims (Jahiliyya) and the orthodox necessary and inevitable. The Jihadists' dream of getting into the past and recreate the Caliphate has to fully evaporate.
- They want to create a world order in which the non-believers would be totally subjugated or destroyed—and Muslim leaders who do not strive to restore the supremacy of Allah would be judged as apostates, and be condemned.
- The connection between terrorism and religion is very old. The term Zealot which meant a **'fanatical enthusiast'** can be traced back to the days of the Roman occupation of Jewish lands in AD 66. They used assassination as a tool of terror. Today's terrorists who spill the innocents' blood through bomb blasts are even worse.
- Such people are possessed by a "Fundamentalist Mindset" as they oppose secular ideologies on the

grounds that the latter defies God's sovereignty.—and his laws as revealed in the scriptures.

- These radicals or fundamentalists have a single minded goal to establish or strengthen Islamic states or a chain of the same. They employ terrorism, brutal force, and inordinate violence to achieve their objectivity—as they can not match the power of opponents (Christian-Jewish forces). In case of India, primarily in Kashmir, they even dream of matching security forces with Pakistani support. In both the cases, their terrorism or Jihad ends up becoming an act of weak and foxy character.
- Sayed Qutub,[13] of **Muslim Brotherhood** of Egypt, who highlighted the revolutionary character of Islam, considered Jihad an essential component of revolutionary Islam. His methods were primarily reactionary and revivalist—and hence, despite spilling a lot of innocent blood, Islamic terrorism has not done any good to Islam and/or its followers.
- Qutub [14]divided the world into the party of his God and the other of Satan. He considered Islam as the only true system and others as Jahiliyyas (uncivilized, pagan and ignorant). Such a one directional delusion is the key character of Islamic terrorists and/or fundamentalists.
- Maulama Maududi of Pakistan too had similar ideas and actively exhibited his mental imbalance.
- Bin Laden[15] went even further than his radical predecessors and declared, **"One of faith is the Muslim camp, and the camp of unbelief is led by the United States of America under the banner of Christianity."** He came nearest in provoking a "Clash of Civilizations."
- Osama Bin Laden, through a fatwa in 1998 virtually declared an Islamic war against the Americans. He said:

"The ruling to kill the Americans, and their allies, civilians and military—is an individual duty for every Muslim who can do it in any country in which it is possible to do so, in order to..." It was a long fatwa encompassing multiple objectivity—and it clearly revealed his **unstable rabid mentality**.

- **Evil pronouncements do find evil ears**—and hence, to many Muslims today, Osama bin Laden appears as a mahdi-like figure that would restore the pristine glory of Islam. Something in his style and communication seems to appeal to the wounded or distracted Muslim mind.

- Osama bin Laden, like Qutub, sees the Christian world, Jewish nationalism and secularism as three anti-Islamic forces combining to destroy Islam. In his views—and also those of his followers, the moderate Muslim states are just the puppets of the anti-Islamic powers. In his own way, Osama Bin Laden has unfolded the parameters of the **"Clash of Civilizations."**
- The Islamic revolution of Iran in 1979 contributed significantly towards genesis and spread of Islamic militancy: it gave religious imperative for terrorism. By 1990s, the Islamic terrorism spread to all Muslim majority countries or where Muslims had geographical concentrations even in non-Muslim ones. That Islamic laws could be implemented only through jihad was the rationale of armed/violent movements. Though totally non-Quranic, in this formation they saw terrorism, resultant violence, and coercion, as necessary for establishment or practice of Islamic laws. Employment of inordinate force and/or violence was deemed to have divine sanction.
- Hussein Mussawi,[5] a leader of Lebanese Hizbollah (eliminated by Israelis in 1992) preached, **"We are not fighting so that the enemy offers us something. We are fighting to wipe out the enemy."** His evil mental orientation was suitably read by the Israelis.
- Islamic clerics and fundamentalists have greatly abused their own Islamic laws. While suicide is totally forbidden by Islamic laws, the fundamentalists, clerics and terrorists are increasingly employing this tool against their own laws, by brainwashing young innocent minds: they make great promises to suicide bombers and terrorists for benefits in paradise.
- Antar Zouaberi[5] from Algeria considered killing of **'apostates'** or those not cooperating with Islamic movements, though otherwise innocent, a duty sanctioned by some Quranic verse which he quoted obviously out of context.

- Rabid hatred towards Jews and their establishments has really done the Islamists in. Without having and/or generating capacity to compete with the Jewish community , the misguided terrorists and their mentor ulema have pushed the Islam on a destructive path—retreating from which is unpleasant for them while succeeding there does not seem possible because their God is not so injudicious as to help them when they are on an unrighteous path.
- Some of these Islamic fundamentalists do even display the 'lunatic belief' that some divine assistance will emerge in their favour to finally destroy or subdue all the unbelievers. The founder of al-Jehad Abd-es-salam, Faraj propagated the idea that a prophetic messiah or mahdi will come to their help. Thus, these fundamentalists, irrespective of their place of origin, do have strange logic and formations to pollute innocent minds.
- Some of them believe that they have to do jihad with sword, with cannon, with grenades, with missiles…against God's enemies…to break and destroy the morale of the enemies of Allah… It exhibits their **mentally-challenged state (MCS)** because God or Allah is omnipotent, and He definitely does not need outside help in dealing with his enemies…existence of whose is extremely doubtful.
- In context of India, several Pakistan based Islamic militant groups have played havoc with innocent lives and property since late 1980s. The terror tactics of these Pakistani based **hawkers of violence** (HOV) included hurling bombs, indiscriminate firings, and fidayeen suicide attacks against security as well as civilian targets. Lack of decisive success of and support to these efforts is now confusing them into a mad fringe. And the recent admission by their present President Mr. Asif Ali Zardari that it is terrorists and not militants who are spilling the innocent blood in J&K, has compounded their confusion and delusion.
- **Quran was a divine gift to mankind**, particularly to the Islamic or Muslim world. Over the past 3-4 centuries, when the Muslim/Islamic countries came under the stress of colonialism and lost dominant role of governance, a

gross mis-interpretation of the holy work has occurred by default or probably more by design. Revivalists and hardliners have derailed the caravans of progressive Islam. In larger interests of mankind, and Islam and Muslims in particular, the leading intellectuals must attempt a softer and more understanding interpretation of it, in view of the demands of the time and the march of science and provable logic. Christians, very wisely, have re-interpreted their holy book to be in line with demands of the time. Why can't Islamists do it? Don't they want their people to modernise and benefit from the changes that are being brought in by science and technology, and thus exhibit tolerance and cooperation in the spirit of globalization? They should collectively jihad to bring out a 21st century compatible version of Islam, which should be difficult for misinterpretation.

Another assessment of Islamic terrorism's contribution towards **"Clash of Civilizations"** is offered by Jonathan Paris[16] who asserted that the four-fifth of the world, that is non-Islamic, can not tolerate the violent jihad against it by a one-fifth section that is Muslim by faith. In his views, Islam not only presents itself as enemy of the West—but as **"Enemy of the Humanity."** It is a strong comment which in intensity of feelings equals or even exceeds **Huntington's** views on **"Clash of Civilizations."**

The fear in mind of Western thinkers, as per author's assessment, seems decidedly over-rated; yet, it clearly exhibits the extent to which the mental screen of the major and more powerful sections of the world has been substantially stained or disturbed against the Muslim community.

In view of the above, it is imperative that the whole Muslim community, particularly its politicians, clergy and the intelligentsia genuinely declare terrorism as **un-Islamic** and denounce the radical groups engaged in fanning the fires of terror, covertly or overtly, as evil elements interfering in the internal matters of other countries. They should also agree to pursue and eliminate such groups, irrespective of their locations, in joint efforts without letting the question of sovereignty interfere with it. Further, they should not behave like Pakistan i.e. first becoming a partner in fight against terrorism, accept huge funds and weaponry for this professed objective, and then drag its feet while being forced to meet its commitments.

Terrorism's Damage to Islam

Terrorism is such an evil creature that it bites the hands which feeds it. It is a pampered guest who puts holes into the very plate in which it is served delicacies of its choice.

Often it behaves like the legendry Durvasa Muni who often got angry for minor discrepancies in his welcome and care on part of his hosts—and was always ready to punish them without any logical analysis.

Finally, terrorism's promoters end up looking stupid and lunatic.

Pakistan and Afghanistan, or the Af-Pak as the Obama administrations prefers to call the two miscreants, which actively promoted terror, have tasted the bitter fruits of having hosted the Islamic terrorism. While the former is a now a failed and bankrupt state with thousands of mini-universities of terror, in form of its madrasas, spread all over its territory, and the active danger of its nuclear WMDs falling in hands of jihadis, the latter has conclusively proved its total non-governability. In both the cases, they are reaping the fruits of their **evil karmas** indulged into while being enamoured by the anticipated fruits of terror.

The Islamic terrorism and fundamentalism, which promoted conflict and violence, employing brutal instruments of terror to kill innocent non-combatants, has had a devastating impact on the right thinking Muslim minds and, in one great blow, it has tainted the whole community with the black paint of violence that is difficult to wash off. In brief, it has left the following adverse/ negative impacts on the Muslim community:

- Political isolation of the Islamist countries and governments;
- Economic backwardness of those not having substantial black gold or narcotics;
- Greater ethnic and sectarian warfare within the community;
- Dangerous confrontation with the secular and democratic world;

- Genesis of dangerous confrontations like the India-Pakistan, and Palestine-Israel situations;
- Catastrophic amalgamation of Talibans and Osama Bin Laden followers;
- Narcotic trafficking and gun-running that is ruining societies in Afghanistan and Pakistan, beyond easy repairs;
- Development of criminalized economies;
- Putting question marks on patriotism and integrity of Muslims where-ever not in ruling majority;
- Travel restrictions and humiliations on all Muslims;
- Development of harmful economic barriers; and, among others,
- Causing internal dissensions in most of the Muslim communities

Muslims' Victim Syndrome

Has a small section of the Muslim community victimized the whole world? Many non-Muslims seem to think, and believe so.

On the other hand, a substantial section of Muslims think that they have been victimized unfairly. Is there truth in it and how much?

Truth is what is verifiable by one and all. It does not change colour or form if a Muslim is speaking it, or whether a Christian speaks it.

But one can not come to grips with truth if his/her thoughts are coloured by sectional and/or religious considerations. In fact, thinking a truth or thinking truthfully is not difficult—admitting it to oneself is—and it is still more difficult to admit and express it, particularly under stressful situations.

This is called the **"dilemma of truth admittance and expression"** as per the author's considered perception.

And many times, especially in times of crisis, communities lose the capacity for facing the truth. In difficult situations you need a Gandhi or Mandela to face and express it.

The Muslim community does not have one such soul at the moment—and hence the difficulty.

Recently, this difficulty arose when Mushahid Hussain,

General Secretary of the centre-right Pakistan Muslim League (Q) and Chairman of the Pakistan's Senate Foreign Relations Committee recently joined the *Indian Express*, New Delhi, in an idea exchange program. On being faced with the truth, he attempted to escape by saying as under in response to one of the several questions which he attempted to answer:

"There is a deep sense of victim-hood in the Muslims of the world. They feel that after 9/11, Muslims are being targeted, that the so called war on terror has become a war against Muslims. Pakistani bomb is called the Islamic Bomb. Nobody says Israel has the Jewish bomb or America the Christian bomb. So, people ask: are we the only terrorists in the world?

Seeking and seeing truth is not difficult: Wash yourself clean of anger and hatred for a moment. Say to yourself that you are only a human-being and not a Muslim, Jew or...and seek only truth; it will come to you like a small child comes to its mother.

Muslims need to seek inside themselves and not tend to blame others—because the facts are not with them. Assuming a sense of victim-hood is no solution or escape to admittance of blame—and seeking to forget and forgive, in a wider process of reconciliation.

For this they need the help of the Gandhian Philosophy.

Is Islam anti-democratic?

Is Islam anti-democratic or does it harbour or nourish dictatorial tendencies? It needs to be examined, in order to fully understand the Islamic mind and Islamic terrorism.

One Amir of Lashkar-e-Taiba, a Pakistan based terrorist outfit, while commenting on their bloodshed in Jammu and Kashmir, commented in 1998;

"It is not possible to establish an Islamic system within a democracy..." and, "Democracy is among the menaces we inherited from an alien government. These are all useless practices and part of the system we are fighting against. If God gives us a chance, we will try to bring in the pure concept of an Islamic Caliphate."

Out of the over fifty odd Islamist or Muslim countries, not

even a single one could come up with true, vigorous and performing democracy. This fact needs some honest explanation.

It is little baffling in view of the fact that almost all of them had long interactions with colonial powers most of which are healthy and durable democracies. Many Muslim countries do have elections but basic essentials of tolerance, treatment of minorities, freedom of worship, equality of sexes, voting right to women, female education, free press, other human rights, and scientific temper are missing in most of the cases.

Some of them are having halting experiences with democracy—and most of them seem to love monarchies, autocracies and dictatorships. And change of governments with the force of ballot is often deceptive.

Muslims seem to love a good, long-lasting dictator! Where from did they acquire this mentality? Is it the residual tendency lingering on from the 7th century when they learned to follow commands of the Prophet?

Did the spread of Islam that occurred primarily under force of sword, inculcate this tendency? Or is it the residual characteristic from the nomadic Arab tribal culture where the following the leader was very important? Detective suspicion also extends to assume that some effect, environmental or otherwise, has rubbed upon them a herd mentality i.e. being herded and/or controlled all the time.

Quran allowed considerable opportunity for use of independent mind and choice ; and it is doubtful whether the anti-democratic tendencies in the Muslim communities have any contribution from this source.

Yet, this is a subject of great importance and needs greater research and investigation. A dependable answer to it will help other communities, which by force of location or circumstances have to live and/or interact with the followers of Islam.

Democratic political work environments allow opportunities for substantial expense of mental energies, including evaporation of anger and frustration. New ideas and inputs often automatically spring up in democratic deliberations, which offer expanding opportunities for engagement of mental innovations and initiatives. Alternatives are easily available and accepted.

The chances of anger accumulation and bursting of the same into violent expressions reduce in democratic living and working environments. Leadership change and rotation in democracies is so easy that every sincere effort could be rewarded in due course. Talent does not have to rot or get frustrated in the shade of good or even tolerable democracies.

Democracy also trains participants in tolerance of each others' point of view. It teaches, while being guided and assisted, for being cooperative.

Collective work and effort is the hallmark of democracy—so participants learn to be cooperative for mutual and/or collective interests.

> Since democracy is based on deliberations or acceptance and appreciation of others' point of view, it eliminates/minimizes the need and/or chances of violence.

CHAPTER 4

THE COMPLEX ECONOMY OF TERRORISM

Terrorism is a nefarious human activity (NHA) that feeds upon hatred and money. The machinery of terror does not move even an inch without the fuel of money: In fact, money is even more important for its perpetration than hatred, as for generation of the latter ample presence of the former is indispensable. But the depth of its financial intricacies is not easy to fathom because:

- Perpetrators of terror develop collective hatred for some communities and/or countries.
- And they develop ingenious means for arranging finances for putting their plans into action.

The apparatus of terror needs to be greased, all through, with the lubricants of money, the major part of which is composed of tainted varieties.

As stated earlier, the basic nature of terrorism is foxy—and hence, it employs foxy means and methodologies for funds collection, their transfers and anti-social applications. Mostly, it employs the parallel economy or the black money—the funds of under-world or which are moved on preferential basis in a foxy manner.

The ideal and the low cost **Brahamastra** for slaying the evil animal of terrorism, in a permanent manner, shall be—to actively and effectively dry-up the sources and flow of funds to its numerous operatives.

The economy of terrorism is very large—multilayered and multifaceted; its tentacles are spread all over the world—like

roots of a banyan tree, very few of which are visible from outside, or to a non-discerning eye. Its vast network is often underground and no part of human activity, economic or otherwise, is truly free from its direct and/or indirect involvement and impact. In the complex economic process of terror organization and implementation, funds flow through multiple channels in covert, as well as, overt manner.

It primarily operates through the **parallel economy—hawala** being the main conduit for the flow of its funds. Credit cards and electronic transfers have now become a boon to terror operatives. The open or normal economic channels come to service its interests through cover organizations that are run by terror outfits and/or by their supporters and sympathizers, through the instrument of camouflage. Some critical equipment supplies are paid for through such cover organizations. International charities, arms dealers, and drug lords are its customers as well as benefactors.

In the post-Mumbai carnage scenario the Russian intelligence confirmed involvement of underworld king Dawood Ibraham's deep-rooted networks located at Karachi and Dubai: It controls billions of US dollars worth of narcotics, counterfeited currencies, and extortion businesses.

Some religious organizations, charities, NGOs, non-secular republics or governments, and even banks such as the Islamic ones, are known to make open contributions to the front organizations of terrorism. Some Muslim agencies are known to reward the Muslim males who entice and marry girls from other religions. Funds for conversions, for running and maintenance, as well as, for new additions of places of worship and **madrasas** follow through the covert as well as overt routes.

Terror: Sponsored by Rich and Resourceful

Most dependable and regular sources of terror finance are rich and famous, individuals as well as businesses. They design ways and means of financing it.

And funds, so collected, from rich and resourceful, are partly used and hugely misused by the managers and perpetrators of terror: They are never audited as terrorism is a foxy undercover activity.

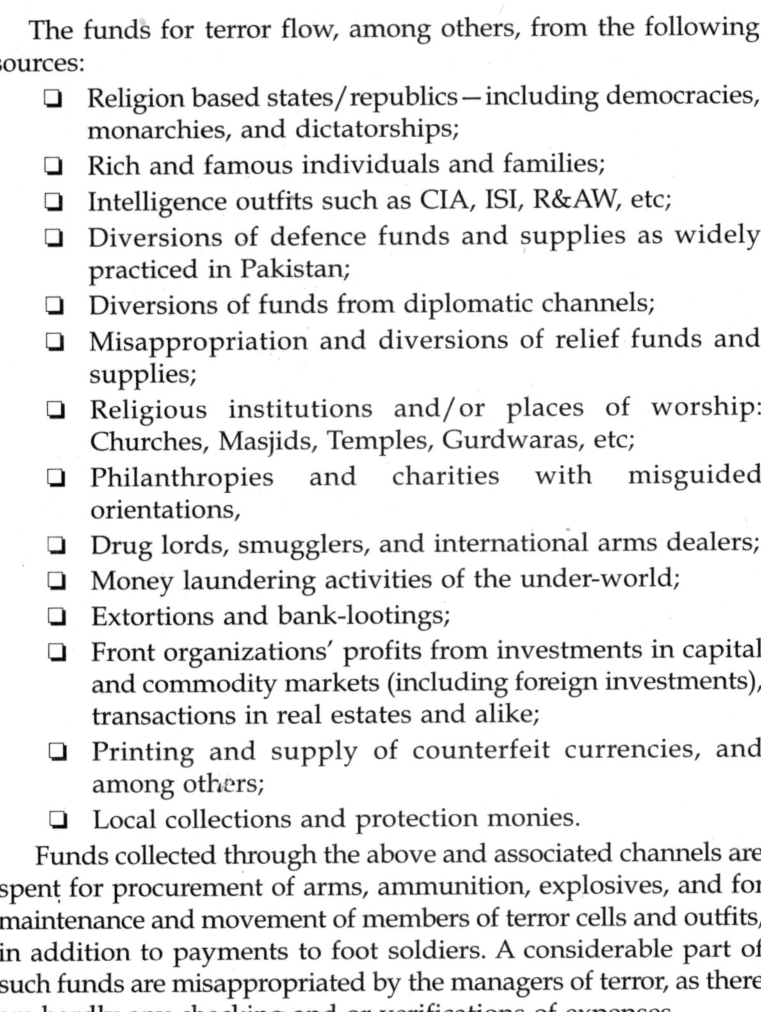

The funds for terror flow, among others, from the following sources:

- Religion based states/republics—including democracies, monarchies, and dictatorships;
- Rich and famous individuals and families;
- Intelligence outfits such as CIA, ISI, R&AW, etc;
- Diversions of defence funds and supplies as widely practiced in Pakistan;
- Diversions of funds from diplomatic channels;
- Misappropriation and diversions of relief funds and supplies;
- Religious institutions and/or places of worship: Churches, Masjids, Temples, Gurdwaras, etc;
- Philanthropies and charities with misguided orientations,
- Drug lords, smugglers, and international arms dealers;
- Money laundering activities of the under-world;
- Extortions and bank-lootings;
- Front organizations' profits from investments in capital and commodity markets (including foreign investments), transactions in real estates and alike;
- Printing and supply of counterfeit currencies, and among others;
- Local collections and protection monies.

Funds collected through the above and associated channels are spent for procurement of arms, ammunition, explosives, and for maintenance and movement of members of terror cells and outfits, in addition to payments to foot soldiers. A considerable part of such funds are misappropriated by the managers of terror, as there are hardly any checking and or verifications of expenses.

Rich Saudis, individuals and charities, are known to having taken a lead in funding of Islamic terror—one because they were centre of origin of Islam and by implication felt that they had a sacred responsibility for its spread—and two—they had the money to spare.

The number of such terror financers is indeed very large; they are found in each and every corner of the world—more densely scattered in Arab and Islamic countries. In recent years, countries of Europe and Americas too have become important sources of terror funds, in overt as well as covert manner.

Yassin Kadi, located in Jidda, the commercial capital of Saudi Arabia, is a case in point. He heads an outfit of businesses, investments, and charities spanning the globe: He was found financing the terror apparatus of Osama bin Laden.

Right after the 9/11, US Treasury designated him as '**terror supporter**', accusing of funnelling money to Osama and his Al-Qaida through a web of businesses, foundations, institutions and universities.

As per an order supported by the **United Nations Security Council** or UNSC, his world-wide assets were frozen—and he was advised by the Saudi government not to leave the country. Though no direct evidence of his involvement in acts of terror is presented by Washington, but a dense labyrinth of associations and business and personal ties establishing Kadi's active linkage with Osama Bin Laden and his infrastructure of terror have been laid open. He being a supporter of terrorism has, however, been confirmed beyond doubt.

Kadi shared a common background to Osama bin Laden, the king of terror. Now in their mid-fifties, they were both born to wealthy families in Jidda, studied engineering and first met in Chicago in 1981. They came together again in Pakistan in late 1980s as enthusiastic backers of the Afghan rebels in their war against the Soviet Union; and they became large investors in Sudan in early 1990s.

Kadi is just one of the numerous enthusiastic Saudi supporters and financiers of terrorism—and underwriters of Islamic-hued causes like hospitals, madrasas, masjids, colleges, and universities, and publication of Islamic literature.

Rich and famous of almost all religions involve themselves into such activities—what they call philanthropy. What is different here is that most of such Muslims have, by design and default, supported terrorism. Without their active financial support it was not capable of being born, what to think of inflicting 9/11 and 26/11 type of damages.

Washington's sanctions against wealthy financers of terror have often gone unchallenged—and only in a very few cases such accused rich and famous have dared to challenge the accusations and restrictions placed in their way.

But their evil ways are numerous and intricate—and flow of terror supportive funds has not diminished in any perceptible manner. A much more tighter and intricate international arrangement to monitor and restrict such evil supportive funds is necessary if terrorism is to be restricted through starving it of funds. UN's financial arms like IMF must become active in this field and, some fool-proof new mechanism is needed be put in place.

Terror Economy: Its Manifestations

It is difficult to estimate the true size of the terrorism's economy but rough estimates by the author indicate that about 15-20 percent of world's total defence budgets get diverted (in case of some countries it could exceed even a 30-40 percent level) for either promotion of terrorism or for its containment. Pakistan for terror genesis, and Israel and Sri-Lanka for fighting terror outfits, decidedly exceed these assessments. While the Islamic countries primarily depend upon outside fund flows for financing terror generation and exports, democratic countries like India, Israel and Sri-Lanka have to squeeze through their development funds to fight this menace. Despite the difference, the two streams of this activity i.e. the funds inputs and outputs for terror promotion flow simultaneously, fully unhindered.

To fully understand the nature and spread of the economy of terrorism, it has to be analysed and studied from the following angles:

- The genesis, collection and flow of funds in support of terrorism;
- Basic motivations involved in such funds genesis and movements;
- Distribution and expenditure of so collected funds—along with their use and misuse;
- Costs of major anti-terror national and international efforts; and
- Effect of terrorism on the world economy; exports, imports, smuggling, drugs trade, counterfeiting, just to consider the key ones.

A brief look at the internet site for anti-terrorism activities of the Canadian Government (SafeCanada.ca—Anti-terrorism Activities) quickly reveals that the major concentration of these anti-terror actions is on the financial aspects of terrorism. It fully underscores the decisive significance of finance for conduct of terror acts and how it could be useful towards its eventual death through asphyxiation.

Several countries, especially the victims of terrorism, are deeply worried about the ever-increasing spread of the tentacles of the terror economy—and its impacts on stability of their economies. India is particularly vulnerable in this respect and signs of unease in its economic apparatus often become distinctly visible. Market sentiments, flow and out-flow of FFI funds, short-selling and cover positions, and all other vibrations of the market response get affected by blasts and explosions. Assessment of these impacts has never been made with any dependable seriousness and accuracy.

Terrorism: Its Multilateral Impact on National Economy

Pakistan's fall into near bankruptcy is a case in point: It has been made into a **basket economy** simply for its misplaced love for terror genesis and its exports.

Similarly, Afghanistan's dominant dependence on the opium cultivation and trade is well understandable. Pakistan was initially not a victim of terrorism. While feeding the wolves of terror—and training them at India, it somehow lost the ropes of their control, and is now experiencing, at first hand, the pain of their bites. The wolves of terrorism have mauled it mercilessly without any regard and/or consideration to the fact that, for long, they were fed and cared for by their unintended victim. It might not surprise any one if the forces of terror finally split Pakistan into small ethnic/tribes-controlled fragments.

Terrorism has not done much good to the economies of Syria, Lebanon, Palestine and Sudan etc. Any terror promoting area or nation has not become an economic bull-work as yet.

Effect of terrorism on economy of a nation could take numerous forms, some of which could be as under:

- Investment slowdown—local as well international;
- Consequent slowing of industrial and other economic growth activities;

- Flight of FFI investments;
- Undisclosed and unauthorised funds deposits by non-residents and influential citizens in foreign, often secret accounts;
- Drying up of non-resident fund inflows;
- Reduced capacity of economy to grow and export;
- Reduction in job creation and resultant unemployment;
- Accumulation of poverty and illiteracy; and last but not the least,
- Community ghetto developments and perpetuation of conditions for cyclic occurrences for terrorism.

All the above impacts have made visible manifestations in case of Pakistan and Afghanistan: Both have become **'basket economies'** and consequently failed states, causing significant dangers for the over-all well-being of the whole world.

Palestine (territory) is another interesting case where terrorism did not allow any substantial development of poverty relieving economy. Here, the people live on donations and contributions from international community, and also from its immediate Arab neighbourhood that attempted to disallow existence to the state of Israel.

It is very interesting to note that while Israel has emerged as a leading industrial and technologically developed nation with the similar terrains and natural resources, its immediate antagonist is deeply steeped in poverty, illiteracy, and unemployment. It is not that technology and finance support could not have become available to Palestinian people, if they so desired—but they, willingly and consciously, elected to devote their total energies into anti-Israeli terror activities.

The Indian economy has encountered several attacks at its vitals. Through the post-Babri demolition explosions of 1993 in Mumbai, the country's financial capital, attempts were made to demolish the main portals of its Dalal Street and associated financial infrastructures. A few years later, a series of bomb blasts attempted to cripple its urban rail transport.

And towards the end of year 2008, precisely on 26th November, a well coordinated attack was made on India's tourist infrastructure, the renowned Taj Mahal Palace and Oberoi hotels in Mumbai. It felt like India's 9/11. Even for a country whose experience with terrorism dates back to its division in 1947, the site of Bombay's Taj Mahal hotel in flames, on the nights of 26th and 27th November, 2008, was totally unimaginable. For, they were the nation's most famous landmarks, including an iconic building that encapsulated both the pomp and grandeur of the British Raj, and the enduring vibrancy of India's film and financial capital. If America can not forget the images of its World Trade Centre, the image of smoke and fire billowing out of the beautiful structures, which represented the very soul and spirit of Mumbai could not be forgotten.

It is to the credit of India's business vitality that, though not the memories, but commercial impacts of all these evil attacks dissipated fairly quickly.

All the above attacks, as per Indian and international investigations (US, UK, Israel and Russia) were traced to Pakistan and its ISI, as truly bitter fruits of its intolerance of India's multilateral progress.

Consistent efforts to damage Indian currency stability, through printing and distribution of large volumes of counterfeits, have been going on for several decades. Karachi and Dubai based underworld has for long run a parallel underground economy, through smuggling contrabands and narcotics. Attempts also have been made to destabilize India's stock markets and realty business. Extortions of funds from rich and famous have been going on for decades. All these funds have been recycled to fund the persistent acts of terrorism in numerous urban centres of India.

Terror Economy: Its Victims and Progress Relationship

Luckily, terrorism does not seem to be very kind to its creators and facilitators. That seems to be the record of the economic development of the countries which have diligently and persistently cultivated and exported terrorism. Pakistan, Afghanistan, Syria, Lebanon, Palestine (territory) Libya, Egypt, Sudan, Iran, North Korea etc, just to name the major ones, have not shown any positive accumulation of gains to their economies on account of terror generated benefits, if any.

Saudi Arabia might look as the only exception to this rule to a non-critical analyst: Its wealth—and resultant developments are products of the unique benefits bestowed by its dis-proportionally favourable reserves of the black gold. It has not excelled in any field of human generated economic activity other than the use and misuse of petro-funds.

On the other hand, a look on the economies of terror-victimized countries and their growth trends, gives clear indications that the activation of resources necessitated, technological and otherwise, to fight and counter the challenges posed by terrorism, has liberated energies of innovation and initiatives. Almost all of them have done better than those involved covertly and/or overtly with unleashing the wolves of terror.

It means the author's formation that economy of a terror-challenged nation, if its citizens are collectively determined to fight the same, shall do well in the long-run, seems to be clearly vindicated.

Size of Terror Economy

Exact size of the economy of terror is difficult to assess, until and unless multi-lateral efforts are made to determine and compile the flow of terror related funds in different directions. Since the subject needs specific international investigations and efforts over a time, it is not considered appropriate for the present work to research into its dark interiors.

In case of India, the gravity of the matter is reflected by the **'Administrative Reforms Commission'** or ARC in its eighth report. It highlighted the need for greater coordination in this regard and added:

"For concerted action on the financial leads provided by information gathered from various sources, a specialized cell may be created in the proposed **'National Counter-terrorism Centre'** drawing upon expertise from Union Ministries of Finance and Home Affairs and the Cabinet Secretariat. Further, different investigation agencies dealing with financial transactions may set up anti-terrorist finance cells within their organizations to augment the efforts of intelligence agencies involved in counter-terrorism activities, and facilitate coordination among agencies."

The ARC also noted that while the normal channels of financing terrorism continued to be active, methods such as online payments, trade based money laundering, abuse of charities, false claims, etc. have assumed centre-stage in the recent years; their magnitude is reaching truly worrying scale. Since probes/ investigations into these and related matters require specific expertise, the ARC prescribed multi-faceted teams in the agencies charged with the responsibilities of conducting investigations under the anti-terrorist law.

The report went on to prescribe various ways of gathering the requisite manpower and expertise. While it is not an easy job, governments like that of India have no real alternative except to incur scarce manpower resources on this indispensable responsibility.

India has multiple terrorism related security concerns in areas such as J&K, Punjab, Gujarat, Maharastra, Jharkhand, Chatishgarh, Andhra Pradesh, Orissa and almost all other states including those in the North East. Security establishments, industrial units, airports, places of worship, residences of central and state leaders, scientific institutions, sports arenas, and innumerable other areas of its commercial and non-commercial life need and attract protection from terror on twenty four hours and 365 days a year.

India's defence budget for FY2007-08 was put at Rs. 960 billion. Some analysts felt that with the clubbing of some associated expenditures, it should touch Rs.1,127 billion: In terms of US dollars it works out to approx. 22.54 billion only, which is relatively small as compared to US defence expenditure. Only about a third of it (author's own assessment) or say equivalent of US$ 7.50 billion goes towards fighting the terrorism in various parts of India, including the troubled state of J&K. If consideration is made for what India's ministry of home affairs spends on paramilitary forces and their deployments, then it might touch US$ 8.00 billion. Yet, it remains only a fraction (below 5.0percent) of what the US is currently spending, each year, on its war on terror in Iraq, Afghanistan and Pakistan.

A better assessment of cost of anti-terror activities becomes visible from the analysis of US war costs, as compiled by the National Priority Project (NPP) and displayed on the internet. It is putting the Iraq related war costs at over US$ 611 billion (by end of 2008), of which FY2008 accounted for over US$ 150 billion. Spending of other agencies such as US Coast Guards, consular programs, migration and refugee assistance, international narcotics control and enforcement, and many other related programs, is additional.

USA's Afghanistan and Pakistan related anti-terrorism war costs are expected to swell to about US$ 5.00 billion a month from the current level of just over US$ 2.00 billion per month (or US$ 60.00 billion per year), if the new Democratic administration has to win this war against terror. Some other sources assess that US Af-Pak operations shall cost it around US$ 100 billion a year.

By end of 2008, Britain faced escalating costs for its limited involvement in Iraq and Afghanistan. As per a report emerging from London (*The Asian Age*, New Delhi edition report dated 27th November, 2008, from its UK correspondent), Defence Secretary, John Hutton told the House of Commons that the cost of Britain's military operations in Iraq and Afghanistan since last six years reached 13.2 billion pounds or approx. US$ 20.00 billion per year (roughly 30 percent of the total spending of the Defence Ministry). For FY2008, Britain would have spent over 3.70 billion pounds or appro.US$ 5.4 billion on these operations

If it is assumed that all nations of the world, other than USA, including NATO countries, Russia, Canada, and India are spending collectively an amount equal to that of the USA, then the annul anti-terror efforts' cost shall add up to over US$ 300.00 billion or roughly a billion a day. It works out roughly to 50 US dollars per head for the whole world population.

Terrorism's own multilayered apparatus too must be spending, directly and indirectly, similar amounts on generating, spread and support of terror activities. Put together, the two sums will add up to US$ 600 billion a year (roughly US$ 100per head per year, for the whole world population), indeed a large sum enough to substantially deliver a world free of poverty and hunger, if spent judiciously on developmental efforts, instead of being wasted on the counter-productive terrorism, i.e. to kill the innocent and unconnected people and in the process get killed.

The Cost of India's 9/11

The three days of terror attack on Mumbai, on its symbols of prosperity and fame, 26th through 29th November, 2008, can not be viewed simply in terms of over 200 deaths and physical damages to the priceless properties attacked. The damages, in terms of pure commerce and money, are estimated to be really huge. *The Times of India,* in its New Delhi edition of 30th November, 2008, front-paged an assessment of losses as under:

"Industry experts believe India's financial capital has taken a hit of up to Rs 50,000 crore and a forex loss of US$ 20 billion during the terror siege. The losses are spread across the markets, entertainment, and shopping and food sectors."

Need for International Efforts and Vigilance

Since finance is the fuel for all terrorist activities, international financial institutions (IMF and others) under the UN should become more proactive in blocking the terror finance channels, and by restraining and punishing the countries and their agencies which engage in generation and transfer of terror supporting funds.

Inactivation and confiscation of terror related funds and deposits, penalties on financers of terrorism, including seizures of their bank accounts need to be actively perused. International banks should observe or be made to observe greater transparency in relation to flow of terror funds through numbered accounts, electronic transfers, etc.

Money laundering and flow of narcotics and extortion generated funds do need to be strictly restricted, if any meaningful success is to be achieved against the demon of terrorism.

IMF and related international finance, and also the central banking institutions of leading financial powers of the world have not done enough to suffocate the channels of finance flow that is employed to sow troubles for the innocent citizens in numerous countries.

Prior to the 9/11, the leading economic world powers were not directly impacted by the terrorism—and as others' pain did not matter to them, no effective measures could be initiated against terror-finance flows.

Now that terrorism is hitting them directly, some measures in this direction have started to emerge.

Often, it is the poor people, and to an extent the middle classes who suffer loss of life and properties through acts of terror, and the same did not adequately excite the deciding powers to take any remedial measures. The situation, however, seems to have undergone a sea change after the event of 9/11 in USA and 26/11 in India.

In view of substantial complexities and intricacies of terror finance flow, the need for constant vigilance and coordinated international attention can not be overstressed.

The need to create a much more powerful **international financial body** for management of terror funds flow should be persistently pursued, as the evil of terror does not see enough teeth in the present anti-terror finance structure. **'Financial suffocation of terrorism'** or FST seems to offer a potential stronger than millions of bullets aimed at it (and saving lives of ant-terror soldiers at the same time) without any un-necessary bloodbath. The international community should examine this way-out very seriously.

Terrorism and Ruined National Economies

Terrorism seems to possess definite **'economy destruction capacities'** or EDCs. The prominent recent-most examples wherein terrorism has ruined national economies are as under:

Iraq's flourishing economy of Saddam Hussein's time has been, almost totally, ruined by the terror related turmoil of the past 5-6 years. What keep it afloat today are its oil resources and inputs from the USA's war or anti-terror efforts. The ethnic differences between Kurdish, Sunni and Shia communities are well-defined—and it is uncertain to assess what turn the same would take after the proposed withdrawal of the US troops in 2011.

Even if the United States fully withdraw by this time, as the Obama and the Iraqi government say they would, US will have to remain very much on a war-like alerts almost all through the new presidency, as situations of alarm shall often arise. It will take the new Iraqi dispensation a lot of luck, and for the US a lot of well-meaning prodding to enable non-eruption of ethnic differences and administrative collapses.

Pakistan and Afghanistan have become bankrupt cases or '**basket economies**'. As per assessment of independent experts, their economies have effectively collapsed. While Afghans face food shortages and economic dis-functions of all varieties, Pakistan is ready to default on its sovereign payment obligations. Both of these are not going to improve very easily, and the USA shall have to bear the fruits of getting too close to these trouble generating entities.

US monthly spending on anti-terror war efforts in these two countries have to grow substantially i.e. from the current US$ 2.0 to about US$ 5.0 billion (possibly these expenditures might peak around US dollars 9-10 billion a month), if the wheels of war efforts are to be turned to winnable directions.

Narcotic Trap of Afghanistan's Terror Economy

To understand why Afghanistan is so ungovernable or why, despite eight years of efforts by US and NATO forces, the world's best-trained and best-equipped, seem to be bearing no fruits, one has to understand this country's unique narco-trap that frustrates all efforts for its disciplined governance. Afghanistan's cultivation of opium and its export earns over a billion US dollars a year as foreign exchange (other unrecorded incomes being extra), on one hand, and corrupts the whole administration beyond redemption, on the other.

On the corruption measurement index, Afghanistan measures 176th out of the 180 nations of the world (Somalia being the 180th or the most corrupt). These two statistics had prompted Richard Holbrooke, the man President Barack Obama had picked up, over a year ago, to handle Afghanistan and Pakistan on his behalf, to write:

> "Breaking the narco-state in Afghanistan is essential or all else will fail."

He had elaborated, as per a report in the Global Edition of *New York Times*, Jan 31–Feb 1, 2009, that over US$ 1 billion that US then spent yearlyto weaken the narco-trade, in fact, strengthened the Taliban, Al-Qaida, and other criminal elements, as benefits of these investments finally found their way to them.

The counter-narcotics strategy that Holbrooke criticized so loudly was based upon payments to farmers for not growing opium crop and its destruction, for several years—and it failed to dent the narcotic trade in any manner, plus it put all the extra funds in hands of the criminal elements. They, in-fact, seem to love the USA's war on terror, as it enriches them faster than ever before. Additionally, it affords them an opportunity to blame the US and NATO forces and also to kill them occasionally.

De-emphasizing drug cultivation eradication through payments would be acceptance of failure of this ineffective US policy, as it has been consistently pursued both by the Democrats as well as the Republican administrations—and no one wants to take responsibilities for change. What now, Obama does now, is to be watched with interest.

Because of the narcotics and corruption complications several analysts in US are assessing that there is going to be no military solution in Afghanistan, even if the US forces level is upgraded by another 30,000 men.

Karzai's holy war against drug cultivation and trade launched with a lot of fanfare in 2004 has made no dent of any type, except enabling a great blossoming of corruption. Prior to the last presidential election in Afghanistan, it was assessed that the Afghan President was not part of solution, but an integral part of the problem that demanded solution in an out of box manner. Nothing however came of such assertions as Karzai again won the presidential battle to the dismay of Western powers.

Looking at the complex problem, some intellectuals are now suggesting that US purchase the whole drug crop in the country at an estimated cost of 2.0-2.5 billion dollars—and destroy the same. It is argued that compared to the over 200 billions that US is reported to have already spent in fruitless efforts in this region for drug and terror control, it will be another small amount, if results could be assured. It is, however, a big if.

Promises from Turning Around the Terror Economy

As a very rough assessment, the over US$ 600 billion strong terror economy of the world is involving roughly 15 to 20 million individuals in the genesis and spread of terror, on one hand, and its containment, on the other. Thus, a large productive population is being put to anti-developmental works. Destruction of property and productive human life, along with the load on society that it had to carry on account of the injured and invalidated people, is not considered in these estimates. It could easily be put at US$ 400 billion a year.

Human attention and energy freed from manifestations of terrorism can, in all possibility, be of help in substantial activation of the developmental process, if collective common sense prevails on part of the actors involved.

Assuming that, somehow, the terror economy is made to take a 180 degree turn—and the sum of US$ 600 billion becomes available for—and put to productive applications, then it can speed up developmental works for health, education, drinking water, poverty amelioration, sanitation, and other related human welfares, in over a hundred countries.

In such an event, it can make human life on earth much more worth living and enjoyable. Only a sense of righteousness, on part of the perpetrators of terror -and their mentors, gurus and financiers is required. How that could come around, lies hidden in the potentiality of the Gandhian Philosophy, as discussed in this work.

Characteristics of Terror Economy

Terror-economy, very much like the terror itself, has its specific characters; it does not follow the normal rules of economic interactions. So, it has to be understood in this reference, if it is to be contained or controlled to a drying-up stage. It would be important to study the following key specificities to the terror economy, so that effective collective international strategies could become possible during the time available:

- It is mostly an underground economy—its depths have to be viewed with a magnifier;
- It does not have to earn its input funds—their flow is often accelerated employing the energies of emotions and/or religious blackmails;
- No account for funds so collected and spent has to be provided;
- It is truly a demand and supply situation—because suitably structured/religion-coloured demands here always bring supplies—people do pay up in face of even misplaced religious perceptions and/or demands;

- It does not suffer from deficiencies of inflation, recession, deflation, and meltdown etc;
- Here, the stakeholders do not have any decisive position once they part with the funds;
- Cost of raw materials i.e. the foot-soldiers is always a very small fraction of the total cost of the product (the terror attacks); and last but most importantly,
- The funds so collected/financial resources employed do not have to be paid back—there is no EMI etc., in this business. The terror funds are written off the moment they are contributed.

It is in deed a lovable economy, and hence it is adored by all those connected with it

What a beautiful business financing situation! Every CEO would love to have it.

The returns to the terror CEOs (or the Chief Terror Operatives) are truly large—position building and social and political status acceleration is a bonus output.

In this economy, there is neither a problem of demand nor of supply: Here, the normal principles of economics do not apply—and the state protection that it often enjoys, is complete and unconditional.

There is no question of any payment of taxes and duties—the tax exemptions for terror economy are total and perpetual.

As a summation, terror economy is a beautiful economy—with all the rights, bonuses, and no responsibilities.

CHAPTER 5

STRATEGIES FOR ELIMINATION OF TERRORISM

There could be several thought and/or action lines in direction of tackling the menace of terrorism. Before discussing the unconventional yet highly promising approach of the **Gandhian Philosophy** or the GP, one should examine the efficacy of the conventional approach that various systems of governance employ for tackling the challenge of terrorism. Its deficiencies and inefficiencies too need to be scrutinized to see what contributes to their intrinsic ability or inability to contain, if not control, the evil of terrorism. How could it be fortified, if such fortification is feasible, to make it deliver the expected results?

While proceeding further in this regard, it will be interesting to examine India's ancient scriptural approach towards terrorism, particularly in light of the great epic of **Mahabharata.** Some of the most evil-intense regimes of that time, just to name the dominant ones, were represented by:

1. Kamsa of Mathura,
2. Jarasandha of Magadha,
3. Duryodhana of Hastinapura,
4. Sishupala of Chedi, and
5. Sakuni of Khandhar.

Lord Krishna,[4] through tactful strategy planning and applications, had eliminated all of them, the first two and the 4th individually and rest of them collectively in the battles of Kuruckchetra. From these instances, four dominant approaches of handling the evil and wicked elements (akin to present day terrorists who traumatize and kill innocents and unconnected people) at that time could be deduced as under:

1. Ugrsena's weak-kneed approach of dealing with his evil son **Kamsa of Mathura**[4] represents an interesting way of functioning. Ugrsena a righteous but weak-willed ruler of the **Yadava dynasty** had allowed an easy take-over of the illustrious kingdom by his cruel and evil son. As Kamsa's evil and wickedness had no limits, an aggrieved **"Mother Earth"** was compelled to appeal to **Lord Vishnu** for finding a way out for lessening the great burden of **accumulated evil**. Having been moved by the genuine appeal of the "**Mother Earth**", the benevolent Lord promised to incarnate for the purpose, and eventually took birth right in Mathura, through the womb of Dewaki who was Kamsa's real sister: She was married to Vasudeva, a distinguished Yadava chief-train. Lord Krishna had incarnated as the 8th child of Dewaki and Vasudeva, for the purpose of freeing the world of that time from accumulated evil and wickedness.

Kamsa became the deadliest evil of his times – and even today his evil acts form part of the long surviving folklore of North India. The weak-kneed approach of Ugrsena is practiced, even now, in several countries, allowing people to suffer at hands of evil manifestations of several types. Afghanistan seems to be a modern example of such a manifestation: Many other countries where evil dictators have grabbed power and are exploiting the masses fall in this category.

> **The moral of the Kamsa story is, "If You have an evil in the family, howsoever close; it has to be destroyed.**"

2. Dharistrastra, this blind king of Hastinapura suffered from '**great love unrighteous**' or GLU for his eldest son Duryodhana, who grew into even a bigger, more illogical and unrighteous evil operator than the Kamsa of Mathura, in several ways. The latter had preceded Duryodhana just by a few decades only.

This blind king, from the great Kuru[4] dynasty, actively promoted his son to takeover the kingdom despite opposition from a great assembly of wise elders and advisors present in the royal court. Pakistan seems to be a case in point: Its rulers, over a period, have actively collaborated in creating a large terrorist apparatus (as their evil child) which is now threatening its creator's own existence, in a very much similar manner to what had happened to the Kuru dynasty in the Mahabharata times.

The kingdom of Hastinapura had enjoyed unique protections of invincibility in the presence of the great warrior Bhishma, Karna – another invincible friend of the regime, the invincible pair of warrior gurus – Drona and Kripa, and Aswathama – the son of guru Drona. In a normal way, all these warriors could not be eliminated by their available contemporaries.

This fact was known to the evil master Duryodhana and he fully capitalized upon the same, while attempting to deny the rightful share of the righteous Pandava brothers, his real cousins. Pakistan's case is somewhat similar to that of Duryodhana, as it sees a lot of invincibility ingrained in its nuclear WMDs. Its hatred towards India and all things Indian does not seem to be inferior to what Duryodhana had reserved for his Pandava cousins.

3. Yudhistra[4], the eldest of the great five Pandava brothers, was an apostle of peace, wisdom, and accommodation: He suffered long exile and indignities at hands of Duryodhana, in an attempt to have a peaceful relationship with his cousins represented by the latter – and his equally scheming father, the blind king Dharitrashtra.

India and its democratic apparatus of governance seem to represent Yudhistra's approach, which brings a lot of suffering and indignities on to its people while dealing with an intolerant Pakistan.

4. Lord Krishna's[4] approach of dealing with the evil and the wicked was most effective; his divine strategy was built upon the five basic elements as inscribed below:

- In-depth intelligence gathering and analysis of evil opponents' (He faced a large accumulation of them) strengths and weaknesses – including their invincibility;
- Active dialogue to persuade them to change course and reform;
- Employment of decisive force to eliminate them and their supporters, if they did not heed the advice;
- Finally, replacing them with wise and righteous descendents, and
- Leaving behind a 'strong intellectual guidance' for the liberated people to be guided by, for a long time.

The, **"Bhagavad-Gita"** or the wise Lord's **"Song of Wisdom"** as it is often called, continues to do this job even after five millennia.

Lord Krishna is the ancient **epitome of effective governance,** particularly in regards to elimination of evil and wicked—and his approach, as briefed above, is the most effective way of dealing with terrorism, even today. The fortified way of conventional approach (FCS), as discussed in subsequent pages, has to reflect the wisdom and tenacity of Lord Krishna.

The Conventional anti-terror Approach

Terrorism, by its basic nature, is **a hard nut to crack:** It is as challenging a job, as the one that **Lord Krishna** had encountered at the time of Mahabharata, for elimination of the accumulated forces of evil and wickedness. In fact, the concentration of evil and wickedness, in form of today's terrorism, seems convincingly more intense and baffling than what the great **Lord** was faced with, over five millennia ago. The universities and crucibles of terror in Af-Pak, Saudi Arabia, Yemen, Syria, Lebanon, Egypt, Sudan and Somalia—along with those of North Korea and Iran, collectively make a formidable formation of evil.

The evil concentrates of the Mahabharata time were **'Kshtriyas'** who could be challenged for an open battle on fields of Kuruckchetra, and they dutifully gathered there, as they were still left with the basic respect for the principle of duties of their profession: They did not attack innocent, unarmed, and unconcerned people.

The forces of today's terrorism, primarily represented by Taliban and Al-Qaida, are foxy in character: They play a hide and seek and are totally devoid of any basic morality or principles, which make the job of tackling them doubly difficult.

Hence, the battle against terrorism, in light of its peculiarities, must be waged on two fronts:

- **One:** Through conventional methodology of physically hitting them hard—and reducing them to an inconsequential level, forcing them to realize that it is no more worth to continue with their old evil ways, and
- **Two:** Through waging a war for totally changing their (those who survive the physical means) hearts and

minds—washing them clean of evil and negativity by employing the Brahmastra of the Gandhian Philosophy.

In brief, a truly effective strategy to deal with the terrorism of present times has to be a judicious mix of Lord Krishna and Mahatma Gandhi's philosophies and approaches.

The **fortified conventional strategy (FCS)** or the approach that should be adopted by victim states/ governments to deal with terrorism shall only suppress it, or even control the same to inconsequential levels—but it is not capable, on account of its basic limitations, in regards to eliminating it fully. **It can't give terrorism a decent burial.** The latter job can be performed by the GP only, which is a form of **Brahamastra** for cleaning up human evils that originate at the level of heart and mind.

In efforts to eliminate terrorism, attention has to be paid to **'mind over matter'** as the origin of the evil of terrorism is from the mind: It is there that thoughts or perceptions of discrimination and/or anger amongst the deviants originate, accumulate and is processed to emerge as actions of destruction—because they are neither trained nor are willing to adopt the ways of dialogue. Lots of falsehood and tainted unrighteous ideas are fed to them by their evil-intense handlers and financers. When the matter in form of evil infrastructure and recruits of terror are destroyed and/or weakened by the FCS, the formations of GP should start to handle the 'mind or thought energies' that have taken destructive form—and cool them through suitable applications of the GP components.

Forces of thought are far more powerful or stronger than any weaponry as the latter is dependent on the former for its birth as well as applications. The GP realizes it and has the capacity to transform the same to positive positions.

Before proceeding further, it seems necessary to examine the conventional counter-terrorism approach, its deficiencies and inefficiencies that limit its success—and how it is to be fortified.

Conventional Approach of Counter-terrorism

The conventional approach of terror management, among others, constitutes of the following action inputs, which cover the processes of investigations and up to prosecutions and punishments:

- Collections of clues of terror in terms of explosives (and other blast components) used by perpetrators of the crime, including the mentors and handlers of the foot-soldiers;
- Interrogation of arrested terror operatives—and also available witnesses to firm up such clues which could be useful in apprehending rest of the members of the trouble creating gangs—and also in reducing future attacks.
- Attempting to apprehend the perpetrators of crime based on so collected clues/leads, including intelligence contacts, informers, and former terrorists/convicts in custody or outside;
- Interrogation of suspects, and raids to apprehend the newer suspects and their supporters;
- Examining communication records of suspected/ apprehended persons for clues of linkages etc;
- Arresting suspects and obtaining their custody for further questioning;
- Corroboration of evidence/leads through narco-analysis, brain-mapping, DNA testing etc of suspected culprits;
- Eliminating non-cooperating yet dangerous suspects through encounters etc;
- Filing FIRs and follow up attempts to get the culprits punished as per laws of the land;
- Providing treatment and offering compensation to the victims of terror attacks, in an attempt to cool down the tempers of the suffering public;
- Managing public outcries, from kin of victims and also from supporters of the suspected/apprehended culprits (like the Batla house case);
- In complicated/controversial cases, ordering/conducting various types of inquiries, judicial as well as non-judicial;
- Intensifying/upgrading security measures;
- Adding/raising more battalions of armed security personnel and ATF etc;
- Examination, review and tightening of anti-terror strategies and approaches;
- Initiating/installing new anti-terror arrangements;
- Training and retraining the staff of security agencies; and amongst others,

- Political management of anti-terror security measures.

All the above actions/aspects of terror management are complex activities, individually as well as collectively—and add to the cost of governance on one hand, and throw up newer challenges , on the other. The complexity of these approaches further grows in secular and democratic systems of governance like that of India.

As a consequence, the security apparatus steadily grows in size as well as its complexities, yet they continue to be ineffective, at least in countries such as India, Pakistan, Sri-Lanka, Afghanistan, Iraq, and Lebanon, etc. What makes the security apparatuses and/or agencies of governance to fail in this job is examined, as realistically and un-emotionally as possible, in the following paragraphs.

Ineffectiveness of Conventional Approach

The main factors which render the present conventional anti-terror measures ineffective, in the opinion of the author, are primarily constituents of the following:

1. First and the foremost, the conventional approach in fighting terrorism is of **'Reactive Nature,'** which is not likely to work in case of terrorism. Terrorists are not normal criminals; they are different, motivated, and indoctrinated. Most of them have lost their capacity for logical thinking and compassion by the time of getting seriously involved in this evil activity. A lot of them do not even qualify to be called as humans—because they do not act as human beings. Their animal tendencies override all logical understandings.

Perpetrators of terror do not have fixed locations, not to think of a fixed approach; hence, in a reactive approach it is difficult to catch or apprehend them after the act of terror is undertaken. Being foxy in character, perpetrators of terror scatter and disappear quickly after undertaking an evil act. They have their safe house, handlers, and protectors for support as well as guidance.

> To succeed against terror, the anti-terrorism approach (a combination of specifically selected measures) has to be **'Pro-active'** i.e. get to the terror outfits and/or their cells before they act and inflict any damage. Through efficient intelligence terror

groups/cells have to be penetrated and neutralized well in time, right in their safe houses and training camps.

Pre-emption and thus prevention through it has to be built in as a crucial component of the FCS.

The means of terror detection and prevention have to be much sharper and efficient than those employed by its perpetrators.

The principle is to kill the terror and/or terror operatives before they strike. Let them worry about the preventives—rather than giving them to cause the damage and get happy about it.

Deny the evil operatives and their supporters the pleasure of succeeding.

2. Secondly, weak anti-terror laws of a country (like in case of India) **act as hormones** for the terrorists and their mentors. Particularly, the mentors and managers of terror, including the foot-soldiers love such weak laws—as they get assured of being quickly taken out of police and/or legal custody, employing vast resources of legal skills and financial means available at the disposal of terror outfits.

In India, after the repeal of '**POTA**' the legal conditions were just right for terror managers to get their front-line people quickly out of the clutches of police and legal confinements. Let us see how effectively and substantially they are changed after the Mumbai episode of 26/11.

While combating terror, '**prevention is always more important than post-incident control measures.**' An anti-terror law, to be effective, must be capable of deterring acts of terror through provisions of strong or '**unacceptably strong punitive measures**' **(USPM)** for foot-soldiers, as well as, their handlers, mentors, and financers.

Terrorists, as a matter of principle, do not respect softness: They love it as a child loves ice-cream! They also do not like to miss opportunities to strike and prove their omnipotence.

3. Thirdly, what negates all anti-terror measures is the **"inadequate quantum of punishment"** or **IQP**, both during, pre- as well as post-terror action periods. Very much like the sub-standard dosages of antibiotics which convert **bugs into super-bugs**, more virulent and non-responsive to future medications,

IQP is loved by terrorism's managers and mentors: It emboldens them in no small measures.

It allows them more space, reasons and stimulus to be active, affording them a visible fact for boasting to their future recruits. And, in this business, nothing works better than a proven evidence of their efficacy.

Democratic systems of governance, which depend on multi-party combinations to form and run a government, as is the case in India, normally become a victim of IQP while dealing with the deadly evil of terrorism. Any **'weak-kneed policy'** encourages terrorism—and eventually it raises the cost of the system in facing this menace.

Terrorism does not respect weakness of action and/or speed in its opponents:

It respects only strength.

This character of evil and wicked has been visible right from the days of Mahabharata, as such forces under command of Kamsa of Mathura, Jarasandha of Maghadh, and Duryodhana of Hastinapura, and also their friends and supporters, responded only to the truly punishing forces of **Lord Krishna**[4] and his allies, the Pandava brothers.

Additionally, the **fear of reaction** from kin and supporters of the evil forces in cases of severe punishments like encounters and pre-emptive arrests keeps several apparatuses of governance in perpetual paralysis of indecision. This too encourages terror rather than diminishing it. India faces several such unhelpful situations.

Procrastination on part of the bodies of governance on need, timing and/or severity of action too acts as a hormone to the networks of terror.

As per one school of thought, it is better to eliminate suspected terrorists rather than allowing them time and opportunity to strike again and kill innocents and unconnected people and destroy their properties. The other school argues vehemently for human rights of those who kill mindlessly innocent and unconnected people and in a democracy such opinions do carry sufficient weight-age and considerations, often rendering responses to terror ineffective.

The case of Maulana Masood Azhar who was released by the NDA government, along with two other deadly terrorists, and was taken to Khandhar, as a VIP, by the then India's foreign minister, Mr Jaswant Singh, is a case in point. In subsequent years, this dreaded terrorist and his apparatus of terror called the JeM, accounted for several massacres of innocents and unarmed in India—and even in the post-Mumbai carnage scenario, he retains a prominent place in the list of most-wanted that the Government of India handed over to Pakistan—and on which no prompt action (or even a delayed one) is expected.

Another such bright example (of desastrous consequences) belonged to the Karzai government in Afghanistan. One terrorist, Maulavi Ghulam Dastagir was personally freed by President Karzai on full assurance from a delegation of elders from his village, who had assured that the subject terrorist now onwards would lead a peaceful life in the village. On 27th November, 2008, in his own north-western province of Afghanistan i.e. Badghis, he led an attack on a large convoy of the Afghan army—killing nine soldiers and wounding twenty seven, and destroying nineteen vehicles, and stealing over half a dozen with arms, ammunition, and other supplies.

This ambush that followed a Presidential pardon to an unreformed terrorist became a matter of great embracement to the Karzai government. It goes to prove that un-reformed terrorists directly released from custody under pressure, irrespective of its origin and intensity, is a great folly that is loved by terrorists.

4. Fourthly, the **unwillingness of the machinery of governance to strike at the roots of terrorism**, like its training camps, indoctrinators, mentors, managers, handlers, and financers, keeps this anti-people system well-kicking and thriving, as there is no dearth of foot-soldiers who could always be attracted by the lure of money or service to their God.

Political interference with the working of security agencies is the greatest '**performance deficiency generator**' or the PDG, as far as the anti-terrorism actions are concerned. Politicians start taking sides of their vote-banks which are hurt or cornered by the anti-terror agencies—and, in the process, they do not care for larger objectives.

In addition to the above enumerated PDGs, a truly successful conventional anti-terrorism policy has to effectively **dry-up terrorism's support base,** for all of its essential causatives and sustaining elements, the major ones of which are:

- Religious and the so called moral indoctrination elements who process the unsuspecting foot-soldiers into committed terror operatives at the grass root level;
- Channels and sources of finance supplies which grease and fuel the terror apparatus;
- Sources of materials, arms and ammunitions which are necessary for converting evil intentions into scenes of blood and gore;
- Sources of manpower, the technically trained ones and raw foot-soldiers for giving the final shape to terror plans;
- Political outfits that hinder in neutralization of the terror perpetrators by giving them political, moral, and financial support; and
- NGOs which act as human rights support groups, as well as the media, the coverage from which the terror outfits finally look for, as proof of their success and efficacy.

All the above elements or impediments should be tackled in a manner that terrorism does not draw any supportive or sustaining incentives, otherwise the war against terror would continue to be inconclusive for a long time to come.

Further, corruption in the systems of governance is a great hindrance and it easily tends to generate conditions similar to those of Afghanistan—where anti-terror funds end up lining the pockets of terrorists themselves.

Moral and/or Immoral Indoctrination

Numerous **'centres of moral (or immoral) indoctrination'** or CMIs, such as madrasas, religious seminaries, religious colleges, universities, masjids, temples, churches, mutts, ashrams, and gurukuls, just to name the major culprits in indoctrination of young minds and raising an army of potential foot-soldiers for terrorism, exist in and outside of the terrorism affected countries.

They are primarily run by the so called men of religion, the primary mischief generators against the peace-loving majority.

Most of these people, in fact, do not have any faith in religion (or at least in elements of true religion) or they just do not understand it. Just reading or teaching scriptures which are 7th century vintage or even older, does not a make a man religious. If one is not able to reconcile today's science i.e. the rules of nature and universe, with the spiritual concepts and be able to put and promote the same to the good of mankind, then how could he or she be called a person of God? It is, indeed, difficult to comprehend for the impartial minds, religious or otherwise.

Superstition and mere ability to loudly recite some mantras and verses—and dressing-up in a peculiar manner, can not make any one religious, or God loving.

Yet, this camouflage or make-believe deception is able to influence young innocent minds into accepting their unrighteous utterances as gospel of truth. All such people of God, irrespective of religion have one single track agenda of creating large followings of misguided and confused people, particularly the youngsters—and amass wealth and socio-political influence in the process. Some of them specialize in indoctrination of young women and exploiting them in all possible manners.

Some of these CMIs in Pakistan, Saudi Arabia, Iran, Afghanistan, Iraq, Palestine, Lebanon, Syria, Egypt, Bangladesh, Indonesia, Malaysia, and numerous other countries work as the "**Crucibles of Terror**" or "**Universities of Terrorism**". Of these, particularly the ones located in Saudi Arabia, Af-Pak, Iran, and Bangladesh are of truly obnoxious nature and they draw substantial official state support, financially and otherwise.

The civilized world has to find a way of destroying these CMIs in a quick and effective manner and not allow any arguments of sovereignty etc to come in the way.

The '**international human work environment**' or IHWE can not be freed of the evil forces of terrorism until and unless these CMIs are not fully neutralized and finally replaced with or converted into teaching of secularism and/or universal brotherhood.

Apparently, to common minds, it looks like an impossible proposition as they do realize and believe that no aspect of terrorism is easy to deal with. Terrorism is decidedly a tough nut to crack and only tough tools could be successful in cracking the same open and scattering the contents into inconsequential fragments.

Any effective apparatus or approach of counter-terrorism should aim at cutting:

(a) Funds supply to such institutions of evil preaching, and
(b) Restricting the flow of the basic human raw material to such places of un-sustainable and evil teachings.

Since it is an international problem, only a supra-national—totally unbiased, and religion neutral programs, under the auspices of United Nations or UNESCO, should be attempted.

The civilized human society (CHS) has to get organized in this respect, if it has to survive and prosper in the near future. Terrorism and terrorists love to be around in an imperfect and unjust society that gives them ample scope to farm their evil designs and indoctrinations—and live and hide there.

Desiccating Terror Support Finances

As stressed earlier, wheels of terror do not move an inch without the grease and fuel of finance.

To go a step ahead, one could say that the seeds of terrorism do not sprout and grow without the life giving elements of finance: Here, the good money is put to bad usage—and the bad one is always eager to show its true colours in hands of the self-seeking religious teachers, preachers, clergy, and ulema on one hand, and the other breeders and managers of terrorism, on the other.

All agencies of governance engaged in anti-terrorism measures have the capability (or are capable of acquiring the same) to uncover flows of finance to the **crucibles and universities of terror,** if they possess the necessary determination to act against the same.

Once the sources or channels of finance to generators, carriers, and spreaders of terror are dried up, their cylinders shall not fire any more—and the seeds or nurseries of terror shall meet definite end right before inflicting any damages. This is the best and a totally bloodless or non-violent solution to the evil of terrorism.

Sources of evil finance that fuel terrorism have been discussed elsewhere in this work.

For a nation determined to fight terrorism, particularly the one with mixed demography and secularism, drying-up of the channels of finance is indeed difficult—and in a globalized market economy, it would indeed need a lot of ingenuity, persistent effort and a lot of international planning and coordination. But, when it is a necessity for securing future of the human race, the peace loving nations of the world should come together to create an effective system for this purpose.

Restricting Supply of Technology based tools of Terror

Denying all tools of terror to outfits that promote and/or carry out acts of terrorism is not possible—as local materials like ammonium nitrate, gelatine sticks, timers, nails etc. shall always be available. What is important is to restrict supply of deadly weapons and WMDs in order to keep restricted their damage inflicting potential. Their means of communication too have to be either restricted or infiltrated into. Here again, international co-ordinations are most vital to be secured and made effective.

LTTE acquired effective elements of airpower and naval capabilities; Al-Qaida and Taliban have anti-aircraft missiles, AK-47s and 57s; and fears are being expressed that these outfits might soon acquire even some kinds of WMDs in the near future. International cooperation, which normally is difficult to achieve, is most necessary for succeeding in this direction.

As per a recent report emerging from the Sri-Lankan governmental sources, LTTE had become the world's **'most innovative terror group'** from technology absorption angles. It is claimed that the outfit had developed a **'technologically superior suicide jacket'** which it had even sold to terror groups in West Asia. The LTTE earned the world's most ignominious record of over 400 of its suicide bombers, male as well as female, having died in suicide bombings since 1982. Rajiv Gandhi too had lost his life to the LTTE's evil technological adaptations.

Only an active international effort could have some preventive or restrictive efficacy in this regard.

Restricting Technical Manpower Supply

Terror outfits need access to high technology for making their acts turn into mass destructiveness. Anti-terror intelligence has to keep track of potentially susceptible students and operatives of high technology. Education and training institutions, including the elite ones, have to be sensitized in this regard.

After the incident of 9/11, USA seems to be exerting an effective surveillance of relevant technology teaching and training institutions, as well as, the students engaged therein, from third world countries, more particularly from the Islamic world. All countries which have suffered at hands of terrorism or those having potential to fall prey to it, need to act in a similarly cautious manner.

Minimizing Political Interference and Double-speak

Political game-playing or double-speak, like that from Amar Singh and Mulayam Singh of the Samajwadi party, and L.K. Advani of the BJP in India, is extremely helpful to terror elements to get bold and be excessively destructive.

"BJP's double-speak is lethal," screamed a news item in the New Delhi edition of *The Asian Age* of 24th November, 2008. The author of the said article elaborated that the doublespeak of the BJP had come full circle; even from its own self-serving double standards, it had plunged to a new low in the politics of summersaults, contradictions, and sifting-sands of disconnected statements.

In reference to BJP's opposition to investigations against the Malegaon terror operatives who were suspected to belong to its Sangh Parivar, and their eventual trial, the POTA for which the subject party, in the past, had been expressing a lot of liking and pleading, had now become **"Prevention of Trial Act"** for it. It did not show any shame or hesitation in taking such a summersault, despite the fact that it led to a loss of its political image in eyes of the Indian people.

Politicians Firmly Believe that Public Memory is short-lived

Keeping that in view, L K Advani, the then Prime Ministerial candidate of the BJP, and the leader of opposition till end of 2009, did not hesitate even in demanding a judicial inquiry into the conduct of the investigating agency called ATS. The fact that some senior officials of his BJP, from MP and Rajasthan states, were seen photographed with a lady conspirator of the Malegaon blasts, had un-nerved Mr Advani out of his judicious balance.

POTA (Prevention of Terrorist Acts), which was in force in India for sometimes, was viewed as highly efficacious in prevention of terror acts but soon a lot of hue and cry arose against some of its provisions and finally it was repealed by the UPA government.

Under this act, presumption of innocence that criminal jurisprudence offers an accused, did not apply and the burden of proof rested with the accused. It allowed investigators unhindered scope for investigation—and perpetrators of crime were brought to justice swiftly and often surely. The BJP and its NDA associates have been shouting in favor of these provisions of POTA, untiringly from political rooftops.

Now, when members of BJP's own Sangh Parivar were caught in the nets of Malegaon blast investigations, it no longer wanted the investigators to be given a free hand, but Mr. Advani wanted, all the way, a judicial probe into the working of Maharashtra's ATS investigators themselves. They wanted the investigation officers to be changed as if they had conspired with the government of the day, for heaping the blame on the BJP supporters. The same officers of the Maharashtra ATS sacrificed their lives on 26th of November, 2008, fighting against the heavily armed and evil motivated terrorists from Pakistan. The BJP had no place to hide its face as it had run out of turns and twists in blaming the apparently honest investigators.

The behavior of BJP's visible partiality raised a pertinent question—whether the security of the nation is sacrosanct or whether there has to be a caste system for the terror investigations, where the suspects related to the BJP and its Sangh Parivar are to be handled with kid gloves, and considered above law since they were from a so called nationalist organizations?

Such thought formations are fully untenable in a secular democracy.

BJP seemed to want application of different yardsticks in case of Muslim and Christian terror suspects than those related to its own family of Sangh Parivar. Such duplicity in a secular democracy is not permitable under any situation.

Additionally, **interference free management (IFM)** of anti-terror activities by people who know the job was highlighted by

K.P.S. Gill, who had successfully handled the evil of Khalistan terrorism in 1980s and 1990s, in his writings in the press after the catastrophic incidents of 26/11 in Mumbai.

The IFM of the counter-terrorism is an absolute necessity.

Doing away with Interference from NGOs of Uncertain Reputation

There is no dearth of NGOs of uncertain and/or unverified reputations, some with roots outside of India. They are seen jumping to help the accused people in all possible manners while none of them is ever seen doing anything for people who fall victim to the evil acts of terrorists. Western human right activists or their henchmen were a pain in the neck before the West was attacked through the 9/11 of New York, London tube blasts, and some other terror incidents. Now, they feel a lot subdued.

For such NGOs, the innocent and unrelated people who fall victim to acts of senseless terror, do not seem to exist. Security forces, which lose a lot of young lives while on anti-terror duties, too do not seem to posses any human rights in the eyes of such outfits. They too, like the politicians, play a game of utter duplicity. The Indian secular intelligentsia and even the nation's judiciary have now commenced seeing through the games of such groups.

Deny Free Publicity for Acts of Terror

The hormone of publicity not only allows terrorism to sustain itself, it speeds up its multilateral growth and reproduction. Terrorists get immense pleasure out of the reportage of their evil acts.

Managers of terrorism are able to justify to their senior religious and non-religious bosses, particularly to the financers that their effort and cooperation was worth the trouble. The media publicity rises in form of a proof that the managers of terrorism were able to deliver as per their commitments. Collection of more funds and recruitment of more foot soldiers and their handlers, including securing cooperation of tech-savvy professionals becomes easier with the availability of the gratuitous publicity from the free media, like the one that exists in India.

Publicity Rejuvenates the whole Machinery of Terror

And, it is free publicity that the media hands over to terror outfits just on a platter. Thus, public funds flow in service of terrorism. This must be curtailed, if not totally done away with, despite the noise that the human rights groups and NGOs might make for overt and covert reasons. Real time reporting of terror acts as was done in case of 26/11 needs to be prohibited in fainess to the victims.

Though not very similarly, security forces too love publicity: Under pressure of media and/or its disclosures, security forces too often dole out half-baked truths and untruths, which in more ways than one help the promoters of terror. The apparatus of terror has so much money that they can plant desired disclosures to misguide or put the investigating agencies on wrong tracks. They attempt and often secure mastery in usage and manipulation of electronic media skills.

During the terrorist attack on Mumbai 26th through 29th November, 2008, twenty four hour unrestricted TV coverage became available to terrorists in hotel rooms which definitely helped the terror creators assess situations and positions of security forces and decide upon more destructive directions.

Subsequently, the Indian NSG bosses admitted that intense live reportage of terror did hinder their operation. They requested the Ministry of I&B to put some curbs on live reporting of acts of terror, in interest of effectiveness of anti-terror operations.

> Why should these evil operators be allowed such unpaid advantages? There is no acceptable logic in the self-defeating approach of the so called free TV media. And the democratic system of India should in principle take a call on it—but political math and likely reactions do not permit it.

In principle, the media coverage of terror and terrorism should be so controlled that the basic objective of subduing this evil is achieved to the maximum extent. Media is for the service of people—not for scaring them and creating near panic conditions.

Some terror outfits show their efficacy and potency by running their own radio stations, TV channels, and even have newspapers to support their cause, whatsoever misguided or unjust it might be. Al-Qaeda, PLO, Hamas and ULFA, just to name a few, have acquired significant expertise in these fields. And LTTE had, at one time, surpassed all others in this field.

Deny them the Facility of Safe-heavens

Hardly, there has been any terrorism movement that grew and/or survived without facility of one or more safe-heavens. Some of the examples narrated below stress the point beyond argument to the contrary.

The Khalistan terrorism of 1980s and 1990s had sanctuaries for support and supplies not only across the border in Pakistan, it could draw massive support from Sikh elements from almost the world over, more particularly from Canada, USA, Norway, Australia, and the UK.

Pakistan, through its ISI, had taken the major responsibility of accelerating the movements of Sikh terrorism. It died an inglorious death primarily for the following reasons:

- The tough resolve of the Government of India to root it out—and the relatively free hand that it had allowed Mr. K.P.S. Gill, in-charge of counter-terrorism in the Indian state of Punjab, during its crucial phase.
- The basic inability of the business and prosperity oriented Sikh community to risk long-drawn conflict that could push it into the ruins of economic destruction.
- Relatively righteous secularist policies of the government of India that made it difficult for any significant world power to render overt support to the misguided elements of Sikhism; and last but not the least,
- The Pakistan's inability to risk a full-fledged encounter with India for a cause that had no logical justification and support from any significant international quarters.

The Sri-Lanka and LTTE conflict, during its initial stages had significant support from Indian Tamils. It almost dried up after the evil decision of LTTE to kill Rajiv Gandhi. Through its foolhardiness, the LTTE not only lost the goodwill of nationalistic Indians, the needed sanctuaries to its terror generating elements became uncertain and ineffective.

The unprovoked and inhuman manner in which the LTTE eliminated Rajiv Gandhi who enjoyed an international goodwill as a good and right thinking politician, reduced a lot of support that the LTTE was previously drawing from the world over. It became the turning point for the progressive downfall of this evil terror organization. Soon after, 2009, saw the final demise of this evil formation. FCS of the Sri-Lankan government finally destroyed it for greater good of all the people involved in the conflict.

The Palestinian terror organizations: PLO and Hamas had support and sanctuaries almost all over the Arab world. While petro-dollars from Saudi Arabia and other oil rich Muslim countries met its basic funds requirements, the ideological support and trainings, including arms and ammunition supplies, came from as diverse sources as Iran, Syria, and Egypt, just to name the few of the sources. The whole Islamic world gave it material as well as moral support which misled the key leadership of the Palestinian movement to take illogical stand—and eventual ineffectivity.

The Chechen militancy enjoyed widespread support from the Central Asian countries and the Arab world, in addition to Pakistan which at that time was engrossed with the dream of assuming the leadership of the Islamic world. The movement failed one—because of the no-nonsense handling by the Russians, and two-due to lack of desire and/or capacity on part of its supporters to earn and face an active Russian ire.

The Irish terrorism in Northern Ireland enjoyed a sanctuary just next door.

Further, large Irish populations in USA and Canada which had moved there as a consequence of the infamous potato famine in the 5th decade of the 19th century, extended a lot of moral and financial support. What took the wind out of the sails of the long and brutal reign of terror was the righteous and accommodative spirit of the British governance, and some good mediating elements from across the Pacific.

There are many more instances of terrorism in the world which, on in-depth analysis, lead to the same conclusion—that whenever safe sanctuaries and support centres are denied, or should they dry-up for one or the other reason, terrorism normally tends to fade away.

CHAPTER 6

FORTIFIED CONVENTIONAL STRATEGY TO EFFECTIVELY FIGHT TERRORISM

Components of Fortified Conventional Strategy (FCS)

From effective counter-terrorism angle, a numbers of specific inputs shall need to be incorporated in the conventional approach to convert the same into an effective terrorism control strategy, of which the important ones are:

- India (or any country for that matter) should stop giving the impression of being a **'soft state'**.
- Toughen the country's anti-terror laws; sink political differences to bring in a **sufficiently tight law**, even tougher than POTA. The possibilities of misuse of a tough law are not an excuse not to have it—when a nation is faced with terror generated precarious situations. Terror perpetrators do not follow any civil law and as such are not entitled for any human rights prompted softness in dealing with them.
- **Fast-track courts** under the new law should ensure that terror culprits are quickly and effectively handled. Punishment delivery should become fast and be visible to people so as it acts as a deterrent.
- The concept of **human rights** of terrorists has to be done away with through suitable legal provisions and the NGOs which howl about it should be examined carefully for their origin and suspected collaborations with terrorism.
- Secularists should stop supporting, by implication or

otherwise, the perpetrators of terror. There should be a tough **religion-independent anti-terror** (RIAT) policy, and the same should not change with change of political parties governing at the centre. It should be a **'minimum accepted program'** (MAP) for all political dispensations.

- Treat 26/11 of India like USA did its 9/11, 2001. Closely study Israeli approach against terror and develop a **long-term anti-terror strategy**.
- Fight terrorism as it was fought in Punjab—each police station should be equipped and its occupants trained to function as an ATS. Raise necessary forces to meet the challenge and equip them to be at advantage as compared with the terrorists.
- Politicians and VIPs should stop to be the priority of security agencies. Technology and economic assets of India should be the priority for protection.
- Improve intelligence gathering to the Israeli level of efficiency; infiltrate terror outfits. There are no substitutes for workable intelligence—and it should be aimed at proactive neutralization of the cells and apparatus of terror operatives.
- India is a growing mass of people, a chaotic situation at rail and bus terminals and in markets and melas: It offers ideal situations for terror operatives to do the mischief and dissolve into crowds. Isolation and identification becomes so difficult. A **chip-based national identification** (CBNI) for all Indian nationals should be developed to facilitate the process of isolation and identification in crisis situations: and India has the technology.
- Since prevention and deterrence is better than cure, a successful anti-terror methodology has to have fail-proof instruments to destroy terror cells, hide-outs and training camps in enemy or potential enemy territory. For this purpose India should develop or procure **pilot-less drone technology**, like the one employed by US in terror infested areas of Afghanistan and north-west Pakistan known for harbouring large number of hardened terror groups. Excuses and explanations for such covert or overt actions could always be learnt or copied from the Pakistan government itself.

- Mercilessly **neutralize terror supportive cells** irrespective of community or religion linkages.
- Leave the anti-terrorism job to **competent security officers** and let politicians refrain from commenting upon and interfering with issues of utmost significance.
- De-link anti-terror responses, policies, and infrastructure from **vote bank politics**. Some provisions to de-register or punish political parties for not worrying about national security or for disregarding any steps in this direction should be made in the anti-terror law itself. Long-term disqualification of terror supportive politicians too needs to be looked into.
- Develop and implement a strict **code of behaviour** for politicians in respect to terrorism and national security. There should be limits to what they could say and those defying the same be treated as offenders under the anti-terror law itself. Politicians' current liberty to say unwanted and base-less things needs to be curbed with iron hand.
- Have a **federal agency** like FBI in USA; not allow states to interfere with anti-terror matters. Varied political interests of some states, in a soft democracy like India's, tend to encourage terrorism and separatism.
- Media should be restrained from doing the job of terrorists—spreading fear, far and wide, and not letting it subside through their 24/7 blaring. A code of conduct in regard to what and how much they could say and reveal is a must.
- Our **anti-terror approach should become pro-active** rather than reactive. The terrorists must be made to run for their lives and finally go out of business. It was K.P.S. Gill's approach that succeeded in a vastly more complex situation of Khalistani terror in Punjab.
- Supporters, financers and **sympathizers of terrorists** should be treated more harshly then the terrorists themselves; suitable provisions in the anti-terror law should take care of it.
- A code of **conduct for religious leaders** that could force them to de-link religion from politics and terror needs to

be brought in. Educate clerics of all religions in the practice of secularism.

- Education at primary level, particularly in madrasas and other institutions run by religious agencies, sanghs and mutts must be made **terror-neutral;** it should discourage communal differentiations of any type.
- Initiate persistent international efforts to **dry-up terrorist finance flow**. The free flow of money, covert or overt, as fuel for terrorism must be stopped.
- Correct the **Indian democracy's minority syndrome**—develop some arrangement preferably through a code of conduct for politicians for refraining from the needless use of minority and majority terminologies.
- Religion based naming of institutions, educational and otherwise, be stopped and all existing ones be forced to re-name themselves in a secular ways.
- **Religion and caste-based reservations** be replaced with income-based ones. The purpose of reservation has to be improvement in economic and employment standards only.
- The Constitution needs to be amended to **outlaw conversions** which always create tensions. Secularism could mean your assured freedom to observe a religion, not to convert others and create tensions.
- A code of conduct for **religious celebrations** be developed and implemented: They make a lot of noise and create tensions. Religious exhibitionism and symbolisms that offend or create reactive responses must be legally disallowed.
- Bureaucracy and the law and order agencies should be made to practice fuller and bias-free **inclusion of minorities** and economically disadvantaged people.
- Develop and implement the concept of **collective punishment** for local terror perpetrators and their supporters. Strong social condemnation can be an effective anti-dote against terror.
- And last, but most importantly, police reforms must be undertaken in a manner that the law and order apparatus of the country is made free from possibilities of interference from politicians—and politically camouflaged criminals.

In addition, for effective development and application of the **"fortified conventional strategy"** or FCS against terrorism, it has to incorporate, in suitable measure, the followings:

Superior Technology – An Essential Input for Effective FCS

Terrorists have international roots and linkages, which enable them gathering of modern technology of attack, communication, and coordination. The November 2008 Mumbai terror attack by ten terrorists from Pakistan, trained, motivated and equipped by the Lashkar-e-Toiba or L-e-T, had a significant input of **superior modern technology** (SMT) in terms of fire-power, communication and other enabling inputs. Against the SMT of terrorists, the Mumbai police had to make do with vintage rifles most of which were not fired for over a decade; their communication tools were even of greater vintage.

Comparative inputs and training deficiency always bring out the worst in trying conditions like facing well-equipped terror groups. There are no acceptable excuses in being unprepared or under-prepared.

In case of India, it was not the first case of being unprepared or under-prepared. Our police apparatus in states affected with Maoist terror too suffers from the same deficiencies and inefficiencies. Going a few steps back in the history reveals that the IPKF in Sri-Lanka too was surprised to find vastly better equipped LTTE forces, for which the former had to pay a disproportionately higher price in terms of more than unavoidable loss of Indian soldiers.

Why should a country like India, which is an acknowledged leader in information technology, on one hand, and not too short of funds, on the other, face such a situation of disadvantage, while dealing with situations of terrorism?

There is no simple and acceptable answer, except being infested with situations and practices of inefficiency and irresponsibility. But, if the **"Idea of India"** is to be effectively protected, then this attitude of stupid irresponsibility must change without any further loss of time.

Internationalization of Anti-terror Efforts

When the apparatus of terrorism grows too big, as that happened to the "**Pakistan-Afghanistan's Crucibles of Terror**", control and containment efforts have to be truly intense and extensive.

If India does not possess the means of destroying training camps, terror cells, and other relevant components of terror apparatus without physically moving into the terror-spewing territory and running the risk of a full-fledged war between two nuclear capable adversaries, then either it has to acquire the same without loss of time or get into a pact with some country like USA, which is endowed with proven capabilities. Joint multinational campaigns do have greater credibility and sell-ability for international audiences.

USA made significant efforts to internationalize the anti-terror efforts in Iraq and Afghanistan, but unfortunately it attracted over-criticism, on one hand, and on the other, missed the real centre of evil genesis located in Pakistan. Smooth talking and cunning diplomacy on part of the latter duped the originator and controller of **"War against Terror."**

In fact, the international efforts against terror have to get much more broad-based and intense, harnessing resources, capabilities and cooperation of all peace loving nations, if situations that could encourage initiation of an atomic war between rogue Islamist elements, on one hand, and India or Israel on the other, is to be avoided.

An intelligence study undertaken in this regard and submitted to US Congress for consideration by the new Obama administration, already predicts use of atomic WMDs by rogue Islamists by end of the year 2013.

International cooperation against terror outfits and countries encouraging the same through their actions of commission and omission has become a must and can not be delayed for long.

Application of the Concept of Collective Punishment

Terrorism is never an act of individual: It does not sprout in individual loneliness. It is a group activity; someone does the job of indoctrination while another provides finance and resources, and there are people to do the organizational and control jobs.

Foot-soldiers are the last link, in-fact the least important one from the point of anti-terror activities—their initiation as well as control.

There is little value in catching and punishing the foot-soldiers. The real culprits related to indoctrination, financing and management of terror must be tackled on priority. Since, terrorism is a collective evil manifestation, the anti-terror actions also should concentrate on collective punishment, even including strong community condemnations.

Social and community pressures are normally highly effective. Hence, the locations and communities which are found to promote terror should be strongly dealt with to make them desist from the same, through a measure of incentives and dis-incentives.

Lord Krishna[4] when he was faced with massive accumulation of evil and wickedness some five millennia ago had designed an approach of collectively punishing an errant community of wrong doers: For him there was no use of eliminating one Duryodhana or Jarasandha; all of their supporters, collaborators, friends, colleagues, and even gurus had to be dealt with for achieving a long-lasting solution to the accumulated evil.

Similarly, in the modern times too anti-terror activities should concentrate with means and actions that stimulate collective refraining on part of communities, from getting involved in evil acts of terror. Almost all human communities do have capabilities and practices of collective decision-making—and these age-old systems should be made use of for discouraging terror involvement of its members.

Honesty and Righteousness—An Essential Input for FCS

One cannot succeed against terrorism by being continuously untruthful; by apportioning blame where it does not belong or attempting to persistently shield its perpetrators, or allowing someone else do the inglorious job.

For the past over two decades, Pakistan has been consistently breeding terrorism by training and indoctrination of its foot-soldiers, handlers, managers and financers. It was directed at India with the objective of bleeding it white. Since, its basic objective was unrighteous and inglorious, the question of its success, beyond a level, did not arise.

Duplicity of approach i.e. saying something and doing something else or reverse of what is preached, does not work for long—as cat always tends to come out of the bag—making a situation embarrassing. It happened to Pakistan for its terror genesis and support to terror elements in India's Punjab and J&K. It could not remain covert over a long time.

Pakistan's efforts to take the leadership in the spread of **Islamic terrorism** did succeed but in the meantime, it could not escape the ire of USA, the sole current superpower in the world. Now, it is paying for its own follies perfected and practiced over a long time.

Truth came out when it got trapped in the US sponsored **'war on terror'** and was compelled to act against the very instruments of terror which it had diligently crafted and trained. Pakistan's own '**pets of terror**' started attacking its vitals to the extent that a severe conflict sprang out in the form of terrorist attacks on Pakistan's politicians and institutions of governance.

Blaming India or any outsiders did not help, as facts were otherwise, and people knew the same. When fully foxed by terrorist/suicide bombers attacks and not knowing what to do, the Pakistan authorities realized the futility (but only temporarily) of constantly telling the untruth. Its interior ministry's Chief Advisor, Rehman Malik, in a seminar in Lahore on 11th October 2008 (report from *The Indian Express,* dated 13 October, 2008) was reported to have said:

> **"Those carrying out terrorist attacks in Pakistan are neither Indians nor Americans—rather, they are our own brethren while those who were training them to do so were also our own people." But such admittances are often rare on part of Pakistani officials and/or politicians.**

This candid admission could not be held back any further because the cancer of terrorism in the Pakistani society which its leaders, political as well as religious ones, had nurtured for long with evil designs on their neighbours, had started having its toll. And some confusion and delusion had set in the Pakistani apparatus of governance.

Almost at the same time, the Pakistan President Asif Ali Zardari too had taken initiative to admit the truth and said that those spilling the blood of innocents in Kashmir were terrorists.

Several constituents of terror apparatus in Pakistan did not like it—nevertheless, truth even when coming out late has its own value.

Since Pakistan's civil administration is not the boss of the situation, Zardari was soon forced to take an about turn. It exhibited the conditions of confusion and delusion that had started to set in the Pak apparatus of governance.

If the evil of terrorism is to be fought effectively to its final burial, truthfulness in our utterances and dealings has to be one of the principal weapons to be employed. Blaming innocents and attempting to place blame where it does not belong shall not help. Terrorism has no friend or relation or religion—it will bite (as soon as an opportunity arises) the hand that feeds it: It will destroy the countries/religions that grow and promote it.

It will indeed be appreciated by the international community, if the Pakistani government or the official and unofficial managers of terrorism, come clean in regard to the ghastly Mumbai terror attack of 26-29 November, 2008. But, as per the currently visible symptoms, such energies of righteousness are not ready to emerge unrestricted in the deeply soiled socio-political environment of Pakistan.

As per considered views of the author, terrorism is a very inefficient weapon of grievance resolution or settlement. It is least suitable for employment against a neighbour. Why Pakistan faced difficulty in comprehending such a simple principle, is indeed difficult to understand.

Reform Education to Dismantle Universities of Terror

Education on communal/religious lines plants seeds for discrimination instead of reducing it, often being the advocated objective. Temporarily, it might increase opportunity—but, simultaneously, it strengthens perceptions of discrimination and eventually its practices, by people on both sides of the divide that it acknowledges and perpetrates.

The remedy, particularly for multi-cultural societies like India, UK, and USA, lies in totally secularizing their education systems—purging the same of all references/materials/practices related to religion, caste, minoritism, etc. The need for such a reform is most acute for the Islamic countries a number of which are working as **crucibles of terror genesis and spread**.

To persuade education/ training institutions, irrespective of levels, in regard to naming, manning, and managing them in a purely secular manner is the only effective way to minimize the chances of **anger and/or fear accumulation**. Religion, caste, creed, and community should have no role in preparing future citizens of any nation.

Any attempts to make designed misuse of religion, which is said to be the opium of masses, by itself, is an unrighteous approach and its results, all over the world, have not been peace and cooperation generating.

Freeing the curricula of all educational/training institutions, from madrasas to universities, of all the non-secular elements and/or biases will be an essential detoxification exercise. Secular contents that promote peace, harmony, tolerance, and universal brotherhood should be given a dominant place in the curricula.

No institution should be allowed to display and practice a minority or majority tag and/or character. It does not help a nation and/or a society effectively, in the long run, if adequate secularizing measures are not built in.

Staff and students inclusions/inputs in any institution should not assume a visible or perceptible communal and/or segregating character. All teaching faculty should be transferred/rotated on a compulsory basis within certain geographical limitations of a town or district in order to avoid genesis of conflicts of interest or undue areas of avoidable influences.

Such a reform in Islamic countries, particularly those currently acting as "Crucibles and Universities of Terrorism" will need concerted international or supra-national efforts.

Some UN organization should take lead to see that educational contents of all countries—at all levels are freed from conflict generating materials, historical and/or otherwise. In the interests of having a peaceful world community, such an effort can not be ignored for long.

Disallowing Criminals becoming Agent of God

God can not be so naive as to appoint criminals as his agents for change. Why should an almighty God depend upon unscrupulous Jihadis to do His bidding? He could have better recourse—as he is said to be so resourceful and omnipotent. If He accepts jihadists help and rewards them in paradise, then how can He be omnipotent?

Those who kill Allah's own innocent creations can not be dear to him! So, there is no way that the jihadists could be dearer to the Lord than his other creations, particularly the law abiding innocent people. They are definitely deluding themselves—or it is just an evil way that the terrorists employ for justifying their evil acts.

Secular and righteous clerics from offending communities and/or nations should be employed in **de-toxification** of affected communities—they should be made to correct the wrong done earlier by them and/or their colleagues:

... this too will need concerted international efforts.

Force Transparency on Part of Terror Tolerant or Terror Promoting Regimes

The apparatus of terrorism as assembled by the evil Islamist elements located in Pakistan, Afghanistan, Saudi Arabia, Iran and several other Muslim countries is likely to prove as a hard nut to crack because of their oil and narcotic money, on one hand, and a free flow of rabid clerics from numerous mosques and seminaries, which compete to overdo each other—and foot-soldiers from a chain of madrasas with 7th century curricula, on the other.

Governments of such terror supportive or tolerant countries have to be pushed into observance of total transparency in terms of activities and flow of terror emerging from these and related sources, through persistent international efforts. By any standards, it is not going to be easy— but there is no way except regular crystal clear feedback on their machineries of terror perpetration.

Condoleeza Rice, the US Secretary of State for the pre-Obama administration, while on a visit to New Delhi on 3rd December, 2008, after the Mumbai terrorist attack by Pakistan based elements that left over 180 people dead—and over 300 more in hospitals, amongst others said:

"If non-state actors operate from the confines of a state, it's a matter of responsibility if it relates to your territory ... Pakistan's response should be ... cooperation and tough action. That is what we expect."

The above remarks came when she responded to press queries in regard to Pakistan President, Asif Ali Zardari's unsuccessful attempts to disassociate the state of Pakistan from the evil elements such as LeT and Al-Qaida, reared and pampered there for long by successive governments and the ISI. He had used the term **'non-state actors'** for the Pakistani terrorists who had attacked Mumbai in the last week of November 2008.

The trouble generating countries like Pakistan do not have to be left lightly, if any success has to emerge from terrorism containment efforts.

In the post-Mumbai terror attack of the last week of November, 2008, **Madeline Albright**, the ex-US Secretary of State, called Pakistan **"an international migraine,"** saying that it was a cause for global concern as it had nuclear weapons, terrorists, religious extremists, corruption, extreme poverty, and was located in a very important and vulnerable part of the world.

While none of it made a pleasant reading for Pakistan, Ms Albright's analysis is hard to dispute. Pakistan's nuclear WMDs could fall into the hands of jihadis, any time, in presence of a weak and collaborative government in place. Unfortunately, most Pakistanis, instead of gathering courage to face the reality, are resorting to the perpetual denial. When faced with truth, they wanted to bury their heads deep in sand—and attempted to say that no such danger existed.

For most of them, not in private as they knew the truth—but in public space, the Mumbai terror attack was a handiwork of Hindu terror elements located right in India. All proofs of Pakistan's and its ISI's involvements, despite acceptance of the same as true by USA's CIA and other international intelligence agencies, were fabrications indulged into by Indian apparatus of governance. This approach of a thief rebuking the watchman could not be tolerated for long.

In final analysis, the international community shall have to find a befitting treatment to the **"international migraine"** that Pakistan has allowed itself to grow into. Is Pakistan going to heed the international worry? The chances of such a change of heart, as per the analysis of the author, are almost non-existant. The treatment to this obnoxious disease, most likely, is to emerge from ruins of Pakistan, which neither strategically nor economically seems to be endowed with energies for long-term survival.

As per Indian and international intelligence, Pakistan and its ISI run over a hundred terrorist training camps (40 in Pakistan, 50 in POK, and another 30 across the unmarked border in Afghanistan), all of which have to be destroyed if the international community desires any relief from fear of Pakistan's WMDs raining on select urban centres of business and tourism.

Does the international community have a choice? Most likely none, other than, dismantling the Pakistan's apparatus of terror—and assuming control of its nuclear WMDs.

Neutralize Terror Sponsors' Super-expertise in Lies and Untruth Fabrication

Pakistani perpetrators of terrorism, particularly its organisers and enablers, both inside and outside their government, have perfected most superior expertise in telling untruths and lies, and in fabrication and presentation of camouflages for the same.

"Do—and deny" has become the 'mantra' of Pakistan's genesis and export of terrorism. Even when being face to face with you, they are capable of saying that they don't see you.

For them Dawood Ibrahim, the renowned international criminal and under-world operative, despite his big bungalow and even bigger business in Karachi, does not exist there.

Further, none of the 42 India origin criminals who committed most heinous crimes in India before escaping across the border—and the list of whom, with addresses, was again given by the Indian government after the 26/11 Mumbai terror attacks, is traceable through their all-pervading police and security networks.

Pakistani government officials could lie to US diplomats, and the whole world's assembled representatives at the recent UNSC meet that considered banning of LeT and other terror organizations responsible for the Mumbai carnage, without even lowering an eyelid. They are so well-trained and experienced in the intricacies of lying. Most probably, lying is very handsomely rewarded in the heaven, as per the scriptures read by them, if any.

They seem to literally believe in the Nazi government's formation that a lie, often repeated, automatically converts into truth.

Constituents of such an apparatus, as the official and non-official (or the non-state actors as they prefer to call them) organizers and supporters of terrorism from Pakistani territories, do not easily respond to application of the soft correctives to be effective: These evil elements need a thorough pulverization, employing a heavy dosage of force as envisioned under the FCS, before application of the softer inputs of the GP.

Apply the Principle of Selective Destruction

A cancer which does not respond to medication has to be surgically removed—and the same needs to be done before it spreads to adjoining body organs, creating unmanageable situations and/or emergencies. The same principle applies to the people, organizations, and regimes of evil dispensations.

Lord Krishna,[4] over 5,000 years ago followed the well-accepted **'principle of selective destruction',** as a vital tool for management of evil regimes concentration. He destroyed cruel and public unfriendly regimes and replaced the same with more humane and efficient ones. Evil and wicked rulers were hunted with uncommon regularity in preference to good and righteous.

The long-drawn destructive feud of cousins, the Kauravas and the Pandavas, was settled through the **grand 18 day battle of Kurukchetra,** wherein approx.60 percent of over 4.5 million battle participants were killed. Major part of the evil and wicked dispensations were destroyed in one go. What was left, decided to cooperate under the righteous Pandava dispensation that came to power after the battle.

In the present situation of terrorism concentration in the Indus and Hindukush range of South Asia, the international community or the sole superpower shall have to exert itself to destroy the **'crucible of terrorism'** so wickedly assembled in Pakistan and the adjoining areas of Afghanistan. And, any delay or hesitancy in executing plans in this regard will not be in the interests of the world community.

Pakistan's WMDs will have to be removed and placed securely at some hundred percent safe locations. The evil terror generating regime shall have to be broken into four or five small inconsequential units, in addition to the destruction of evil organizations such as ISI, LeT, JeM, Al-Qaida, Taliban etc.

It has to be a component of the FCS for effective management of terror generating apparatus in the Af-Pak region. It will cut off, or at least reduce, the supply of terror managers and indoctrinators.

Employ the Brahmastra of Corruption-free Society against Terrorism

Corruption is an ardent ally of terrorism.

This association has been re-certified in Afghanistan in terms of US policy failures in regard to narco-trade, for control of which it has been spending large funds for the past several years.

In the past six post-independence decades, India always had a parallel economy that was often patronized by politicians and a large section of small traders who had perfected the art of staying out of the tax net. Similarly, the big business's crony capitalists, senior bureaucrats, and almost the whole senior babudoom, the underworld mafia, terror perpetrators, and its managers, and most significantly, the police who are assigned the delicate responsibility of curbing the great menace of terror, took full advantage of the situation.

At the grass-root level, each time a RTO is issuing an irregular driving licence for a consideration, or a passport or ration card is being made, the forces of terror take a new leaf, invigorating the whole network of the apparatus of evil.

And, the process of corruption, on daily basis, serves delicacies of opportunities to the vicious elements of terror to strike at the roots of our largely secular society.

The Mumbai carnage, and many others which preceded it, were caused, fed and fuelled by active corruption in our apparatus of governance and public control. Corruption helps terrorists and their managers to hire or acquire **safe houses, transport, new identities and a string of supporters and collaborators.**

In a corruption-less society terrorism can never germinate and/or grow: Hence, a successful anti-corruption drive could be a Brahamastra against the disturbing evil of terrorism. But it is neither easy to acquire nor operate.

Can the civilized society, especially in South Asia, take the challenge of cleansing itself from the diet of corruption? The increasingly informed public of the region has a right to agitate in this direction—and persist to design a platform to hang the devil of corruption. Terrorism will then die an unsung death.

Develop FCS into a bi-polar Approach to Tackle Terrorism

In order to fight terrorism with any perceptible success, a victim state should firm-up and implement its **FCS with a bi-polar flexibility**.

It means, in other words, that **the hard nut of terrorism is served with strong-enough direct and destructive response, not only to crack open but to crush it, along with its roots and shoots of supporters, financers and enablers.**

Terrorism does not respect weakness, hesitation, and knee-jerk responses; it mocks at them. So, the direct response has to be really hard and destructive so that the managers of terrorism are forced to change their evil thinking, in interests of their very survival.

Simultaneously, on the opposite pole, the people who serve as roots and shoots of terrorism, not so much from the force of hard conviction but circumstantial conveniences, have a chance to retreat and reform. **For them the provisions and facilities of Gandhian Philosophy should be made available in an easily and extensively accessible manner. Such a provision shall work as an escape route on one hand and on the other, a genuine opportunity to forgive and forget—and start a new line of mutually supportive engagements.**

Terrorism: Need for a Supra-national Approach

Since terrorism is a product of deficiencies, deliberate and/or otherwise, in the international governance, its control too will need '**supra-national efforts**' which transcend the boundaries and sensitivities of sovereignty. No country, whether Pakistan and/or Afghanistan, should be allowed to raise the invalid question of sovereignty, as the impact of this evil product of the demonic perpetrators is running across the international boundaries, on land and across the seven seas.

Both the approaches discussed herein, the FCS and the GP have to be rigorously applied where-ever needed—and the supra-national cooperation needs to break the resistance in the name of national boundaries. USA is already debunking the Pakistani bogy of sovereignty in regards to its drone attacks on the elements of Al-Qaida and Taliban, deliberately sheltered in the hilly regions of the latter. More such efforts need to be initiated and supported if this greatest threat faced by the humanity is to be effectively tackled.

Not only the physical destruction of the infrastructure of the terrorism needs supra-national efforts, the applications of the GP for preventing the re-greening of the ideology of terror shall need co-ordinated international efforts,

Some FCS Success Stories Against Terrorism

With the application of FCS, terrorism has been contained, and even controlled, in several cases, of which the following ones are worth attention in the current international context.

- ❑ Post 9/11 US security scenario;
- ❑ Israel's tight safety belt; and
- ❑ K.P.S. Gill's Indian Punjab.

1. For the lone super-power, 9/11 was an attack on the very "**Idea of America**"—and the strongest pillar of capitalism and the free civilized society. It was not only a wound on the psyche of the giant of the free world but a hand-full of salt was rubbed into the same.

USA took sometime to emerge from the shock of 9/11: It was very difficult to accept the curbs on the body and mind of care-free civil life. Equally tormenting was the idea of American infallibility falling apart in public view and the might of great state looking helplessly at its classic structures.

USA took all the pains and insults in its stride; did its sums thoroughly and decided that 'enough was enough'.

It tightened its security procedures and practices to a level that certain inconveniences so caused could be tolerated with the dream of a promise of terror free future. The US public cooperated, though a little grudgingly; and even foreign visitors suffered the same with inconvenient dignity.

A committed George W Bush took the war on terror to the home of terror genesis (the Islamic world); though a mistake in targeting the same made it go a little off the mark. A more befitting and rewarding target than Iraq, the "**crucible of terrorism**"—namely Pakistan was left out through an error of judgement; it is difficult to say whether it was done intentionally or otherwise. In the ensuing years, the left-out culprit of terror genesis and nurture converted itself into an open "**Furnace of Terrorism,**" which is now ready to ash a significant part of the international community.

Terror-proofing the territories of USA was decidedly successful as a result of application of the FCS—and slaughtering the evil of terrorism in larger context will take much more international effort and resources. It has a good chance of coming through if the new US administration of Barack Obama turns out to be equally committed.

2. Israel lies in the sea of antagonistic Arab world, which has not forgiven it for the brief war of 1967. It left Israel with much extended territories into Syria, Jordon and certain other areas. Though, it has not seen much of peace since then, it has successfully protected itself from any catastrophic terror attack, **through a proactive usage of FCS.**

Israel's intelligence gathering is intense and responsive—and its response to terror often proactive. Whenever terror succeeds in striking any of its territories and/or citizenry, the response is swift and punishing.

Its army is fully and perpetually prepared to face the expected, as well as, the unexpected. It has not allowed Hamas, PLO or any other terror group to grow too big for its shoes—and, whenever needed, leaderships of such enemy groups have been eliminated in numerous successful initiatives.

Israel learnt to respect the lives of its citizen long back—and it is for this confidence that Jews from world over still continue to arrive and settle in a hugely risky environment.

Despite odds stacked against it, Israel has not given any signal of weakness, overt and covert. Its political leadership has remained firmly committed to the **"Idea of Israel"** and its security. Technologically, this small nation has succeeded in collecting and creating all that it takes to give a great impression of serious security.

Despite being small and of very limited resources, it has conveyed the massage of no nonsense to its belligerent neighbours.

Is it not a great success story worth emulating in full?

3. Not long ago, we had a great success against the evil forces of terror in India's Punjab, thanks to the uncommon leadership of K P S Gill and late Beant Singh, who was the Chief Minister of the state at that crucial time. The latter provided foolproof political leadership to the no nonsense field leadership that Mr Gill had provided to the anti-terror police and paramilitary forces.

KPS Gill, as per his own expressions, believed in snatching the initiative from terrorists: He made them run from one hideout to another and no time in day or night was safe for these merchants of terror, to venture out and commit a misdeed.

He modernized and trained the Punjab police as per requirements of the situation—converting each and every police station or **"thana"**, as it is called in India, into an ATS.

Politicians were not allowed to interfere and those supporting terror or sympathising with it, were given a tough massage, which made them retreat to non-damaging positions.

A very clear objectivity, good leadership, and a well-defined responsibility assignment made the terrorists and their foreign supporters to retreat and or get eliminated in the long run.

CHAPTER 7

GANDHIAN PHILOSOPHY FOR ELIMINATING TERRORISM

Lord Krishna's Approach Towards Management of Evil

Can Gandhian approach be effective in tackling the menace of terrorism? Experts, as expected, have varying views in this context. Some of them jump to comments even without understanding it.

The author, however, is firmly of the view that for any long-term success against terrorism, FCS should be combined in a right and persistent dosage with the Gandhian Philosophy (GP), because as per **Lord Krishna's wisdom concentrate approach** to management of **wicked and devil** tendency people (very similar to today's terrorists), the following five approaches were tried and tested for fuller success. These are:

(a) In depth analysis of situation;
(b) Intense dialogue to dissuade the evil minded ones from their anti-people activities;
(c) A harsh dose of force to crush those evil and wicked who do not listen to logic and persuasion;
(d) Replacement of so eliminated evils with virtuous and righteous rulers; and
(e) Finally, leaving behind a 'wisdom concentrate' to guide newer generations for a long time.

The last two of the measures to deal effectively with the evil of terrorism have to come from the GP, while the first three are taken care of by the FCS described earlier in this work.

It is, however, necessary here to warn that the GP is not a **bullet-proof jacket that can hold AK-47 or 57 fusillades of bullets:** It is a **cooling and cleansing device** (CCD) that frees human mind, heart and soul from manifestations of evil of anger, terror, fear, revenge, and bitterness. GP can be employed:

(1) In the pre-anger explosion stage, to cool down tempers, and

(2) In the post-anger explosion situations, it helps both the victim and the terror perpetrator in forgiving and forgetting—and finally in wiping off the traces of bitterness and discord.

GP operates on depths of mind and heart, freeing human spirit or soul from limitations of anger, hatred, greed, attachment and non-inclusiveness.

Further, GP is not a tool for weak and coward: It is an instrument of brave and righteous, or the true kshtriyas (warriors for righteousness) who know how to sacrifice for good of humanity.

Let us recollect, origin of **ahimsa or non-violence** is not new: It was clearly visible in **Arjuna's**[4] forceful arguments with Lord Krishna on the battlefield of Kurukchetra, some over five millennia ago.

Arjuna, the great Pandava warrior, did not want to fight for regaining the kingdom of Indraprastha from evil Duryodhana, his cousin—as the same involved fighting against and killing his own cousins, friends, relations, gurus, and even grandfather. The whole certainty of large scale blood-shed did not appeal to him. He argued hard and for long with Lord Krishna who had elected to be the charioteer of the great warrior, in favour of non-violence, and this whole argumentation is enshrined in the great work of wisdom called the **"Bhagavad-Gita."**

In final analysis, **Arjuna** was not able to convince the great Lord about the suitability of abdication of one's duty as a warrior when faced with an evil accumulation that was not receptive to arguments of righteousness, compromise, and collective welfare. Attempts to persuade the evil Duryodhana for not insisting upon his wicked ways had been a failure.

Further, it was a great chance for **Lord Krishna**[4] to eliminate the vast gathering of evil and wicked people, the rulers and their supporters, who had for long traumatized righteous and virtuous people. He had to meet his own commitment and promise as a '**mission incarnate**'—and, as such, it was not possible for the great Lord to let this opportunity slip away from his hands. Hence, he argued hard and convinced **Arjuna** that, in those circumstances, violence was justified.

In this chapter, attempts are made to analyse and assess individual components of the **Gandhian Philosophy** from the standpoint of their applicability, as well as, the GP's potential efficacy in handling the great menace of terrorism. Its instruments of '**ahimsa, universal brotherhood, and truth**' are looked at with a degree of priority as these can be highly effective as preventive as well as curative measures, if taught and promoted on large scale in areas and communities where potential for germination of terrorism exists or which have already been taken over by the evil.

Being Home Grown: Essential pre-requisite for Effective Applicability of the GP

For GP to be effective it must be 'home grown', as an outside input is not easily accepted in troubled and/or unrighteous communities. The term **'home grown'** does not mean that Gandhi has to take birth in such troubled communities—it would suffice, if some persons of righteous thoughts and behaviour are able to study, absorb and practice the GP in an intense and committed manner—and spread the same to components of their community with a sustained persistence . These passive resisters of violence or the soldiers of non-violence should essentially be locals who understand the terror perpetrators well enough and are identified as constituents of the same community. External help for emergence and training of such people could come from outside.

GP or any of its components does not work in isolation, or with remote control. GP's soldiers or passive resisters must be supported in their initial growth phase till local support makes the movement self-sustaining —as it sets the terror perpetrators and promoters thinking, and such a thought genesis finally leads to their imbalance from the path of evil and unrighteousness.

On 17th of January, 2009, Dalai Lama, the current leading light of Buddhism, while speaking to a gathering of intellectuals at New

Delhi, was reported to have observed that non-violence was not the tool to encounter the terrorists. This comment emerged from the learned speaker either in an isolated context or in light of inadequate thought inputs given to GP's action methodology, as non-violence is just one of the several components of the GP, which works best when used in form of appropriate situation specific capsules of action inputs. There could also be reporting deficiencies on part of the press, in this regard.

Where-ever the GP has worked effectively in the past, whether South Africa, USA or India, its action inputs were spearheaded from internally germinated and reared passive soldiers. Outside inputs were limited to ideological stimulations and/or inspirations. And results did take time to emerge as change in human thinking and behaviour patterns is a slow and pains-taking process.

> And as said earlier, GP or any of its components is not a bullet proof jacket which one could sport and straight-way jump in front of terror and humble it.

Ahimsa or Non-violence as a Tool Against Terrorism

> During the struggle for independence of India, the renowned Gandhian leader Khan Abdul Ghaffar Khan had successfully converted the fearsome Pathans and other tribes of the NWFP, into totally non-violent, cooperative, and community serving **Khudai Khidmatgars.**

Here, the Gandhian movement was home grown in the sense that its leader was a local Pathan who was influenced by the GP and participated in several of Mahatma Gandhi's campaigns.

One has to first deeply believe in a philosophy and undertake experiments with self before attempting to convert others. Same highly disciplined and cooperative people of Pakistan-Afghanistan border areas are now manning the **apparatuses of terrorism**. These changes have occurred due to leadership deficiencies, over the last 2-3 generations that emerged in six decades of post-independence period.

The philosophy of non-violence has to be learnt anew and practiced intensely before it is ready to take on terrorism. It does not work in a half-baked or quick-fix manner.

In view of the current spurt of terrorist violence in several parts of the world—particularly its genesis and spread in the Muslim world, inclusion of **Gandhian studies** as part of curriculum at various levels of education will be highly effective in inculcating **anti-terror temperament (ATT)** in young minds—and, thus, finally it could move towards eliminating the evil of terrorism from face of the earth.

Another great and current success example of '**ahimsa**'s **capability of anger management'** is that of Dalai Lama, who has been able to keep a large mass of Tibetan refugees in India, totally peaceful, in their agitations to secure some functional autonomy for the Tibetans.

Though not much success has been achieved, primarily due to the Chinese leadership's intransigence, the genesis and spread of terrorism amongst these people, which otherwise would have been very easy, has been successfully avoided. Dalai Lama calls himself as a successor and disciple of the Gandhian Philosophy.

> For the effective applications of the GP towards terror management, UN institutions should actively promote this concept, as essential requirement for member countries, for qualifying to receive any financial, technical, and/or any other type of assistance.

In communities/societies affected by terror related violence or influence, such studies could be effectively employed for cooling the tempers and altering negative thought processes on long-term basis.

Thich Nhat Hanh, the great Vietnamese Gandhian, a tireless advocate of non-violence and peace, views **'terrorists themselves as victims who create more victims.'** Their thought process, as per the wise monk's assessment, is vitiated as acts of terror have roots in anger, fear, hate, and wrong perceptions.

> **He recommends preventing anger from becoming collective energy. And only GP has that divine capability.**

> Since the international diplomatic community does not have requisite grounding in the GP, they do not attempt to promote it as an alternate approach towards conflict resolution.

On priority, they should be benefited from intense lessons of the GP.

The only **anti-dote for anger and violence**, as per this great advocate of peace, is compassion—and not forgetting that terrorists too are victims, who create other victims directly as well as through escalating misunderstanding.

As per this **great disciple of Gandhi**, and an ardent advocate of non-violence, terrorists are in their own **self-generated trap** (SGT). Their information, perceptions, and the mentoring that they are getting is not right—these are not helping them—and it is making them angry and violent—they want to punish. It is a confused state of the minds with victim perceptions, wherein evil has overtaken the righteous thought genesis.

They need to be helped—and the best way to help them is that their seniors (who have cured themselves of anger accumulation) from their community should hear them and help them in greater humanised rationalizing. Bringing them face to face with their innocent victims might speed up evaporation of their anger and frustration, This could be done only by their immediate community only: Police cannot help towards this goal, at least not in the beginning.

GP's all applications must emerge and intensify locally, to be acceptable and effective.

With attention and compassion they can start understanding their folly. He added:

> "Peace negotiations will be successful if both parties have mutual understanding and know how to use deep listening and loving speech. This kind of training should start at the earliest level of education. This is 'peace education' and it is the way out of war and violence."

And peace education is nothing but exposures to the principles and practices of the GP.

Non-violence can never be taken in absolute sense. It can, however, be employed to make aggressive violence less violent, like avoiding loss of innocent lives or minimising reactions to acts of violence.

For greatest effect, it has to be employed in conjugation with several other tools and inputs (a report in New Delhi edition of *The Times of India*, 2nd October 2008).

Outside India, in Mahatma Gandhi's first Karma-Bhumi, the South Africa, **Nelson Mandela** and numerous other leaders of the **African National Congress** or the ANC came under influence of the Gandhian Philosophy, which had several significant manifestations of its effective instruments in South Africa's struggle against its white rulers' intense apartheid and segregating discrimination.

As per Mr Mandela's own admission[18] the **Natal Indian Congress** (NIC) sponsored and managed non-violent agitation against the white rulers' discrimination and atrocities heaped upon the Indian community there, influenced him and his colleagues a great deal. A small reproduction from the great revolutionary's autobiography illustrates the contention with adequate illumination.

> "The Indian campaign became a model for the type of protest that we in Youth League were calling for. It instilled a spirit of defiance and radicalism among the people, broke the fear of prison, and boosted the popularity and influence of the NIC and TIC.
>
> They reminded us that the freedom struggle was not merely a question of making speeches, holding meetings, passing resolutions, and sending deputations, but of meticulous organization, militant mass action and, above all, the willingness to suffer and sacrifice.
>
> The Indian campaign hankered back to the 1913 passive resistance campaign in which Mahatma Gandhi led the tumultuous procession of Indians crossing illegally from Natal to the Transvaal. That was history; this campaign was taking place before my eyes."

The practice of GP helped the ANC a great deal in keeping the **pot of anger** of the suffering and discriminated against black majority from violent boiling. It kept violence down and restricted and helped Nelson Mandela and other leaders of the ANC survive long-terms in white-men's jails, for a long period, without really breaking their will and determination.

After end of the white minority rule in this strife-torn land, GP helped a great deal in **forgetting and forgiving** perpetration of numerous inhuman atrocities committed under conditions of unmanaged or mismanaged human thought eruptions.

Further, some of the great applications of non-violence by Mahatma during the four decades for which he ruled the political skies of British India were:

Application of Ahimsa in Riot-terror Management

In September 1946, following Calcutta as if it were a well-planned effort, wide-spread violence and rioting irrupted in numerous villages of Noakhali in East Bengal, caused and aided by the elements of Muslim League, under patronage of its apparatus of state governance (it ruled Bengal at that time), against the minority Hindu community, leading to a lot of killings, mass conversions, and rape.

This district of East Bengal was flooded with Maulanas, Maulvis, and Hajis, a lot of whom were brought in from north of the country. Fanatical passions of the majority Muslim population were aroused by evil preaching and prodding of the clergy present there in large number. Muslim politicians had joined hands to oppress the Hindu population who were living there under conditions of terror and dread.

These riots seemed an organised response to the call for direct action, as issued by the Muslim League, under directions from Mr M A Jinnah, with the overt call for getting rid of the slavery under British and fear of losing dominance to the Hindu community after independence.

On 10th October, well-organized mobs led by Muslim clergy and politicians, engaged themselves into large scale killings, lootings, and rapes, as they roamed a large number of villages, creating unimaginable devastation of human life and properties. The fabric of multi-culturalism and tolerance was torn-off mercilessly.

In some villages regular classes were held to force the converted Hindus to recite kalmas and ayats from the Holy Quran: People were compelled to eat beef. The team of Sucheta Kirpalani and her colleagues were made to witness and hear most of it, as they had proceeded to these centres of rioting before Mahatma went there. When Mahatma Gandhi came face to face to details of the misfortunes of the suffering victims, he said:

> "My ahimsa will have to pass through an ordeal of fire this time."

The Mahatma was shocked but his faith in his own preaching was strong enough to confront terror heads on. He persisted and succeeded because he was a master of dialogue and a skilled craftsman of his own GP.

But, this terror was different than the organised and over-armed terrorism of today.

In the meantime, an independent and impartial team of Indian Civil Service officers had confirmed the extreme inhuman-ness of the atrocities committed on the Hindu population of a number of villages in this area.

Mahatma Gandhi reached Noakhali on 7thNovember, 1946, and immediately dispatched his volunteers to go to some villages and attempt to cool off the communal situation. The Muslim clergy and the League politicians were not happy to see Gandhi there, and a lot of efforts were made to see that he retreated from the trouble spot. He was a great fire-fighter and the Muslim clergy feared him.

> He had to fight his way through an anti-Hindu administration of the Muslim League, but the Mahatma was not made up of elements who gave up easily.

At long last, army was called in and the combined efforts of his team introduced some temporary order in the fluid pre-partition period. Gandhi organized mixed prayer meetings of the two communities, every morning and evening. And about the situation in Naokhali, he said that his motto was, **"do or die."** And he came out of it alive and at least partly successful, despite the ganging up of the whole state administration and also the Britishers against him.

By early March 1947, Gandhi was in Patna to review the riot situation in Bihar, as the Muslim League was blaming him for not caring for Bihar's Muslims. Soon, the unfolding partition scenario forced him to proceed to Delhi but he was not destined to stay there for too long.

On 7th August, 1947, Gandhi again left for Noakhali in view of renewed deterioration of situation, but he had to stop at Calcutta for handling the communal situation in the city. Though his experiments at Noakhali did not get completed , he had to stop at Calcutta on request of Muslim Chief Minister who earlier had not hesitated in calling him the **"No-1 Enemy of Islam,"** for restoring peace: He resorted to fast at Calcutta to bring riot situations under control. He, thus, remained out of Delhi when partition of the country was officially announced.

Mahatma's approach of non-violent persistence had demonstrated that the worst variety of Islamists could be handled and mollified with application of his practices.

Without Gandhi's **"ahimsa,"** loss of human life and property in Bengal, Bihar, Calcutta and Delhi would have been definitely far beyond imagination. That the two communities were able to talk to each other, and pray together during the difficult times of partition, was a direct miracle of Mahatma's presence and his **"ahimsa".** It gave a lot of healing touch and did unimaginable wound dressing.

Bidyut Chakrabarty[19] in his work entitled, **"Mahatma Gandhi: A Historical Biography,"** elaborated, as under, on the vital tool of **non-violence**:

"Semantically, non-violence means refraining from causing harm and destruction to others and is thus a negative concept. For Gandhi, however, **non-violence connotes positive resistance**—probably an appropriate method to politically mobilize Indians against the British at a particular juncture of history. Not only is the method well tuned to the Indian situation, it is also a means to build character in conformity with the well-entrenched Indian tradition. So despite its apparent negative content, non-violence, in its positive and active sense, results in organization for political action, which is grounded in compassion and love. Drawing on the Hindu, Buddhist, and Jainist tradition, Gandhi seems to have arrived at an all-compassing definition of non-violence by means of three crucial steps:

(1) non-violence in Gandhi's explanation, is compassion which is equated to love;
(2) like all other emotions, love constitutes a formidable force, and
(3) love is thus an alternative to the prevalent ideology of political mobilization."

In this reference, Gandhi implied that we should not aspire to subdue an opponent without pushing violence out of our own system. He [21] said:

"Until you are sure you have an overpowering love at heart

for your enemy, don't think of driving him out. You must generally forget the term "enemy." You must think of him as a friend who must leave you. You must train yourself to become a 100 percent ahimsa soldier."

For Mahatma, non-violence was not only an individual value: It could also be a rule of conduct for the society, if it were to live consistently with dignity. He had made non-violence obligatory for all of his followers—and he wanted common people too follow it.

Gandhi had no doubt that **'the power of unarmed and non-violence'** is any day far superior to that of the armed force. He had realized the strength superiority of non-violence in South Africa, where he was pitted against substantial organized violence and prejudice. And subsequently, in several Naokhali type situations in India. His tool of **ahimsa or non-violence** always came out of these situations successful and un-dented.

Non-violence was thoroughly field-tested against the mighty British imperial power.

Gandhi saw non-violence as a way of taking a fight to enemy camp: He had argued that non-violence did not mean meek submission to the will of the evil doer but it meant pitting of one's whole soul against the will of the tyrant—and he often elaborated through his writings in *Harijan*, a part of which is reproduced below:

"Non-violence is not mere disarmament. Nor is it a weapon of the weak and impotent. A child who has no strength to wield lathi (stick) does not practice non-violence. More powerful than all the armaments, non-violence is a unique force that has come into the world. He who has not learnt to feel it to be a weapon infinitely more than brute force has not understood its true nature."

It has to be felt and cultivated in heart of a seeker through the grace of God.

Non-violence, thus, was the weapon for those who possessed tremendous mental strength. It's adoption and application was not strategic consideration contingent on the situations because

Mahatma never allowed any space for violence in his conceptualization and the practice of satyagraha.

Mahatma Gandhi wanted all of his followers, Indian Congressmen included, to search for any residues of violence in their hearts and minds, and come forward to participate in satyagraha only if they were sure of their total freedom from violence, even when faced with grave threats of it. It was a stringent requirement—and most of his followers passed the test.

For Gandhiji, ahimsa was a conscious choice, because according to him, the use of violence was fruitless as it did not generate a genuine change at all. In his own words:

> "Violence may destroy one or more bad rulers, but like Ravana's head, others will pop up in their place for the root lies elsewhere. It lies in us. If we reform ourselves, rulers will automatically do so."

Gandhiji's faith in non-violence's ability of changing the rulers like the British imperialists did look inadequate to many leaders and followers of that time and the same could be said about its utility against terror. But teachings of **ahimsa and satyagraha** can definitely help a lot in cooling and cleansing off the minds of terror perpetrators to a considerable extent, if a right dose of these divine inputs is delivered.

For Gandhiji perception and/or practice of the non-violence never had any shade of cowardice—and hence, on occasions he upheld use of violence in preference to cowardice. He observed:

"Where there is only a choice between violence and cowardice, I would advise violence." The logic for such a preference lies in the fact that cowardice only encourages manifestation and magnification of evil acts.

Gandhiji justified the application of violence if an individual can not defend himself or his nearest and dearest or their honour by non-violently facing death, he may and ought to do so by violently dealing with the oppressor. In his views, he who cannot do neither of the two is a burden.

In views of the author, the role of non-violence in management of terrorism, in the present context, lies in its preventive or pre-genesis contextuality. Right inputs of education laced with the principles and practices of non-violence have the capacity of dissuading a lot of partly or newly indoctrinated minds from being pushed into active inflictions of acts of terror.

Further, teachings of ahimsa have profound utility in cleansing the evilly indoctrinated.

For Gandhiji non-violence was a well thought-out strategy in the political campaigns in South Africa, as well as, in India in view of white-man's methods of repression and his massive apparatus of oppression, against which neither terrorist nor revolutionary, nor the normal civil methods seemed effective.

For issue based campaigns non-violent methods had proved their efficacy in Champaran (in Bihar) for benefits of Indigo farmers, in Ahmedabad by textile mill workers, and most importantly for the success of the salt campaign at Dandi and several other places.

Combined Tool of Satyagraha and non-violence

Satyagraha means, **"Insistence for Truth;"** often also referred to as, **"Civil Disobedience."** And when combined with non-violence (or ahimsa), it converts into an omnipotent **Brahamastra.**

Gandhiji coined the term **'Satyagraha'** in 1906 at Durban in South Africa while fighting against the racist registration laws of the white minority government. While thousands of agitators refused to get registered as per Gandhi's guidance, he was dissatisfied with the usage of term, 'passive resistance' in the agitation. He wanted a more forceful term that could convey a lot of moral force and meaning of righteousness.

The term, **'Satayagraha'** evolved with the efforts of inhabitants of **Phoenix ashram** near Durban, and it eventually imbalanced the British empire on both sides of the Indian Ocean. The resulting word combined the **twin themes of truth and firmness**. Sataya, as noted, means truth and agraha means, **'forcefulness or grasping.'** Satyagraha, thus, is persistence for truth, firmly holding onto or striving for truth.

> At times Gandhi defined Satyagraha as, "pure soul-force or truth force."

Writer George Orwell was not an admirer of Gandhi, yet he was morally forced to admit Gandhi's uniqueness: He wrote,

"Gandhi's attitude was not that of most Western pacifists." He added, "Satayagraha was a sort of non-violent warfare, a way of defeating the enemy without hurting him and without feeling or arousing hatred."[22]

Mahatma Gandhi had employed it at numerous critical occasions in South Africa and in India during the first five decades of the 20th century, to successfully fight and subdue the forces of discrimination, apartheid, repression, intimidation, exploitation, violence, and terror—and, almost in all situations, he came out with flying colours.

The two ends of this weapon, namely **Satyagraha and Ahimsa** are of equal significance but the former has decisive significance in determining its efficacy—because it is able to boost impact of non-violence several folds, as truth can not be resisted for long even by the mightiest oppressors.

The tool of Satyagraha gained decisive currency during Gandhiji's campaign against the Rowlatt Bills, beginning with 1919 and it set the tone of anti-British campaign in India: It enabled Gandhiji consolidate his leadership as an undisputed leader of India's political assault against the oppressive British imperialism. This **'non-violent non-cooperation'** infused significant energies into the otherwise stagnant nationalist politics of the then India.

During the next phase of non-violent civil disobedience or Satyagraha, from March 1930 to 1934 (with intermission during 1931) had its significant manifestations in form of attacks on the British Raj policies towards government's salt monopoly and the boycott of. foreign cloth. The **absolute non-violent resistance of the salt Satyagraha** volunteers against unexpected brutalities perpetrated by the British controlled police apparatus had amazed the world that had watched this campaign with interest.

It had effectively loosened the roots of British control over the people of India.

The unarmed non-violent salt volunteers had defeated the British terror: The energies of truth and ahimsa had a symbiotic manifestation, thus creating a moral outrage towards the alien administration.

The campaign against purchase and usage of foreign cloth, or its boycott, was of much greater economic significance, as its impact adversely affected the economic viability of British textile factories back home. While the British authorities were tormented, it created a vibrant constituency for Indian National Congress amongst local textile business houses and trade. Without even a gram of gunpowder, Manchester was bombed to dust by the non-violent boycott of its products in the British imperialists' greatest textile market.

Non-violence had triumphed in this case as a **means of political action**. Having been alarmed by these successes, the British worked extra hard to break the Hindu-Muslim cooperation by igniting the **two nations' theory**; they fed the baseless anxiety in minds of Muslim leadership—and were successful in their nefarious designs initially in the Muslim majority provinces of Bengal and Punjab.

In view of Mahatma's proven experimentations with the Satyagraha and Non-violence, this combined tool of grievance redressal could be very useful for those harbouring accumulated anger and frustration, and even accumulated ill-will, which eventually tends to erupt into acts of violence and terrorism. They can, forcefully, put across their point of view—and, if truth is on their side, the same is most likely to be resolved without loss of life and property.

It is, however, dependent on a forceful and persistent presentation by a community's seniors—the parents, teachers, and the clergy to the young minds. Proper and timely teaching and learning will determine the efficacy of this Brahamastra—as nothing operates without adequate preparations and resultant stress balance.

Thus, the terrorists do not know the worth of Gandhi's methods; otherwise they could have achieved a lot more of their objectivities without creating any bloodbath.

And, the apparatuses of governance, national and/or international too do not have any exposure to—or grounding in the GP's technology of conflict resolution—and hence, no initiative has emerged in direction of applications of the same for blunting the forces of terror.

Truth and Righteousness

'Satya' or truth had its manifestation in Gandhi's **"Satyagraha."** It was the '**moral force**' behind the Satyagraha, in its all forms and manifestations—such as non-cooperation, civil disobedience, and/or peaceful dharna (meaning strike); and also the non-violence that went along to make all this effective and irresistible, was based **on inner truth and strength** only.

In final analysis, terrorists tend to lose their struggle because either it is not based on truth or the same, even if presenting it to some extent, gets soiled by blood and gore. It loses its visibility as well as appreciation in cloudy situations of violence.

Lord Krishna[4] championed the cause of righteousness and truth all through his long struggle intense life, and was successful in banishing the evil and wicked from face of the earth, for the forces of truth, in final analysis, are always victorious.

In all human societies, teaching truth and righteousness is never difficult as scriptural pasts of all religions and communities are full of them. Only difficulty arises on part of parents, teachers, and clergy who are either not efficient in practice and communication of the same—or due to accumulated evil and unrighteousness have lost faith in the same. Narrow selfish interests and desire of quick gains or unrighteous leadership propel them on to such wrong paths.

Gandhiji had said, **"Truth is God."**

Search for truth excludes the use of violence; and in this reference he added, **"Because man is not capable of knowing the absolute truth and therefore is not competent to punish."** Thus, the terrorists and/or their masters have no justification in hurting and killing people, except for their multilateral confusion and clouding of logical thinking.

Only exposures to the GP could help clean up their mental cobwebs.

In regard to truth and non-violence, Mahatma Gandhi had further elaborated:

> "There are two ways to achieving God. They are truth and non-violence. If you follow these principles, you can reach God."

Can here be any simpler path to God? The perpetrators and preachers of terror need to be taught this through the unique instruments of the GP. They might develop a liking for Gandhiji's divine method as it is so simple and effective—with absolutely zero loss of human lives.

He even said that in ultimate analysis, "Truth and Non-violence' are God. Though it is difficult to follow them in an absolute sense, one should keep on working on these lines to achieve the ultimate."

Since Islamic terrorists are so enamoured for pleasing the God by fighting for him, the GP's ways could be most rewarding to them if, the same are properly taught to them.

Intense teachings of GP should make terrorists and their masters see logic in final approaches—but a lot of patience and persistence shall be necessary in such efforts. It has the basic capability for all conflict resolutions; the two sides of the evil coin should, however, make or be pushed to make genuine efforts.

Had the Palestinians and Israelis invested even five percent of efforts that they have put into conflict genesis and its continuation, into studies and practice of the GP, the history of the Middle-East and, by implication, of whole the world would have been different.

Samvada or Intense Dialogue as a Tool of GP

Dialogue has been an important tool employed by all great personalities, prophets and incarnates in human history, written or otherwise, that often helped it change its course.

Lord Krishna[4], through-out his event intense life, employed dialogue in dealing with even the leaders and rulers who represented the evil and wicked. He tried his knowledge and divine communication skills, even his special **madhura technology**, to dissuade the unrighteous rulers from engaging into anti-people policies and practices. Since, as per the manifesto of his being in this world, he had to decisively deal with the evil and wicked forces, those not responding to logical persuasion through dialogue or '**Samvada**' were physically done away with through the use of his preferred **Brahmastra, the "Sudershana"**.

Mahatma Gandhi too was a great believer and practitioner of '**Samvada**' or its expanded form, the Sarva-Dharma Samvada, whenever he healt with communal forces. Even with the leaders of the Muslim League who were a difficult nut to crack, their leader MA Jinnah who was bitten by the **two nation theory** bug, the equally tricky Britishers, B R Ambedakar on demand for separate electorate for India's dalits, and numerous other equally demanding and inflexible negotiators, Gandhi engaged into intense dialogue using moral force and facts as resources to back his point of view.

More often than not, he was fairly successful in his missions; and wherever success did not come easily, he persisted with renewed efforts. Even when pitted against evil communal elements during riots in Naokhali and Calcutta; he did not let his logic, fairness, and persistence desert him in any manner.

How would he have dealt with the terror perpetrators of today, is a matter of conjecture. Since he was not averse to employment of violence when it becomes unavoidable in right contextual situations, he would not have hesitated in use of force in Mumbai carnage like terrorist created situations. But, if and when opportunity allowed, he would have had recourse to dialogue, as a first choice.

Thith Nhat Hanh, a renowned Gandhian of Vietnamese experience, was recently posed the following question by the media in relation to terrorism (*The Times of India*, New Delhi edition of December 6, 2008).

"What would you say to a terrorist?" His GP-based reply was as under:

> "First, I would listen. Why had he acted in that cruel way? I would try to understand all of the suffering that had led him to violence. It might not be easy, so I would have to remain calm and lucid. I would need several friends with me, who are strong in practice of deep listening, listening without reacting, without judging and blaming. In this way, an atmosphere of support would be created for this person and those connected so that they could share completely, trust that they are really being heard.

After listening for some time, we might need to take a break to allow what has been said to enter into our consciousness Only when we felt calm and lucid, would we respond in such a way to help them discover their own misunderstandings so that they will stop violent acts of their own will...

When we react out of fear and hatred, we do not yet have a deep understanding of the situation. Our reaction will only be a very quick and superficial way of responding to the situation and not so much true benefit and healing will occur. Yet if we wait and follow the process of calming our anger, looking deeply into the situation, and listening with great will to understand the roots of suffering that are the cause of the violent actions, only then will we have sufficient insight to respond in such a way that healing and reconciliation can be realized for everyone involved.

In South Africa, the **Truth and Reconciliation Commission** has made attempts to realise this. The presence of strong spiritual leaders is very helpful to support such an environment."

Dialogue by knowledgeable and spiritually respected people, thus, can be a great tool for dealing with terrorists before they commence their evil acts. A gap of hope, to make them understand their folly, does always exist: Whether the evil-filled individual, at that critical moment, is able to disconnect, is a deciding question.

Lord Krishna had made even a last ditch effort to dialogue with the evil Duryodhana in the latter's court of Hastinapura, to allow a small accommodation to his Pandava cousins, so that the clouds of war could be wiped away from the horizons of Hastinapura. Duryodhana not only failed to disconnect from the evil that had taken hold of him, he attempted to harm the great **Lord** for having attempted the impossible reconciliation, for which he was given a befitting rebuff and reply.

Duryodhana had not attempted listening because he was an evil concentrate; he could not connect to Krishna—and had to pay with his life and that of a large number of those who supported him. Finally, truth and righteousness had prevailed.

Mahatma Gandhi was a great listener: He could quickly connect with the target person or persons of dialogue. His dialogue expertise emerged with flying colours during the renowned **round table conferences,** and several multi-party and/or multi-religious interactions. He could communicate without saying anything or through small chits of paper when he observed mon-vratas, the non-speaking fasts.

Righteousness or the soul force energises the dialogue process: Mahatma Gandhi was not only aware of it; he made its productive usage in several situations.

Peaceful Mass-action as a Practice of GP

Peaceful mass action, by involving all sections of societies, particularly those with proven spiritual strengths is highly useful in resolving issues of larger interests. Mahatma Gandhi applied the forces of mass civil disobedience, peaceful dharna and strikes, collective peaceful actions to break discriminatory salt laws of British India, and also for the sawedeshi campaign i.e. boycott of foreign made cloth and clothing, including filling jails whenever such an action was deemed necessary.

Gandhi was a man of masses: He understood strength of **'collective peaceful mass action'** early in life when he spearheaded campaign against certain registration requirements for non-whites, as imposed by the then South African government. He knew how to make masses move as he never hesitated in leading from front, and by himself setting examples.

Recently (in last quarter of 2008), in Thailand peaceful citizens collected in large number and took peaceful control of Bangkok's international airport that is known by the name of "Svarnabhoomi," thus compelling the government to accept their demands.

The Thai public was agitating for removal of their Prime Minister, whose performance was not to their satisfaction, and who resisted resigning from his coveted office.

Pakistani public too, if they elect to act in a peaceful collective manner, can easily force perpetrators of terror by marching in large number to the terrorist training camps and occupying the same till they are inactivated. It will be the simplest and most effective Gandhian method of terror management.

> And if Palestinians can learn and practice the GP technology, then they should be able to get all that they want from the reluctant Israeli government, at zero cost in terms of human lives.

There is a lot of power in a society's collective action: The feeling of righteousness in masses needs to be ignited through a meaningful dialogue based on truth and collective welfare. The leaders engaged in counter-terrorism activities need to study and understand the **Gandhian Philosophy,** and once some basic understanding of it is achieved, employing it for subduing the forces of terror shall not be difficult.

Most of the programs and campaigns of Mahatma Gandhi, including hunger strikes or fast unto-death were collective mass actions. He was not a loner; he could easily excite people into massive actions at short notice, a measure of a great leader's true popularity.

Programs such as untouchablty removal, khadi spinning for self-reliance, bonfire of foreign cloth as a symptom of boycott of products which were not benefiting the local public, non-cooperation with authorities of governance on various issues, quit India campaign, and numerous others, which broke the back of the British Empire, were all mass action programs.

Love, Compassion and the Healing-touch

"Love is the greatest instrument of Gandhian Philosophy."

Other components of it such as non-violence or ahimsa, satayagraha, dharna, non-cooperation, sanvada, untouchability removal, etc emerge from application of love in socio-political interactions.

Manifestation of true, selfless love and the love without fear and favour can win even substantially clouded and biased minds. It helps people to see reason. Love and compassion initiate the great process of healing-touch in people who hurt—or are victims of injustice: Those affected by terror too can benefit from it.

For putting at peace the aggrieved minds—the harshly treated ones and/or the wrongfully confined suspected militants or their kin, is very necessary for breaking the chain of continuity of acts of terrorism. It is best achieved through application of the **'forgive and forget principle'** of the Gandhian Philosophy.

Forgiving is a very difficult action—it is not the job of the weak. Only a mentally strong and righteously thoughtful individual can forgive the person or persons who committed unreasonable acts of hostility or terror.

Forgiving but not forgetting too is an incomplete act in the process of conflict resolution.

In the interests of long-term peace (for both the parties—the victim and also the tormentor), the process of reconciliation must end with forgetting i.e. wiping the imprints of undesirable events from mental screen.

In recent times, South Africa employed this **Gandhian technique** through establishment of a **'Truth and Reconciliation Commission'** before which appearance of the perpetrators of terror and associated crimes, as well as, their victims was encouraged: People openly admitted their crimes, shed tears, and forgave each other; it cooled off a lot of accumulated enmity between the whites and the blacks.

An honest act of mere admittance on part of the wrong doers and an expression of repentance cools off the residual fires that otherwise tend to linger within the victims.

For cooling the **accumulated anger** in terror affected youth, **fermenting Muslim minds** and correcting the **'Victim Syndrome'** of the community could be effected by application of this unique methodology of the GP.

In India, Andhra Pradesh police recently admitted wrongful treatment and torture of some two dozen suspected Muslim militants, in regard to the May 18, 2008, Mecca Masjid blasts in Hyderabad, in which nine people had died. The state government admitted that they were innocent and, as a healing touch, the sufferers were offered a rehabilitation package of Rs. 30,000 as compensation, and Rs. 80,000 as loan for starting a new life, as some of them had lost jobs and others found it difficult to get employed for the stigma of being arrested in such a manner.

For resettlement of not only the victims of terror but also those who give up terror and decide to merge with the mainstream of society, need inputs of love and compassion.

Thich Nhat Hanh, the great **Vietnamese Gandhian** has said that the only antidote for violence was compassion, which is made of understanding. To understand, we must find paths of communication so that we can listen to those who are desperately calling to be understood. This great Gandhian refers to Lord Buddha in this context as under:

> "There are people who want one thing only: revenge. The Buddha said that by using hatred to answer hatred, there will only be an escalation of hatred. But if we use compassion to embrace those who have harmed us, it will greatly diffuse the bomb in our hearts and in theirs..."

The technique of Buddha is to look deeper within our hearts and minds: It can help us answer inconvenient questions—some of which could be as given below:

- ❑ Why did the violence happen?
- ❑ What responsibility do we have in that happening?
- ❑ May be they misunderstood us?
- ❑ But what has made them misunderstand us so much to make them hate so much?

In brief, as the author believes, the Gandhian Philosophy can help us win the battle of minds—and then the battle of hearts too.

Religion Neutrality of the GP

Ghandian Philosophy is primarily based upon **truth and love and it is fully religion neutral**. It's all other virtues and constituents emerge from these two principal branches—the truth and love.

Since clergy of all religions have influence on people, especially on young and forming minds, all these religious leaders should volunteer or be persuaded to read and understand the finer aspects of the GP, so that the same could be further disseminated to students, even in madrasas and primary schools.

Mahatma Gandhi was killed for being partial: It was decidedly a misunderstanding as he had washed himself clean of bias and partiality long back. For perceived appeasing of Muslims, in the tension intense situation of partition, he lost his life. It will be in fitness of things to employ studies of his philosophy to wash our society free of terror genesis and its spread.

GP a Great Tool of Re-indoctrination

For de-indoctrination of arrested/surrendered or de-activated terrorists, GP could be a great tool of a long-lasting, rather life-long reformative impact.

Saudis are reported to have established some schools to retrain a large number of former jihadists who have been netted in anti-terror campaigns. These schools are intended to bring the misguided people back to mainstream of the society, preferably productive and responsive citizens. Once jihadists are given correct and unbiased religious training, means of establishing productive civil life, and are married, most of them are said to shake off the jihadist tendencies in a permanent way.

With close cultural connections, Pakistan can easily draw upon the Saudi expertise in this field.

Concepts of GP should help a great deal in this regard. The irresistible formations of this field-tested philosophy should be aimed at the following sections of the society, which determine and guide genesis and spread of terror tendencies:

First Priority: The clergy or the priestly class of all major religions, covering the mullahs, maulanas, hajjis, pundits, pujaris, saints, sadhus, sadhvis, preachers, reverends, priests, etc.

Second Priority: Key politicians at state, district, and block levels, irrespective of party of affiliation.

Third Priority: Youth in madarsas and schools.

It is no secret to any right thinking person that clerics—priests, and religious operatives of all religions, and more so in Islam, have the capacity to play a positive role in putting young people's thought process on right rails. It is well known that jihadi terrorism has emanated from radical and backward-looking strains of Islam such as **Wahhabism** and **Salafism**. It is also no secret that the dominance of these hard-line ideologies can be traced to Saudi backing and money.

The world-over mushrooming of madrasas and mosques that preach the ideology of hatred and conflict, is the outcome of this unholy connection. In Pakistan, LeT and several other apparatuses of hate and terror are known to have received the Saudi money. Pakistani state patronage is an icing on the cake. And, undoubtedly some in India too are receptive to the same ideology and finances.

All of them, without exception, including the saffron parivar, should get an intense and persisting dose of the GP. Substantial incentives need to be offered to people to study GP and excel in it—as the same is bound to result into a productive environment of tolerance and cooperation.

Islamic clerics, who are a figure of authority, when exposed to the GP, are bound to become highly productive assets for the nation in building a congenial working and living environment. A GP-exposed or influenced social environment will make it much more difficult to the merchants of terror to gain acceptability.

Soul-force for Effective Countering of Terror

Mahatma Gandhi never believed that the East India Company captured India by the dint of physical force. Instead the company was lucky to get the support of Indians in achieving its goal. Gandhi, in his own words, had described the phenomenon as under:

> "The English have not taken India; we have given it to them. They are not in India because of their strength, but because we keep them."

Same is the situation with the actors of terrorism in the Af-Pak and other countries afflicted by this disease. Terrorists are not there because of their strength—but because the locals tolerate and keep them.

Similarly, as per the author, violence has not overtaken our society because it is really potent in conflict resolution or has some miraculous powers, but because we have allowed it to get within us.

Mahatma's logic was very simple: Indians contributed to the company's (the East India Company) mercantile interests and hence the company prospered.

He explained the phenomenon with the help of the sale of 'bhang,' as unless the consumers' habit was kicked off, the seller will continue to be in the business. So, instead of blaming the seller one should change one's habit. Similarly, if Indians had not cooperated with the Britishers, they could not have taken over the country. It would have been impossible for them to survive here even for a day.

The communal divide of the Indians had come as a handy tool for them to divide and extract benefit. As per the Mahatma, the Hindus and Mohammedans were at daggers drawn, which had given the company its control over India.

In the present scenario of terrorism, terror represents the scheming East India Company, which is being helped by us to spread its wings into India, Pakistan, and Afghanistan, and beyond. By itself, it has no independent energies and resources for growth. We, the people of the region, are feeding this evil with resources, indoctrinations, and foot-soldiers, to do the nefarious job of killing innocents and unconnected.

We have to stop blaming the consequence (as terrorism is one) and look for its causatives within ourselves. Only unbiased and intense studies of GP can allow this to us.

Mahatma Gandhi, after analysis of the causes of spread of the East India Company, had concluded that it was not possible to throw away the British rule simply by physical force. He was dead convinced that the physical force was not the right means to defeat and repeal it. At that time the British had a great accumulation of physical force and to assemble an effective counter force for the freedom fighters was not possible. He searched hard and came to find the **"Soul-Force"** that, in his assessment, the Indian could assemble more—and the British being the intruders had none of it.

Having been so convinced, Gandhiji employed the Soul-Force against the British with a devastating precision and efficacy: They did not know how to react. His ahimsa, non-cooperation, passive resistance, dharna, fasting, charkha, khadi, boycott of foreign goods, sawadeshi, and all other tool and methods composed of this unique force only, helped defeat a large empire.

Against terrorism, we are, in fact, in a slightly better position than what Gandhi faced against the British rule. We have the adequate force and physical means to destroy the apparatus of terror. But its sole application will have two undesirable consequences.

One: The application of the needed amount of force will result in loss of a lot of human life and property; and

Two: The leftover roots, branches, and residues of terrorism will tend to re-assemble and re-grow with the passage of time.

Forgetting is not an area of strength for terror oriented people and their mentors—and even when defeated, they are likely to harbour an acute grudge for a long time.

Hence, the best strategy against terrorism shall be to employ needed force through the FCS, as described earlier and couple the same with application of the Mahatma's tools of GP, to cool the agitated minds, wash clean the indoctrinated ones, and apply the balm of love, compassion, and inclusiveness to impart a healing touch. An effective application of the GP can stop any regeneration of terror tendencies because it will rob its evil indoctrinators of the divisive tools that they employ.

There is no bigger or stronger force in the world than the 'Soul-Force' for combating evil and wickedness (including terrorism).

Employing the arguments inherent in the Soul-Force, **Lord Krishna**[4] had convinced the Pandava warriors to fight against the evil forces of Duryodhana, and his friends and supporters, on the battlefield of Kuruchetra. And the results were magnificent—the evil forces were wiped out from face of the earth and they took very long time to emerge and assume threatening positions.

Inclusiveness as a Tool for Terror Dissipation

Inclusiveness, which means inclusion of people from all strata of society in **programs** (welfare oriented or otherwise) of mass-action, was Gandhi's standard approach for activating human cooperation and collective action. It reduces or even eliminates the feeling of **not being consulted or left-out,** and as such, invites and catalyzes cooperation.

Mahatma was a great strategist: He had developed a **'multi-class model'** in all of his approaches and strategies of action against the British Raj. They were all superior works of inclusiveness.

The principle of inclusiveness was very distinctly elaborated by **Lord Krishna**[4], while delivering a **"Discourse of Wisdom"** to Arjuna before commencement of the battle of Kurukchetra: Later on, it came to be known as the **"Bhagavad-Gita" or the "Song of Wisdom." It still continues to guide and illuminate billions of lives in righteous living or at least efforts in that direction.**

The wise Lord had said:

"Everyone is dear to me."

He had elaborated to add:

"Everything is in me and I am in everything."

It epitomised the every concept of inclusiveness, which for human relations management, with common people or terrorists, is the most valuable **"Brahamastra."**

Mahatma Gandhi had studied works of most of the great people, incarnates and prophets included, and he made a very practical use of the "Principle of Inclusiveness" in his long and arduous campaigns against the colonial rulers in South Africa and India.

Gandhiji had perfected the technology of making effective usage of the relaxed and chaotic plurality of the traditional Indian life into an effective instrument of united action: It was the case of a '**vast span of inclusiveness**'. He constructed a viable nationalism out of a chaotic plurality of the Indian society, with the application of democratic glues of his thoughts and practices or the GP.

> Gandhiji was well aware of the fact that God's own creation—or Darwin's unique process of evolution is the supreme epitome of the manifestations of the Principle of Inclusiveness." He greatly valued and respected nature which is the supreme example of inclusiveness. Earth does not tell any human not to walk on it even if he or she is totally wicked and undesirable.
>
> And no animal is ever told not to graze the grass that grows on earth's surface. Gandhi had understood nature as the most unique example of inclusion.

It seems Allah is a great practitioner of inclusiveness: He did not want whole of his creation to be Muslim. He wanted a variety even in the faith fabric of the human race.

Allah or God created universe millions of years ago. He created a diverse mass of animals and vegetation. Similarly, for his human population too he wanted a good variety, some blacks, some white—and some brown. The religious variety too added to the beauty of its diversity.

For the faith of his human creations too the God did not want everyone to be a Muslim, or all of them to be following Islamic laws. Had he desired or designed a singularity of faith, then he could have sent Mohammad to the earth much earlier, right in the beginning of the human race on face of the earth. Since he did not do that right in the beginning, then why should he now want to disturb the equilibrium of living of his creations through the acts of some misguided jihadists or clergy?

Are not we, or particularly the jihadis, acting against God's own design of diversity, for our own unsustainable personal reasons and biased perceptions?

Righteous inclusion is the best way for not allowing the feeling of discrimination to build around.

Through this process of inclusiveness, anger accumulation gets no opportunity to work itself up to dangerous levels.

Through the process of inclusiveness, blame apportioning in a society of any unwanted happening of commission and/or omission, is very much minimised.

GP is very rich in elements of inclusiveness. Mahatma's activities of sarva-dharma samvada, mixed religion prayer meetings, collective agitations, padyatras, just to name a few, were full of the elements of variety and inclusiveness.

Terrorism will get quickly scared away when it encounters the collective energies of people, particularly when the same is spiked with the essence of the GP.

Constructive Programs as Components of the GP

Khadi, Charkha, and village industries were essential components of Gandhi's strategy for struggle against the British imperialism. He sincerely believed that the people had to be, constructively and remuneratively engaged with productive activities as per their capabilities and available resources. A situation of unemployment and/or being without work could aggravate the situations of income, and maintenance of social life.

> Mahatma viewed poverty as being truly de-meaning, or a curse, for the body as well as the mind of the so afflicted persons.

Mahatma's charkha and khadi had effectively destroyed the British textile industry in one clean and swift stroke. Further, he had constructively occupied his volunteer force during intervals that invariably occurred between satayagrahas and agitations.

We don't have to revert to Mahatma's tools in the present case against terrorism; it is cited here for its symbolic value. But, today's youth that is being lured to terrorism, for money and/or other benefits, will have to be suitably occupied even after they are helped to come out of this destructive quagmire.

Constructively occupied minds, if they are not intensely polluted by evil indoctrinators, are not easily preyed upon by the forces that are promoting terror. Once the religious clerics and politicians are suitably sensitised by the powerful elements of the GP, the provision of constructive occupation shall definitively help in frustrating the forces of terror because it will make the restorative forces stronger than the residual destrucive ones.

The author has a firm opinion as to why the commercially well-occupied Sikh community could not sustain the terrorism in Punjab for long; its inability to sustain the economic disturbance that was the result of it, allowed the agitation and terror to evaporate.

Further, the excellent occupation of Punjabi youth in productive works made regular supply of foot-soldiers really difficult, in the long-term. All Punjabi youth are very mindful of their future prosperity and well-being: They are intensely ambitious and competitive for personal and family growth, which acted as a natural restrictive in the path of terrorism's survival in Punjab.

By implication, the Muslim youth who are often reported to be distracted by the lures applied by the forces of terror, need to be made to understand the implication of future and prosperity—and the best people to do so are the parents and elders in the society, if they themselves are well informed and free of toxic or terror friendly afflictions.

Contextual Approach as Dynamism of GP

Interestingly, the Gandhian ideology—and, also the strategies emerging out of the same were never stagnant, except for its basic ingredient of ahimsa and truth. He constantly refined and redefined his formations, safeguarding the basic core of non-violence and truth, as per emerging situations.

Gandhi became a **'metaphor'** shaping the nationalistic

campaign in accordance with what the participants deemed fit at a particularly historical time. That is why the GP has been devoid of a standard formations; his responses had to be contextual—and, thus, sometimes it used to become difficult for the second rung of leaders of the India's freedom movement to fully convert the mass responses to comply with Gandhi's basic requirements.

In 1922, the Chauri-Chaura movement was a case in point—as, the moment participants of the non-cooperation movement became violent, Gandhiji suspended the movement. He could not tolerate any deviation from the basic core of his philosophy of work—namely, the **non-violence**.

Similarly, while applying the principles of GP for encountering terrorism, situation based formulations will have to be worked out, keeping its basic core compositions intact.

Optimism as a Productive Tool of GP

Gandhi was an incorrigible optimist:

> Despite partition of the county and a great loss of life before and after it, he had not lost faith in the goodness of human mind and heart.

To his restless mind, the Indian masses represented a resurrection of hope. His non-violent resistance provided a viable alternative in the struggle against colonialism, where force had become both illegitimate and ineffective.

The Champaran Satyagraha of 1918 gave some productive hope to impoverished farmers without really invalidating interests of the landlords. Here too, the campaign was managed in a manner that aspirations of multi-layered society were kept alive: Inclusiveness had its vibrant and majestic manifestation.

> Gandhiji was a builder of excellent thought structures—he was not a destroyer like leftists and militants. He saw synthesis as a way out of complex challenges.

Almost at the same time he superbly handled the agitation of Ahmedabad's textile workers, getting them benefits, and at the same time not destroying the economic viability of the industry. Gandhi, thus, was a **synthesizer** of immense proportions.

Gandhi gave hope for amelioration of the living conditions of the Harijan community, including sweepers, daily wagers, and artisans. He had considerably diluted the load of untouchablity, which gave the suffering masses a bright hope for eventual relief. Many dalit organizations in India strike critical positions by asserting that Gandhiji did not do enough for the dalit population—because they forget to appreciate that 20th century's greatest conflict manager was not a destroyer; he always attempted to build on existing structures—strengthening and modifying them—and not blasting them to ground like the communists—who destroyed a lot and built little.

Mahatma was a true leader of people: He could read their minds as open book and interact with them constructively. He led from the front—and always through self-example. It was irresistible not to follow him, if you ever came near to him or heard him speak.

His getting easily related to people gave the latter hope of being understood—and eventual relief from poverty and mismanagement.

GP: For Wining the Battle of Heart and Mind

In all religious or even in secular living environments, clergy plays a vital role in keeping people's thinking on track, or in derailing the same, if the former by itself gets unrighteous and biased.

All clerics: Muslims, Christians, Hindus, Sikhs and others, need to be educated in management of secularism through the applications of the Gandhian Philosophy. The areas of emphasis, among others, for this purpose could be:

- That God (or all Gods, if multiplicity is necessary) is omnipotent—He does not require human help in eliminating or fighting his enemies. First of all, he does not have any enemy and, if one or some exist, he is capable of dealing with them.
- That there can not be more than one God, one for Muslims, another for Christians, separate ones for Sikhs, Buddhists, Jains, and Jews, and several ones for Hindus.
- All Gods integrate into the finality of **"Truth and Non-violence."**
- If Gods were different then why have they not created their followers in different morphologies and

physiologies? The identity of all human beings in structure and composition proves that they are all products of the same artist.

- **"Truth is God"** said Mahatma Gandhi: Untruth and evil can not be God; follow what the Mahatma said and the world shall remain perpetually in peace. It will then progress in leaps and bounds.

Lord Krishna had said some five millennia ago, when there were no Hindus, Christians or any practicing religion that, "**I am in everything and everything is in me"**: He implied living as well as non-livings.

Now, scientists of the world are trying collectively to prove what the great Lord had said while preaching the merits of action or Karma to Arjuna, on the battlefield of Kurukchetra.

As soon as the presence of God particle or Bosson is proved, Lord Krishna's revelation will be established irrevocably. With it will be cleared the concept or existence of dark matter or dark energy that infuses life into non-life entities. Uniformity or unity of every-thing and hence, the uniformity of all religions shall be established.

Application of GP for Management of Terrorism

The application of GP for management of terrorism has to proceed in the following three stages:

- Intensive study by the clerics, politicians, intellectuals, and senior bureaucracy;
- Converting it into programs and formations suiting actual social and cultural situations;
- Organising teaching of GP or its specifically designed formations to the above mentioned critical groups of population.
- Spread of the GP to younger levels of population; and
- Periodical evaluations of its formations and subsequent improvements on continuing basis.

One: Prime initiators and spreaders of terrorism in any community, irrespective of religion, are its clerics, the preachers and pujaries, and mullahs and maulvis who, these days, are creating confusion and inflaming passions through biased and untrue scriptural expositions. They love the resultant chaos and confusions as it brings to them a lot of attention and money—and finally dominance and control over the masses. They love power because it gives them double benefits; material well-being and perception of service to their God.

At least the perception of service to God by self-centred clerics is totally false—as no unrighteous person is acceptable to the great Lord to do anything on his behalf. God does not practice outsourcing His work to humans of evil nature and practices.

The first attempt of intense GP study and teaching should concentrate on this most vital group of citizenry. If our state apparatus of governance succeeds in focussing the torch of GP on this section of population, then more than half of the battle against terrorism should be taken as won, without fail.

Politicians in our democratic set-up control allocation of funds and passage of schemes for any purpose. Additionally, the use and misuse the **'licence of free speech'**, to inflame passions, create perceptions of discrimination, disaffection, and anger accumulation, rightly or otherwise—and in this manner they sow seeds of terrorism. Clerics take away from where politicians leave it and give it the camouflage and masking of religions.

This process, sometimes, might be visible operating in the reverse order i.e. where clerics take evil initiatives and politicians follow up with their magnifications.

> In opinion of the author, over 90 percent of responsibility of terrorism genesis and its spread lies on clerics and politicians as the two evil promoting units of the society.
>
> GP must be utilized first to neutralize their evil production energies.

Two: Intellectuals who include, teachers, professors, and middle and senior managers, as a group, do influence public opinion though they have no capacity to indoctrinate youngsters to get into the muck of terrorism, but if they are exposed to the elements of GP, then in a substantial manner the civil society can safeguard itself from the mischievous teachings of clerics, on one hand, and exploitative manipulations from politicians, on the other. Hence, their exposure to GP is vital: They can be of decisive influence in situations of crisis.

Three: Bureaucracy runs the apparatus of governance:

Planning for various sections of society and resources allocation remains always in their hands. A degree of righteousness in their thoughts and actions is necessary for peace and balance in a society.

Further, they train and control the politicians. Additionally, they exert operational control over the security agencies and are directly responsible for law and order. GP as an element of terror management can not be successful, if this vital component of society is not favourably disposed towards it.

GP's program formulation: For positive indoctrination of all the above groups, the rich literature of GP, including the Mahatma's own writings, have to be studied and the concerned apparatus of governance, namely the Ministry of Education or Human Resources, and NGOs active in this field, have to develop course components and teaching/reading materials, which should work as GP-indoctrination capsules for different groups of the population.

Critical groups' intensive exposure to GP: The above three critical groups have to be taught or exposed to the so prepared GP capsules and/or teaching/learning materials, through suitably designed training/ re-education programs. How effectively this job is done will determining the efficacy of the whole GP component as a constituent of the terrorism neutralization campaign.

Spreading GP to younger population is the next vital job, which in view of the availability of so many channels—such as schools, colleges, universities, films, theatres, media like TV and radio should not be difficult. We have large proven capacities in the field of information dissemination.

Not only one-time indoctrination in the GP would be essential, its continuous pressure on young minds, coupled with suitable incentive and rewards to those who not only excel in absorbing the GP but produce projects and confirmed evidences of having practically put the same into productive action, shall need to be built into the system.

Continuous evaluation and strengthening the GP exposure to various levels of population, in living and working environments, shall have to be achieved. It will have to become a perpetual process of managing human populations (all its sections) in a cooperative non-violent and secular mode. And GP can definitely do it; it is only a question of making a beginning. It can kill terrorism permanently—including its roots, shoots, and seeds.

In opinion of the author, GP is the most effective herbicide for not only killing—but eradicating the weed of terrorism that presently infests a major part of the world.

Brahmastras Emerging from the GP

Elements of the GP relevant to their employment towards combating terrorism can be arranged into the following four combinations of non-failing efficacy—or the Brahmastras:

(a) Truth and non-violence;
(b) Satyagraha and mass actions;
(c) Inclusiveness; and
(d) Constructive programs in contextual relevance.

Since all the above elements have been discussed earlier in this chapter, any further deliberations in this regard are avoided in interest of repetition avoidance.

GP: It Cements the Forces of Introspection

Intensive application of the **FCS** that crushes infrastructures of terror, normally leads to emergence of the forces of introspection at thought level—as the process of negative returns sets in under pressures of **FCS**—leading to realization of the futility of evil actions of terrorism. And a concurrent environment of active **GP**, or its inputs' applications, will further concentrate such 'thoughts of introspection' into **'potential action capsules'**—and cause, though slowly, so affected terror operatives and/or their political masters take corrective 180 degree turns. It permits an easy shift from evil and untruth to righteousness, truth, tolerance and inclusiveness.

Some media elements are attempting to nudge the evil terror operatives in Pakistan to take this way out from the tight mess into which this Islamic entity has landed itself. One political commentator by the name of Ayaj Amir, in Friday's (12 December, 2008), *The News International* argued for the need for Pakistan to give up the **diplomacy of 'jihad'**, as a lesson from the 26/11 Mumbai carnage. The unified international response to the horrific Mumbai incident fully cornered Pakistan, which in view of this political commentator, could turn into a blessing in disguise for the Islamic republic. He wrote:

> "It may be time to bid a final farewell to the diplomacy of 'jihad'. There was a time when Pakistan could get away with the sponsoring of cross-border jihad. Profiting by the Afghan experience, and indeed spurred by it, we did it again in Kashmir. The concept of 'jihad' may be alive and well in Afghanistan but it has become passé, a dangerous fad to nurture, in Pakistan."

In Amir's opinion, Pakistan faces a double task: exorcising the ghost of **'jihad'** and at the same time, while seeking American friendship, saying goodbye to the military alliance with the United States, which sits like a yoke around Pakistani necks. The Mumbai incident, though terrible for India, if well handled, should turn into a blessing for Pakistan, helping it to concentrate its efforts on taking a full circle turn—which otherwise was very difficult for it.

Muhammmad Asif, another political commentator, writing in the *Frontier Post* prompted Pakistan for self-introspection.

"Instead of looking at our problems, we as a nation have chosen to burry our heads in the sand and blame India, the US, Israel, and almost everyone but do not realize how and why we have landed in such problems," he said in this Peshawer-Quetta based daily (as per a Times News Network report that appeared in *The Times of India* of 13 December, 2008). He raised several other uncomfortable questions for Pakistan and its thinking section of population. He traced the terror related problems of Pakistan to the Zia regime—and did not spare those who followed him, from the charge of abusing Islam and 'jihad' for their narrow personal and/or political interests.

Further, **John Negroponte**, the tough talking US Deputy Secretary of State's, no-nonsense personal message, in 2nd week of December, 2008, to the Pakistani apparatus of governance, set it on a course of forced introspection. Such introspections, on part of politicians, diplomats and/or terror perpetrators, if supported by adequate exposure or knowledge of the elements of GP, are capable of pushing the political and terror habituated operatives into deeper thinking, in respect to the futility of violence and untruth. Once some intense chain of thoughts starts and some of these operatives gather courage to face and speak truth, the process of introspection begins to cement into concrete responses and actions.

Emergence of introspection within an individual or even its intensification is not enough; and as per its tendency, it should grip a group—and from there spread to a whole society, intensify and comenting therein to the extent that it explodes into open admittance of feeling of guilt, in such a dose, that a wave of **'forgiving and forgetting'** or (FAF) sets in. Several terror prone communities, especially in Pakistan, Afghanistan, Saudi Arabia, Palestine, and several others, (if they have to become terror neutral) have to pass through this process of active introspection and the responses, which normally follow such a development.

Introspection is one of the essentially most positive manifestations of the GP. The **force of silent majority** can introduce introspection amongst the most biased and subjective minds, probably even in the evil ones. The high and peaceful turn out in the December, 2008 polls to the J&K assembly re-stressed this phenomenon.

The high voter turn-out and the unexpectedly peaceful conclusion of these assembly polls in defiance of a loud and persistent boycott call given by the separatists, forced the leaders of the so called azaadi movement in this state of India into an **"introspection"** mode, though despite the unexpected, they continued to insist that it was not a vote against separatism.

"There is a need for us to introspect," said Mirwaiz Umer Farooq, chairman of the All Parties Hurriyat Conference, in the aftermath of the high and peaceful turn-out of the electorate.

Now, suppose the separatists who are a miniscule minority financed , supported and misguided from across the border, give up their disruptive objectivity, do you think that the same silent majority would ask for and force them to return to their old game that brought tremendous sufferings to people for no fault of theirs? The answer is obvious no.

The GP when attempted on large scale, right on young minds and upwards, over a period of time, is bound to set in much faster introspections and pave ways for bloodless resolutions of conflicts.

Once a process of righteous thinking or introspection is forced in or ignited, the **GP's Brahamastra** of **"Truth and Non-violence"** assumes active capabilities to be effective on hearts and minds, generating and cementing thoughts and action capsules which give courage even to those possessed by evil to get into the process and forgetting and forgiving, or even asking for the latter, in case of former perpetrators of acts of terror. Getting out of situations of terror perpetration needs as much courage, if not more, than what was consumed in performance of evil acts. And the divine components of GP do help in garnering such courage.

Islam and the Gandhian Philosophy

Gandhian Philosophy is religion neutral—as neutral as the truth, which forms the foundation of all the religions and philosophies of the world.

Does GP contradict Islamic tenets? Why Muslims did not get attracted to this new art and science of human relations management on long-term basis? Was Gandhi discriminatory in selection of his disciples and/or did his morphology and expressions deter them?

It is deemed necessary to examine these issues, before assessing the GP's suitability to and adoptability by Muslim masses who are suffering today the greatest blame for **initiating, supporting, feeding, and perpetrating terrorism** world over. Only afterwards, the issue whether GP could effectively help in elimination of terrorism, particularly of the Islamist variety, could be answered with substantial weight-age and conviction.

During the three decades prior to partition of India in 1947, Gandhi tried his best to bring in Hindu-Muslim unity. Efforts in this direction were particularly intensified during the Khilafat movement. But, the centuries long mistrusts of the two communities, Muslim clerics' penchant for conversion, Swami Shraddhanand's murder by a Muslin in1926, RSS and Muslim League's incompatible politics, and British Raj's divisive diplomacy frustrated Mahatma's persistent efforts.

The Raj came in the way of Gandhi and Ali brothers' joint efforts to subdue communal tensions resulting from Kohat (located in NWFP), and clerics on both sides of the divide foiled Gandhi's persistent striving in the direction of peace.

When Gandhi went on a long fast at Ali brothers Delhi residence, the whole Ali household had turned vegetarian as a mark of respect to the Mahatma. They had developed at one stage deep reverence to the Mahatma, but the politics of British Raj and some of its Muslim cronies proved too much for the positive energies of the GP to keep the two communities cooperating in the desired direction.

Britishers greatly feared the Hindu-Muslim unity or any type of cooperation amongst them.

The two nations theory or TNT became the handiest tool in their hands—which they employed with decisive efficacy.

While the Khilafat leaders, the Ali brothers, Maulana Zafar Ali Khan, and others slowly drifted away from Gandhi, as the question of forced conversions for the Muslim leadership had become a frog and snake story: They loved the pray but could not handle the ill-will that it created. Kohat riots in NWFP had created such a situation that the two sides had to issue conflicting reports.

Despite Gandhi's failure to retain the mainstream Muslims with his movement, men like Abdul Kalam Azad, Aruna Asaf Ali, Hakim Ajmal Khan, M.A. Ansari, Khan Abdul Ghaffar Khan, and Rafi Ahmed Kidwai remained as his steadfast followers. They had seen ample merits in this association's fairness and secularism: They did not believe that the TNT would cure the Muslim community of all of its ills. Further, out of religious bias and long-held prejudice, the community had developed incapacities for appreciation of truth and/or those who persisted with it.

The violence of the partition times had saddened Gandhi to the extent the he gave up his plan for a 125 years' long life, in favour of being freed from being a mute witness to the violence—and his wish was granted by the wise Lord, who had sent him to this earth with a purpose.

Often, Gandhi faced criticism for obvious Hindu content in his approach and life style; the use of words like Rama, Ahimsa, Satayagraha, etc had not pleased a lot of Muslims. And on the other side, he was charged that he was not Hindu enough, that he appeased Muslims at each and every occasion.

Muslims took advantage of him whenever it suited them—and criticized even when he was trying to be impartial and righteous. They wanted that he should always favour them out of the way.

They wanted to extract an unfair price of associating with him—and in the process lost the opportunity to learn value of truth and non-violence from the great soul. Their own selfishness failed them like it had happened to the evil Duryodhana some 5,000 years ago when he had refused to listen to the sage advice—and even admonishments of Lord Krishna.

The Muslim community too during the struggle for India's independence was overtaken by the evil of TNT; and Britishers were playing the role of evil intentioned Sakuni who had imagined his importance only in conflict of cousins.

Some people, from the other side of the divide, did not hesitate in charging Gandhi that he brought religion into the struggle for independence—but this charge too was not sustainable.

At around turn of the 19th century, **Sayyid Ahmad Khan** had charged that the reforms advocated by the newly born Indian National Congress (INC) would benefit Hindus and harm Muslims; it demonstrated the existence of elements of religion and consequent divide in the polity of undivided India. Gandhi only attempted to manage the divide, but failed as the force of circumstances were grossly against his divine efforts.

By providing the non-violent alterative of fighting the British Raj, Gandhi prevented a lot more deaths and deprivation on both sides of the divide, though in a number of cases his presence did not stop the same. But, no one could deny that his presence diminished occurrence of violence and its intensities to a very large extent.

Muslim League had built the case of TNT on fear of facing the Hindu majority after British leaving India—and this fear, as fanned by the interested parties, became the long-lasting cause of the problem of mistrust, which even the partition could not wash away. Britishers had enjoyed covertly and overtly instigating TNT loving Muslims to insist and persist with the obnoxious demand of utter non-inclusiveness.

> Gandhi was faced with an impossible situation: He could not accept to retain the Britishers for ever, and they did not want to give the keys of the nation to one; their scheme was to divide. It was probably the design of the destiny, which is un-fightable.

During the Khilafat movement, Gandhi through his wise advice to Muslims to be firm in their demand against imperialists' design to dismantle the privileged status of the Turkish Sultan attained a position of leadership among them. He was able to tell them to select and follow the path of non-cooperation. Gandhi had moved a step closer to the Hindu-Muslim unity and it was very much visible in the Amritsar session of the INC. By then, M.A. Jinnah had turned Gandhi's admirer.

The Khilafat movement eventually failed due to Turks own infighting, Mustafa Kamal's disinterest in it, and the allied imperialists' own special designs. With this, the Muslim cooperation too pattered away from Gandhi's non-cooperation movement, as the community came under growing allure of the TNT.

In subsequent Gandhi-led agitations, namely salt satyagraha and open rebellion, Muslims hardly participated and that brought confirmed visibility to the Muslims falling prey to the Raj's policies of divide and rule. Muslims happily hanged to Jinnah's TNT as the same seemed to offer the Muslim leaders of various hues a scope, for becoming a ruling class. So, it was their opportunism that had pulled the League and its sympathizers away from the GP.

In fact, the Muslim fundamentalists and the clerics did not want the Hindu-Muslim unity or cooperation to last for long, as they saw dual disadvantage in it; and they formed the deciding force of the community at that time.

One—the dropping the idea of the TNT—and two, losing the lure of conversions, could be the consequences of co-operating with the Mahatma. The Hindu-Muslim unity was neither in interests of Muslim League, nor those of the managers of the Raj. And Gandhi had to face persistent opposition of the RSS and other hard-core Hindus organizations too.

Even after partition, Gandhi fought with Vallabbhai Patel and undertook fast to get Pakistan paid Rupees 55 crores (equivalent to today's over Rs 5,500 crores), a lot of money at that time—and, as a result, he lost his life for the alleged act of appeasing the Muslims.

Muslims lost the chance to own Gandhi, learn the value of truth, non-violence, peaceful resolution of conflict, tolerance for others views, and other vital components of the GP and they are today the losers. Even the opportunity that had unfolded in the NWFP, through the unique success of **Frontier Gandhi's peaceful agitation**, his **Khudai Khidmadar** movement (or the Red Shirt movement) and inter-tribal cooperation—an example of live inclusiveness was lost in an utterly careless manner. Had the post-independence governments of Pakistan given due respect to the Frontier Gandhi, his ideals and works, the situation today in this Pakistan's western border area would have been entirely different.

On the other hand, for Tibetans their leaders' deep understanding of GP and freedom from evil thoughts and designs benefited the community. Though it has not won freedom to the Tibetans, but the community's violent disintegration has been avoided. Their moral fabric remains unpolluted and unaltered. They have appreciation of the world. Despite being refugees for so long, they have not lost the virtue of logic, peace, and dialogue. There was and continues to be much more justification for the whole Tibetan people for turning to terrorism, than that had by any of the Islamic community, any where in the world.

The difference lies in the culture and traditions—and the choices that they dictate.

GP: The Holistic Approach

For its long-term solution, terrorism needs a **'holistic approach'** that is capable of handling;

- The causes of terror genesis and spread,
- Its promoters—financial, religious and political ones,
- Its foot-soldiers who do some-one else's bidding, and
- Its victims.

Except the immediate need to eliminate (or suppress to acceptable level) the non-cooperative and illogical elements in the apparatus of terror, through the use of force (as discussed under the FCS), all the four above aspects of terror management need application of soft forces which target the energies of minds and hearts of the people involved i.e. to get them into the process of introspection, finally leading to appreciation of the futility of bloodshed for conflict resolution. The GP is decidedly most suitably equipped to meet all these challenges.

Not long ago, the Chief Justice of India K G Balakrishnan, while speaking in an international conference of jurists stated the necessity of the holistic approach in management of terrorism, instead of pitting one nation against the other. And the Pakistani media (*The Friday Times*) liked it a lot, probably without realising that constituent actions of such an approach have to be initiated from its soil. Decidedly, it has to be a persistent international approach, concentrating upon the countries which are operating the universities and crucibles of terror propagation.

GP: Scepticism about its Applicability and Efficacy

The other day a friend of the author while discussing the GP and terrorism quipped, **"It has not worked against terrorism."** I corrected my well-meaning friend by saying that GP, for that matter any philosophy or strategy, was not going to work by itself. It has to be understood in correct perspective and then implemented at a certain scale to exhibit its impact. No one has made any intensive and/or planned effort to use GP except the Mahatma himself. Terrorism, in its present avatar, is just about three decades old and GP, in this reference, has not been tried.

Only worth mentioning use of the GP has been made in South Africa through the "Truth and Reconciliation Commission" which helped a lot of people of both the communities to come clean, unload their guilt for wrong doings in an open court, and attempt to forgive or ask for forgiveness—and then try to proceed on the arduous journey of forgetting i.e. cleansing your own soul free from the dirt of communal and/or racist violence, perpetrated and/or endured for so long.

Dalai Lama, the Buddhist head of Tibetans has for long attempted a non-violent approach for solving the Tibetan problem but he failed primarily for (a) the Chinese irresponsiveness of not talking to him, and (b) he being away from the site of action. **The components of GP can not be easily applied with remote control yet, for so many years, he succeeded in keeping his followers in a non-violent mode, which the Chinese authorities show no spiritual maturity to appreciate.**

Palestinians could have benefited a lot from applications of the GP because they were near to the conflicting party and the two sides to the conflict had to interact on day to day basis.

Additionally, this theatre of conflict was open to the media from which application of GP could draw a lot of practical support. Tibet and China being closed to independent media did not offer such an opportunity to the Tibetan case of Dalai Lama.

Since terrorism represents negative manifestations of the energies of thought and actions, generated and governed from mind and heart, its solution too can emerge only through such measures which are capable of impacting the two centres of its origin.

And only GP has that capability.

> For right mix of anti-terror measures, FCS components need to be used for controlling the acute manifestations of terror, while the GP has to be targeted for correction of chronic causatives as well as the effects.

As discussed earlier in this chapter, terrorism is a four tiered apparatus, primarily comprising:

(1) Its financiers,
(2) The politicians, clerics and managers/ handlers, etc.
(3) Its foot-soldiers, and
(4) The religion.

GP's components are effective on all the four layers of Terrorism, and when employed properly with right intensity and persistence they are expected to act as true **Brahmastras.**

GP: Its greatest USP

GP's most unique USP is that when employed as a counter-terrorism measure in any combination, it creates '**zero negative response**' amongst the elements of terror on which it is targeted. They might remain slow in their initial response but the reactions set in amongst the target population are never negative or conflict enhancing.

On persistent application no element of terror shall be able to resist it for a long time because it hits the soft centres of thought and action genesis.

GP: Its Exposure to the Western World

Gandhi never travelled to America.

Spread of the Gandhian thoughts in the Western world [22] is primarily credited to the adoption and interpretation of the GP by Martin Luther King Jr. who was deeply impacted by the discrimination that the non-whites were faced within the United States, the democracy of unequal rights, which this young Gandhian wanted to remedy.

The non-believers of non-violence often raise persistently troubling questions. They say: Non-violence is nice in theory, but is it practical? Are the principles of Gandhi and his disciple Martin Luther King Jr. still relevant? Is non-violence feasible in a world gripped with terrorism? Will non-violence work against adversaries without conscience? These are valid questions on part of non-believers—as they neither know the powers of non-violence—nor the methodology of its working. Some of these were answered by King's interpretations and applications of the GP in his short but eventful life.

- The hesitation to try non-violence comes basically out of the lack of its study—and some non-violent agitations fail to achieve correct results for lack of efforts, persistence of actions, and their defective management. Either people use sub-normal intensity of actions that are inadequate for initiating a critical mass or reaction for change, or give up efforts too early.
- Non-violence should not be seen a method but a philosophy—and, it has a set of associate elements which together are known as the GP; it is a philosophy of life as well as action.
- King modernized Gandhi's methodology and applied the same to American situations, the civil rights movement among them. And some of King's followers, colleagues and contemporaries took it even to rural settings.
- On collective level, GP is fully religion neutral: Gandhi was as much a Muslim as a Hindu or Christian. He had distilled the goodness of all religions into the religion of mankind, and gave it a form through his philosophy. He had digested scriptures of all major religions and, whenever in any doubt, he referred to the "Bhagavad-Gita," the brightest gem amongst Indian scriptures.
- Gandhi's Hindu origin did not come in his way of being most Christ-like. He was very fond of going through the Gospels before any dialogue with his Christian adversaries. He considered Christ the planter of the seeds

of his non-violent philosophy.

- Jim Wallis,[23] a Christian leader of social change has termed the Gandhian way as a **"form of spiritual politics."** Gandhi persistently attempted to reconcile the coarse demands of politics with the higher principles of moral beliefs and practices. He is known to have observed, "Men say I am a saint losing myself in politics." "The fact is that I am a politician trying myself hardest to be a saint." This spiritual foundation of Gandhi's politics assigned the GP immense power of opponent's behaviour alteration—rendering the GP as a matchless "Brahamastra of spirituality."
- According to American activist Dave Dellinger,[27] **"The genius of Gandhi and the basis of his remarkable success lay in his insistence that religion and politics could not be separated."** He had the technology to employ the soft energies of religion to influence public opinion in favour of righteous collective action. It compels even the most adamant and unrighteous to look within and see what is right and what is wrong.
- The GP initiates action from within—and often it is unstoppable: Evil tends to melt when adequate pressure of GP is applied. But its practitioners have to be well versed, patient and insistent.
- GP's political methodology emerged from its perpetrator's concept that politics (for a righteous person) was an expression of spiritual commitment, as a way of seeking truth. He applied non-violence to develop unique and highly effective forms of political struggle.
- George Orwell[24] in his reflections on Gandhi said that **"inside the saint or near the saint was a very shrewd"** political leader. In Gandhi's political campaigns there were three stages of activity:
  1. Dialogue for persuasion,
  2. Self-sacrifice, and
  3. Non-cooperation.

  Before engaging in direct action, a GP activist has to engage in intense dialogue, through presentation of facts and rational arguments. When factual argument fails to bring desired results, as often is the case in the dialogue process, the next stage is that of self-sacrifice like fasting, willingness to suffer arrests and inconveniences. The final stage is for mass action of non-cooperation, which could be disruptive to the interests of the reluctant adversary.

- Gandhi was master of dialogue but he had an **aversion for coercion**. He always preferred negotiations over confrontation, though often it was not productive enough because the issues involved were intricate.
- **Satyagraha was a means of moral persuasion for him.**
- **Gandhi refused to countenance** an armed response by Jews, Czechs and other subjugated people against Hitlerism in Europe.
- When Japanese knocked at India's doors in Burma, he was reluctant to consider armed struggle against the invaders.
- He was sickened by the barbarism of war and armed struggles—and became greater pacifist as he advanced in years.
- Non-violence, a major component of the GP has potential to generate positivity in adversaries as was evidenced from Gandhi's warm welcome by the textile workers of Lancashire in 1931, who were the worst sufferers of his Sawadeshi movement which primarily was targeted against the British government policies.
- **Moral justifiability of an action was very dear to him in all circumstances.**
- The Gandhian method, whether as pressure or persuasion, requires a willingness to suffer. Gandhi believed, **"Purer the suffering, greater the progress."** The readiness to sacrifice is the key requirement of Satayagraha and primarily accounts for its political success. Commentators on the Gandhian thought and practice have differed on the need for suffering to be interregnal part of the non-violent action.
- Though suffering is directed primarily at **moral persuasion**, Gandhi also saw it as a path for self-realization and spiritual fulfilments.
- Suffering can also be the dramatization of the evil being challenged as Martin Luther King Jr. and his colleagues had demonstrated in the civil rights movement. Their

submission to police violence dramatized the brutality and moral unfairness of the segregationist system. However, it is not assured that suffering will wash away the deeply ingrained prejudices.

- GP can be a **chosen path for the strong, not the weak.** It takes strength and determination to suffer for a cause—and not to respond with violence.
- Gandhi did not like or **tolerate cowardice and is reported to have asserted that if there was a choice only between cowardice and violence, it was better to choose the latter.**
- Non-violent sacrifice is never demoralizing while cowardice had such an effect.
- Strength to struggle non-violently is a necessity for the GP.
- Subdued and controlled anger leading to indignation has a role in the GP towards pushing one towards action and persisting with the same.
- Gandhi often emphasized the need for courage and readiness for sacrifice. Only by **forgetting the fear for retaliation can one be free of the power of oppression.**
- GP turns an activist into a fearless campaigner. The ultimate test of our commitment is, **"Are we ready to die in defence of our non-violent action?"**
- Gandhi always **believed in updating a view**. He is reported to have said that he was not fully a Gandhian—by which he meant that he was constantly revising and updating his formations and approaches.
- When he did not know answers, Gandhi diligently looked for truth in every setting—**there is nothing better than truth,** as a weapon of defence as well as aggression.
- King was the brightest disciple of the GP; he had a sort of divine inspiration that the **non-violent social change for justice was God's work**. King had proclaimed that the arc of the moral universe was long and it bent towards justice.
- The idea of human beings working to fulfil God's will was the bedrock of King's **"Concept of the Beloved Community"** or the kingdom of God on earth.
- King had said that he **discovered Gandhi through Christ,** which could be the greatest compliment to the Mahatma and the GP.

- King, very much like Gandhi, emphasized the importance of action: He did not believe that justice could come to the black community automatically with the passage of time. For him action was most important; he was indeed a follower of **Lord Krishna's principle of Karma**.
- Like Gandhi, King believed that a non-violent activist must be prepared to sacrifice and **suffer for the cause of justice**. He wrote in 'Stride Toward Freedom, "the non-violent resister is willing to accept violence, if necessary, but never to inflict it."
- King's fundamental inspirations for non-violence came from the Gospel. About his attraction to Gandhian methods as he said, **"I went to Gandhi through Christ."**
- Like Gandhi, King came to understand the social implications of Christ's teachings; he placed increased emphasis on the obligation to care for the oppressed and overcome injustice.
- King also came to realize that ethical appeals alone could not guarantee justice and that **coercive pressure** might be necessary to achieve social change. Gandhi, however, was not favourably inclined towards use of coercion.
- King appreciated Neiebuhr's [25] emphasis on **reality of evil in human interactions.** As an African American, he had sufficiently experienced the social discrimination at hands of evil accumulated humanity. He understood that, often, it is not reason but power that determines politics.
- Christ's injunction to **"love your enemy"** is the most difficult of his commandants. King believed it to be the most important. Through the power of love, we appeal to the divine spark of goodness even in our enemies: It is supposed to exist in every human-being.
- The love that King emphasized was not aesthetic or filial but pure, spontaneous, creative and selfless one. It is a **"disinterested love"** he wrote. Like Gandhi, King too considered the selfless love to be proactive, an affirmative commitment.
- Gandhi had also cemented King's belief in the **"essential compatibility of ends and means"**. Non-violence demands that the means employed must be as pure as the ends that we seek. The notion that ends justify the

means—that an equitable and just society could not be built and sustained through usage of unjust means. Here, Gandhi as well as his distinguished disciple differed with **Lord Krishna** who had said that, under certain exceptional situations, somewhat unjust means too could be employed while dealing with evil and unjust of disproportionably huge capabilities.

- King believed that non-violence had the **capacity to turn adversaries into allies**—as the goal is not to defeat but to convert the adversary—or to forge unity out of division and discord. King had realized, like Gandhi had done earlier in case of his complex situations of Hindu and Muslim differences, that whites and blacks had to live together—and that not segregation but cooperation was the solution to their long-held differences. That was the prime reason why Gandhi had painstakingly resisted the two nations' theory advanced by the advocates for creating a separate nation for the Muslims of undivided India.
- In his conviction towards non-violent social change, King saw a divine purpose or God's work. While King saw the omnipotence of God, he was careful to distinguish between **the perfection of divine and the imperfection of man**. He persisted with a belief of divine guidance of history, with an insistence on the necessary commitment of human-beings to help bring about this divine purpose.
- King did not believe in the immense **power of time to bring in change**: He did not like the idea put forward by some whites that the segregation would disappear with the passage of time and that the blacks should show patience. He saw no certainty that communities of love and harmony would emerge by themselves or unaided.
- Like Gandhi, King believed that a non-violent activist must be prepared to sacrifice and suffer for the cause of justice. He wrote in the *Stride Toward Freedom*, "the non-violent resister is willing to accept violence if necessary, but never to inflict it." King frequently emphasized that the unearned suffering was redemptive and found a theological support in Christ's sufferings. A willingness to suffer is a crucial requirement to the moral power of non-violence.

- Sacrifice requires courage, King emphasized. Like Gandhi, he believed that **overcoming fear was the essential** requirement for non-violent action. It had both political as well as theological manifestations for the King. Non-violent method is not for cowards, he often emphasized.
- Like Gandhi, King too sharpened his non-violent formations through practice. He often admitted in discussions with friends and colleagues that he knew very little of Gandhianism or the GP.
- King came to India in 1959 to learn more at first hand about the GP and about this travel he said that it was **a pilgrimage to him**. After returning from India, King established the **Institute for Non-violent Resistance to Segregation**, in order to provide a more serious study of the GP and train activists for the purpose of intensifying his non-violent campaigns. He even talked about organizing an **"American Salt March."**
- This institute trained a large number of activists in practical applications of the GP. The principles of the GP were also taught in the citizenship schools set up in 1961. Through the citizenship schools, the Nashville workshops, and the Institute for Non-violent Resistance, King and his colleagues in the civil rights movement recruited and trained a huge core of committed workers.
- Cesar Chavez[22] stands next to Martin Luther King Jr. as one of the greatest non-violent American leaders in the US history. He founded the United States farm workers movement and led it for over thirty years with outstanding results. Chavez had been greatly influenced by Gandhi after seeing a news reel about Mahatma's great work against the British imperialists. He read a lot on the GP and mastered its fine points.
- In Gandhi, Chavez had found a leader who **could inspire poor people to challenge** the rich and powerful, a formula of immense utility for the farm workers who were faced with greedy rich farmers. What had most appealed Chavez in the GP was Gandhi's **method of leading by example:** the Mahatma never asked any one to do something that he did not do himself or was not ready to do.

- In gatherings Chavez often echoed Gandhi's sayings and practices. Through intense study of the GP, he had fully integrated the principle of non-violence and truth into his work strategies. The **principle of means and ends appealed a great deal to him.**
- Chavez and his farm workers movement burst on to the US national stage in 1965—and it was known as the **great grape strike or *la huelga.***
- In January 1968, the national boycott of Californian grapes became famous nationally and internationally. It was later described as the **"most ambitious and successful boycott in American history."**
- In addition to the boycott, Chavez became famous for application of his frequent fasting methodology of dispute resolution. He fully emulated Gandhi, who had often resorted to fasting while attempting to subdue the Hindu-Muslim communal violence. Chavez too subscribed to the Gandhian concept of penance; he viewed fasting as a great communication tool.
- Dorothy Day [26] was the third great adherent of non-violence in USA. She was a gifted writer, committed political activist, pacifist, suffragist, and an ardent advocate of the poor and under-privileged. Dorothy Day has been described as the **"most significant, interesting and influential person in the history of American Catholicism."**
- Day had much in common with Gandhi and was thoroughly familiar with the Mahatma's life, works, and writings. In Gandhi's style, she saw a role for herself. True faith, she said, is expressed in our love for others, especially our love for "least of these."
- Her eulogy at the time of Gandhi's death **portrayed him fully a Christ-like figure.** She said, "There is no public figure that has more conformed his life to the life of Jesus Christ than Gandhi; there is no man who carried about him more consistently the aura of divinized humanity." He was assassinated, she wrote, **"because he insisted that there be no hatred, that Hindus and Muslims live together in peace." She described him as "pacifist martyr."**

- Day was outraged by the war in Vietnam and greatly admired the willingness of Catholic youth to go to jail instead of joining the US army.
- Unlike King and Chavez, she was not credited with any big political achievement—as she did not strive for immediate results the way most activists do. As her purposes were different, she sought to change attitudes and moral principles. Her definition of success was more personal.
- Barbara Deming[22] of the War Resistance League was another significant Gandhian. In February 1968, she had written a very persuasive and intellectual article on the Mahatma, which was widely appreciated. She was deeply involved in the civil rights movement all through the 1960s.
- Deming's Gandhian urge crystallized after a visit to Cuba and her very uncommon encounter with Fidel Castro: To an extent, she attempted to strive for Castro's objectivity for social change through Gandian means.
- Deming wrote *Revolution and Equilibrium* in order to refute the violent methodology that was advocated by the writer of *The Wretched of the Earth* by Frantz Fanon, which she had read.
- In defence of non-violence, Deming had often said that people criticized it without adequately understanding and practicing it. As per her perception, non-violence in her times was only in the initial stages of its development – and Gandhi, for non-violence, was as Edison for electricity. It had to develop, like electricity did, to realize its full potential. So, many more people should work with this high potency input.
- Deming believed that to be politically effective, operatives of the GP had to confront and undermine the oppressive powers. She argued that key to assertive social action was knowledge and even embracing coercive elements of non-violence could be employed. Coercion means forcing opponent to act against his or her will. Through mass noncooperation and actions that disrupt the business of the oppressor, non-violent resisters can limit the adversary's freedom and choices. Deming did not have

any of the Mahatma's ambiguity about the coercive actions as part of the GP.

- Deming emphasized the importance of maintaining control in any activist campaign—as by keeping our balance and avoiding the dizzying effect of violence and chaos, we can better control the responses and behaviour of our adversary more effectively if we show concern and respect.
- The unique duality of non-violence was well understood by this Gandhian: It included concern for the person but defiance of the authority, which often throws the adversary out of balance.
- The non-violent action, unlike the physical encounter, eliminate genesis of anger and aminocity, the flow of emotional and psychic energies is altered. The intense energy bursts that emerge in case of physical or violent encounter are tempered in case of the non-violent methodology.
- Non-violent action is also viewed as a unifying force; instead of energies clashing as they do in violent actions, the contending forces positively interact to learn from each other and eventually cooperate.
- Another important feature of non-violence, as per Deming is to win sympathy and support of those who previously were uncommitted. She called it as the "Special Genius of non-violence." As a rule, non-violence attracts third party support and goodwill.
- As per some commentators of the GP, impact of non-violence travels through social media or social distance, very much like the physical forces that move their impact through physical or spatial distance.
- With the progress of this understanding even 'green activists' have realized the undesirability of street trashing and damage to public properties, despite the fact that a number of activists continue to question the efficacy of non-violence since they do not have requisite patience.
- Suitability of the Gandhian methodology of non-violence and satyagraha often came in for questioning in the Western world , especially in context of the Nazi Holocaust and Stalin's mass elimination of opponents.

Jewish leaders of that time questioned whether the Gandhian method was appropriate or even possible in face of the Hitlerism. In response to several queries Gandhi wrote in 1938 that the Jews of Germany could resist non-violently. But, why no one was convinced adequately or attempted decisively in this direction seems to be that the Jews were not adequately trained or exposed to the GP and they had no leader of strong conviction to learn and spearhead the same.

- Additionally, the Jewish community which was intensely engaged in business and trade and that its adherents were engaged with their future, could not assemble resources of thought as well as action to be active with the GP.
- Instances where non-violent methods have been successful, amongst others, included the Velvet revolutions of Central and Eastern Europe in 1989 and afterwards; the people's power movement that brought down Ferdinand Marcos in the Philippines in 1986; the students resistance that toppled the Milosevic regime in Serbia in 2000; and the orange revolution of Ukraine also followed non-violent methods in 2004.
- But, non-violent movements sometimes fail spectacularly—like the Tiananmen Square uprising of 1989 and Burmese Generals' intransigence in case of San Suu Kyi. Here, the problem, most probably was inadequacy of the agitational inputs and its consistence in relation to the magnitude of the oppressing force.
- Some commentators of Gandhism have even commented that Gandhi could not understand the true horrors of the totalitarianism. He could not comprehend the enormity of the evil perpetrated by that diabolical steamroller. It is quite possible that the GP is not a universal Brahamastra, and some obnoxious evils like Hitlerism and Stalinism had to be handled with the technology of Lord Krishna. But, possibly as per another set of views, concerted GP approaches in early stages of these evils could have probably halted their development into such monstrosities.
- Also, non-violent action may not be feasible or viable in every situation, despite its success in numerous

campaigns by Gandhi in South Africa and India, and by his disciples in several parts of the world. The primary reason for some exceptions to the universality of the GP lies in the inability of activists, in certain situations, to come up with the right mixes of the elements of the GP, and inadequacy of their intensities, to be adequate to break the inertia of specific situations.

- Basically, the Western world was unfavourably disposed towards Mahatma Gandhi and his GP because it had challenged the greatest world power of that time—and Americans and most other westerners bought the coloured versions of Gandhi and his philosophy dished out by the British establishment. That was the main reason why the Nobel Prize Committee consistently ignored the '**greatest peace warrior of the world**', all through his lifetime.

GP: It can Soften Hardened Minds

In order to understand terrorism and the inner thought processes of its promoters and executioners, we have to understand the working of human mind, particularly when it is in unrighteous mode.

The mind is meant to receive information, process the same to workable conclusions, which lead one into actions. Action and speech, amongst humans, determine whether a person is in righteous or unrighteous mode.

Some seers have said that the mind of some people can get hardened just to be similar to hard rock that does not absorb anything—and righteous information input, as a result, bounces off such hardened minds like water from a hard rock.

The mind of terrorists and terror perpetrators, including its financers and supporters, is indeed hardened to the extent that information and perceptions of pain of victims, empathy, compassion, and love for humanity get promptly bounced back.

What ends up making mind so hard and impervious, or a closed one? It is said to be an automatic front-line defence mechanism of the wicked mind for protection of its beliefs and perceptions, particularly the egoistic ones, ingrained therein.

When one encounters an idea or a situation that is not in line for receptors to pick up, his/her mental circuits get closed and the incoming inputs are bounced off. The mind is, thus, blocked and such a mode of mind is called a **mind-set**.

Ego is said to create a mindset which is always protected by a self-defence mechanism, because the possessors of such mindsets are scared of what others think and often avoid logical discussion and discourse. A mind-set is often self-destructive, as it is proving in case of terrorists and their handlers. For them a simple discussion, if it does not appreciate their point of view, can quickly develop into a conflict.

GP is very effective in persuasive dialogue process. It softens hardened mindsets and can ultimately assist the terror perpetrators see the futility of their indoctrinations. Slowly, it brings them along towards cooperation from positions of confrontation.

GP: It Enjoys Unique Superiority in Fighting State Terrorism

The human history is full of instances of active state terrorism wherein undemocratic imperialistic forces, local and/or otherwise, employed violence to subdue protesting local populations. The two most significant ones of such instances included the British, exploitative and often violently suppressive, occupation of India and a white minority's violent suppression of the black majority in South Africa. The post World War I occupation of large parts of the Arab world, again by the British imperialists, was another such significant example.

In Indian Punjab, the totally unprovoked massacre of unarmed and non-violent local freedom demonstrators on 13 April, 1919, killing 350 of them in cold blood and injuring over 1,500, at the Jallianwala bagh in Amritsar, was beyond doubt an act of stark state terrorism. It was designed to break the will of the Indian freedom fighters, in which regard, it precipitated only a very strong and persisting adverse reaction.

Similarly, unimaginable atrocities were inflicted by British India's soldiers on peaceful and totally non-violent salt Satyagrahis, at Dandi in March 1930 for several days, where ultimately the non-violent GP had decisively defeated the terror striking forces. In fact, during the over 30 years long struggle for independence under Mahatma Gandhi's guidance, unwanted violence visited non-violent satayagrahis at numerous occasions. And in all these cases, state terror was effectively defeated by the GP's non-violent approach.

Simultaneously, under Mahatma's initiation and inspirations, ANC in South Africa too had succeeded brilliantly against the state terrorism and atrocities of the white minority rulers of British origin.

Additionally, the socio-economic terrorism of British controlled business interests, inflicted upon impoverished Indigo farmers in Champaran, Bihar, and also in Bardoli region of Gujarat was successfully defeated by the peaceful applications of the GP.

On the contrary, the conventional approach of Arabs[28] in fighting the British state terrorism, almost in the same period as that of the India's non-violent freedom struggle, was much less successful, the residues of the failure of which are continuing to trouble the Arab states even today, in addition to having spawned a culture of violence which is highly self-destructive and development obstructive. Palestinian leadership's failure to learn from the GP made this aggrieved community pay a horrible price in terms of human lives, on one hand and, on the other, the persisting politician, social, and economic convulsions that it continues to suffer even today.

The current waves of terrorist violence, in the west and south Asia, that are now threatening to engulf the major parts of the world, in view of the author, are the consequence of the wrong selection of the counter-state terror strategies and conflict resolution approaches adopted by the Arab world. Had they elected to adopt and practice the GP for this purpose, the world today would have been a much happier and progressive place to live and work.

The highest price that any community or country has ever paid for electing to fight state terrorism and exploitation (imperialistic and/or local) through application of the conventional strategy of using force to negate or neutralize state terror, has been paid by Vietnamese people. Its residual scars are visible even today. Better results, doubtlessly, could have come to them, without significant cost of human lives, had the Vietnamese leadership elected to fight the occupying forces employing the GP, by which time it was available in a well-tested and tried form. But, the communist leadership of the Vietnamese resistance was not educated in the GP technology, primarily because their very strong faith in their own technology of violence did not permit them any meaningful exposure in this direction. The Chinese success story of application of violence in throwing away the decadent rulers prevented them from learning the new approach of the GP. And, they had never believed in economising at the human cost of regime change and/or socio-political revolutions.

Presently, in India's immediate neighbourhood, non-violent resistance to state terrorism in Mayanmar and Tibet is not making enough headway as the elements of the GP being applied therein are falling significantly short of assuming a critical mass for a non-stoppable action.

GP: As a Global Phenomenon of Universal Applicability

GP is a phenomenon of global applicability, free from racial, religious, and/or territorial limitations. It is also free from requirements of education and financial developments—as it can be applied in a poor and/or rich country with equal ease. A community with a low level of literacy and economic development can employ it with easy and/or even superior ease.

> It is not very much a philosophy of governance but a philosophy of corrective and reformative resistance—and to be truly effective, it has to be applied from within a suffering community; its applications from outside are not very much effective.

GP, however, is poor in cross-border movements—meaning that outside influence can work only as stimulation as the truly moving force for it has to emerge from within. It can not be easily imported and transplanted from outside. In this case, it is very much different to the philosophy of socialism and/or communism, where individual gains become more visible, and non-violence is not an essential requirement.

> The inbuilt absence of striving for governance and/or dominance has made the GP less attractive for infusion from outside. And possibly for the same reason, political outfits have found it less attractive. GP tends to put more responsibility and accountability on leaders than followers

and this too to an extent seems to have contributed to its unattractiveness to political parties.

In other words, it can be asserted with fair certainty that the GP is, by and large, hard on leaders as they have to follow certain rules and observe a behaviour compatible to Gandhian thoughts and practices. This is perhaps why the GP has not been adopted and practiced by leaders very frequently. Another reason is that unlike communism there was no regular push of a state to popularize it.

GP: Its Ingress into the Barack Obama's Strategy Against Terrorism

Roger Cohen's article on Barack Obama's strategy for tackling terrorism that appeared, by arrangement with the *New York Times*, in *The Asian Age's*, New Delhi edition of 1st Feb. 2009, seemed to confirm that it exhibits a strong tinge of the Gandhian approach to conflict resolution.

In his first White House televised interview that Obama gave to the Dubai based Al-Arabia news network, he threw away the USA's confrontational approach to the Muslim world emphasizing that **"the with-us-or-against-us"** global struggle—the so called long war in which the freedom loving West confronts undifferentiated forces of darkness, comprising Al-Quaida, Taliban and all other perpetrators of terrorism, struggling under the wide banner of "Islamo-fascism," has been terminated.

For him, what mattered most was defeating terrorist organisations: It looked very much a strategic challenge, not so much of a war.

The new President overturned the post-9/11 '**Bush Doctrine**' which had a lot of confrontation and isolationism built into it.

Obama's new approach smelt of inclusiveness and religion or faith neutrality. At the moment, it resolved nothing but opened the way for rapprochement. His self-criticality reflected Gandhian dialogue content, free from the blunt bombasticity of the previous administration.

He clearly separated the people and/organizations that differed and disagreed with US than those like Al-Qaida and Taliban who killed and/or were ready to kill innocents and unconnected people, without discrimination and logic. Obama seemed to make a clear distinction between the people who were bent upon destroying America and other peace loving countries, on one hand, and the ones who just disagreed with them and/or with their policies and approaches, on the other.

Disagreement of all types did not worry him—as the same could be handled though dialogue, a key component of the GP.

He said that the mission, to begin with, was that of listening to those who differed, again a key component of the Gandhian approach. He defined his task as convincing Muslims that "Americans are not your enemy," and persuading Americans that respect for a Muslim world is essential. He said, his objective was to promote not only American interests but also of those who were neglected and ignored, including the Muslims deprived of opportunity. This tinge of active inclusiveness too was totally Gandhian.

The post cold war US doctrine of supremacy stands replaced by a new inclusiveness dictated by the globalization—from the 'decider' to something close to **'mediator-in-chief,'** a significant reflection of the Gandhian realism.

He went ahead to suggest dialogue with Iran too which carried several over 30 years old elements of confrontations.

> What looked certain is that Obama's path shall not be easy, new challenges and hindrances shall emerge with unpredictable regularity, but the very change of approach shall convert several potential confrontations and disagreements into the opportunities for agreements and cooperation.

That confirms his GP orientation.

GP: The Greatest Need of the 21st Century

Today terrorism is casting clouds of senseless violence causing uncommon uncertainty for the world community. Incidents of 9/11, 26/11, the forest fire carnage in Australia and the more recent incident in which Major Hasan killed his 13 colleagues (and any other subsequent ones), on one hand, and the persistent Palestinian-Israeli terror violence in West Asia—and the chaos being caused by Al-Quaida and Taliban in the Hindu-Kush belt of Afghanistan-Pakistan, on the other, throw up ample indicators about the scheme of things likely to emerge in the forthcoming decades of the new century.

Iran's knockings at the doors of the nuclear WMDs' club and the North Korea's reluctance to give up similar dreams do not foretell of any peaceful developments. Situations in Dafor, Tibet, and Myanmar too are not comforting in any manner, except that the Sri-Lankan terror situation has turned a lot less threatening.

For conflict resolution, the instrument of dialogue seems to have decisively lost grounds to violence—the bomb blasts, human bombs, and fodayeen attacks by deeply indoctrinated non-state actors. In the mean time, USA and NATO seem fast losing any meaningful international policing and/or stabilizing capabilities.

International market meltdown and the resultant uncertainties that deepened during 2009 with ominous clouds of global dimensions seem to be diluting in the new decade. As per several respectable analysts, doubts about the new US presidency to have a calming effect on the ominous international scene are becoming stronger by each passing day.

Is not the world barking up the wrong tree in its quest to solve the problems of growing terrorism and the international market crises? Impartial thinking minds, particularly those free from religious ferment and indoctrinations, are increasingly raising relevant questions in regard to this possibility. The methods being applied to cure the twin cancers of terror and market uncertainties seem decidedly inappropriate and hence ineffective. And climate change is adding to international uncertainties.

The true cure, in all possibilities, lies in intense and widespread applications of the elements of the GP. This spark of practical wisdom was seen re-dawning on the US policy makers on 10th February, 2009, while observing the 50th anniversary of Dr Martin Luther King's visit to India in 1959, which he made as a pilgrimage to places associated with the life and works of Mahatma Gandhi. The US House of Representatives passed the following resolution.

"We need Martin Luther King, Gandhi more than ever."

According to the information made available by the office of Jim McDermott, co-chairman of the Congressional Caucus on India and Indian Americans, he made a brief intervention before the above resolution was adopted. Stating that there was much to be learnt from the lives and works of Dr King and Mahatma Gandhi; he said:

"We need them more than ever. And this resolution and our upcoming journey to India will honour their contribution to mankind and rekindle their spirit to seek peace by living in peace."

As per Mc Dermott, these two people changed their countries and the world for the better, and the world today would benefit from a new King or Gandhi. **"They taught us that violence begets more violence, and as Gandhi said, 'an eye for an eye makes the whole world blind'."**

A US delegation comprising Dr King's son Martin Luther King III, and members of US Congress including John Lewis, the last surviving member of Dr King's original team which travelled to places associated with Mahatma Gandhi, 50 years ago, planned to walk down the nostalgic lane.

Let the philosophy of Gandhi and subsequent practices of his brilliant disciple show light to the world in tackling the intricate challenges being thrown up by the global terrorism and the equally, both of which are caused and perpetrated by unrighteous and actively discriminative policies of world leaders.

The GP, in deed, is capable of freeing the mankind of these twin menaces, and many more, if world leaders elect to walk the path shown by Mahatma Gandhi and Dr Martin Luther King Jr.

GP: Impracticality of its Superfluous Applications

It is important to note that any superfluous or piecemeal Gandhigiri is unlikely to work against the hard-boiled terrorism. Early in 2009, in one such effort, the British government attempted to alter the mental make-up of Pakistani terror apparatus, through an advertising campaign on which it had planned to spend over 4,00,000 British pounds via the Pakistani media. In this campaign, well-known UK Muslims were to tell Pakistanis how happy and successful they were in the UK—and so please, would the Pakistani militants stop hating the West? The campaign was to be called: **"I am the West."**

The campaign obviously lacked an in-depth understanding of the process through which terrorism normally germinates and spreads, despite the fact that, not so long ago, the Britishers had first hand exposure to the psyche of South Asian Islamists, as well as the GP.

It looked totally naïve on their part to have believed that the hard-boiled terror apparatus of Pakistan, and the hardened minds of its terror perpetrators, could be washed clean of their accumulated grievancial muck.

Terrorism, as said earlier, is a hard-nut to crack—as it has been created through a laborious process of long-term indoctrination of youth, through local education system, and that the religious clerics have made the maximum contributions in this regard. The logical thinking of terror perpetrators has been made non-operative, and the same could not be revived though a simple advertisement campaign. The foot-soldiers of terrorism—and also their handlers, are captive in hands of senior terror chiefs, for whom terror is a game of achieving and sustaining dominance over people.

> It assures them a good life—and they shall not give up or loosen their hold easily.

The job of weaning away the indoctrinated youth, again, has to be done in a long-term sustained manner, with the help of same and/or similar religious clerics who did the dubious work in the first place. Thus, the road map of application of the GP has to be done a lot thoughtfully, by targeting its components on the key elements namely the religious clerics, politicians, state administrators, intelligentsia, terror financers, and also the army leadership, who suffer from unsustainable grandiose dreams of regional and/or world-wide dominance and leadership. The whole education system and the curricula of the afflicted countries or communities have to be overhauled for adequate impact.

GP: Its Limitations in Relation to Terrorism

No philosophy works by itself: Its formations have to be studied, understood, and applied by a sizable percent of the involved population or the community. Someone has to take leadership and steer the masses in its understanding, cost-benefits, and eventual success.

Such an understanding, and the resultant active confidence of the people in question, has to reach a critical mass where a little spark or stimulus leads to active and sustained actions in the desired direction. This basic requirement is truth for the GP, in even greater proportions than any other philosophy and/or collective action mechanism.

For success against militancy, terrorism, and/or external occupation, the GP must be home-grown; no transplanting from outside sources is likely to be successful, beyond initial idea import and/or material and intellectual support.

GP applications, in all the three challenges and/or situations, do not ensure instantaneous results: It is not a cut and dry capability tool, as impact at the level of heart and mind, which is the action route of the GP, takes time to manifest and emerge. But, in some cases glimpses of success might emerge fairly early.

Meeting violence with counter-violence is the standard response methodology practiced for centuries by human beings—as it offers instantaneous results, positive or negative. The concept of slow emergence of results, as is inbuilt in the GP, needs greater depth of understanding and conviction, for its acceptance as a tool of choice.

GP has been tried and tested against imperialistic violence, suppression of majority by minority apparatuses of governance, and even towards brutal denial of rights to minority by the majority governance, but it has not been tested against extra-territorial non-state terror outfits, which commit violence and disappear—and continue to strike with uneven frequencies.

Hence, for effective applications of the GP, the above peculiarities have to be considered while developing the need-based capsules of its component elements.

GP: Towards a Road Map for its Implementation for Terror Management

The Gandhian Philosophy, when propagated effectively, through all educational institutions/systems and media and intellectual interactions will help create an environment of human cooperation by:

- Forgetting and forgiving on part of victims of violence, as well as its perpetrators;
- Healing wounds and clearing mental cobwebs;
- Removing and negating the causes of contradictions and conflicts, at thought as well as action level;
- Eliminating the interfaith misunderstandings, as and when "**Truth**" as the universal form of God is accepted through its international propagation. The concept of

"Clash of Civilizations" will moult into the concept of **"Cooperation of Civilizations."**

Under influence of the GP, **"Pluralism"** shall be willingly accepted—as disparity of thought, faith, association, and worship will be viewed as useful and constructive attributes of human diversity, than as a cause and basis for irreconcilable positions.

GP should be popularized through an '**international road map**' drawn under the guidance of an international agency.

As a first step, all countries—especially those contributing to the genesis and spread of terrorism and/or the ones having active tendencies in this direction, and also the countries which have been victims of terrorism, should launch into intense studies of the GP through their own groups of experts.

A GP teachers program will have to be activated to create a large number of GP instructors for all types of requirements, which as a side effect shall end up solving the problem of unemployment of the educated to a substantial extent.

Through these efforts, they should work out suitable capsules of GP components —discuss the same widely and then work out an action plan for each individual country for its active implementation. A large international fund must be created to support these efforts.

On priority, GP-capsules specific to politicians, clerics, and the financers of terror shall need to be implemented as they are the key elements without which terrorism does not move even a single step.

Simultaneously, students in all schools, colleges, and mandrasas shall need to be intensely exposed to suitably drawn capsules of GP: It should become part of all curricula.

All existing universities and colleges should be encouraged to open departments and have chairs for the study of the GP.

Intellectual discussions at numerous levels, national and international, shall need to be activated for need based understanding and propagation of the GP, on long-term basis.

A large number of prizes for excellence in GP education, and its spread and practices will have to be created, in order to divert intellectual attention to this divine field of human understanding.

A wave of GP studies should replace and fully annihilate the infrastructure and ideologies of terror propagation. When about fifty percent of the world population is exposed to the elements of the GP, the roots of terror shall automatically decompose and become ineffective.

ATTACHMENT-I

Terminologies Employed

Abhinav Bharat: An organization associated with the Sangh Parivar which was found involved in the Malegaon blasts.

Action-reaction response: A process of reactive response genesis.

Adharma: Refers to an act of unrighteousness.

Ahimsa: The concept of non-violence as popularized by Mahatma Gandhi.

Al-Qaida: The world's most feared Muslim terrorist organization which had organized the 9/11 attack.

Apostates: Those not cooperating in religious movement or renouncing their religious beliefs.

Apparatus of terrorism: An infrastructure or system that generates and spreads terrorism.

Apsara: A celestial beauty.

Arjuna: The greatest warrior of the Mahabharata era who did Lord Krishna's bidding for destruction of evil rulers and princes.

Ayodhya: The birth place of Lord Rama located in the Faizabad district of UP in India.

Azadi: Independence.

Babri Masjid: A derelict structure or abandoned place of Muslim worship bearing reference to the Mungal ruler Babbar.

Babudoom: Refers to the community of bureaucrats.

Basket economies: Economies which are not self-sustaining.

Batla House: A residential house in Jamia Nagar of Delhi made infamous on account of Muslim terrorists' association with it.

Bhagavad-Gita: Record of the divine discourse that Lord Krishna gave at Kurukchetra to convince Arjuna, the great Pandava warrior, to do his assigned karma as a kshatriya, before commencement of the epic battle of Mahabharata.

Brahmastras: Refers to the non-failing celestial weapons, destructive as well as managerial.

Caliphate: Refers to a system of Muslim rulers of Turkey that came to an end through efforts of allied countries after the first world war.

Cancer of Terrorism: Refers to the fast spreading Islamic terrorism.

Chalta-hai: It literally means, "It goes." Figuratively: "It works well enough, so why bother?"

Charkha: The spinning wheel used by Gandhi to decisively defeat the British Raj.

Chauri-Chaura: A small place in central UP that became centre of freedom struggle in certain reference.

Civil disobedience: A Gandhian technique of non-violent agitation.

Clash of Civilizations: A concept of likely conflict between Islam and other civilizations, as postulated by Prof. Huntington.

Conflict of cousins: Jews, Christians and Muslims are considered as cousins on account of their origin from Jerusalem at different times of history.

Conflict resolution potential: Potential of an approach to solve or diminish conflict in collective living and working environments.

Conflict-of-self: Refers to an inner conflict where one is unable to righteously understand oneself.

Crucibles of terror: Refers to a place or location where a concentrated action or actions take place towards creation of terror.

Culture of Peace: A culture or way of living of people where peace is assigned a high value.

Dalal Street: A business street in Mumbai where stocks trading takes place.

Dalits: Refers to the lower castes of Hindus who were deprived of material benefits and social equality for a long time.

Dandi: A sea side location in Gujarat where Mahatma Gandhi and his followers broke the discriminative salt law of 1930s.

Daral-Islam: Means—land of Islam.

Delusions of greatness: Refers to development of misconception about one's greatness, without it being there.

De-toxification: The process of removal of elements of intolerance and hatred.

Deoband: Refers to an influential seminary of Islam located in Saharanpur district of Uttar Pradesh in India.

Dewaki: Mother of Lord Krishna; she was demonic Kamsa's sister.

Dharistrastra: The blind king of Hastinapura who was known for his great love for his demonic son Duryodhana.

Dharma: Refers to duty or way of doing things in a righteous manner.

Dharna: A non-violent way of sit-down agitation.

Directional confusion: Inability to decide which way to proceed.

Discrimination perception: Development of a feeling by a person or a community as if not being treated fairly.

Disturbed thought process: A situation where straight /logical thinking is disrupted.

Dominant evil design: Refers to evil actions emerging in a dominant way.

Duryodhana: A key evil character of the epic Mahabharata.

Dwarka: An ancient town on the coast of Gujarat which was reported to have been established by Lord Krishna as the 2nd capital of the Yadava empire, after abandonment of Mathura..

Evil karmas: Unrighteous and/or injudicious acts.

Evil ruthlessness: Refers to commitment of evil acts with an unexpected ruthlessness.

Failed state: Refers to a country that proves itself ungovernable from law and order as well as economic growth angle. Pakistan is currently referred to as a failed state as it has lost control on its law and order machinery and also on its economic processes.

Fanatical enthusiast: Refers to religious zealots in a community.

Father of the Nation: A title accorded to Mahatma Gandhi for his almost bloodless campaign to gain India's independence from the British Raj.

Fatwas: A term that denotes directives, often unrighteous, issued by Muslim clerics to their followers.

Fidayeen: Those who destroy themselves to destroying others under a false perception that their God will reward them in Paradise for services rendered for its cause.

Flawed objectivity: Refers to a situation where objectivity of a group or community is not sustainable or defendable.

Foxy approach: A terminology coined by the author to describe the evil elements of terrorism who instead of coming face to face for a fight elect to disguise and kill and maim innocent and unconnected people.

Frankenstein: An unmanageable creature or situation that gets out of control of its creators.

Gandhian philosophy: Refers to concepts and practices of Mahatma Gandhi during his over four decades long struggle against the British rule in India.

Godhra: A small town in north-east Gujarat where some train bogies were burnt long with its occupants, which created communal tensions and conflict in the state.

Grievancial muck: A term evolved by the author to describe unjustifiable accumulation of grievances perception by a community.

Guantanamo: A prison location operated by US to detain Al-Qaida, Taliban and other terrorist elements caught by it.

Gurudwaras: Refers to the places of worship for the Sikhs

Hajis: Muslims who have travelled to holy places in Saudi Arabia.

Hamas: A Palestinian terror organization.

Haram: A term often employed in Islam to describe situations not granted or acceptable as per the Shariat.

Harijans: Refers to under-privileged people or lower cast Hindus. This term was evolved by the Mahatma himself.

Hastinapura: A Mahabharata era township some 160 km north-west of Delhi, which was capital of the mighty Kuru dynasty.

Hawala: Illegal and often unrecorded transfer of money and/or valuables.

Hindu Radicalization: Refers to efforts to promote non-inclusive and non-secular behaviour amongst otherwise mild and placid followers of Hinduism.

Hindutava: A term employed to describe hard-line Hindu organizations' approach and non-secular philosophy.

Idea of India: A term meaning the concept of a progressive and upcoming country.

Idea of Israel: The fact of existence and progress of Israel.

Illogical logic: Refers to unsustainable type of logic.

Illogical thought warriorism: Refers to illogical and impractical thought process, like the ones projected by Islamic terrorists, to justify their misplaced objectivity.

India's 9/11: Refers to 26 December terrorist attack on Mumbai.

Indication of fickleness: Indicating instability of mind.

Intellectual dishonesty: Refers to an intellectual practice of a group wherein it does not seem to be honest to its own thought content.

International migraine: An activity that causes persisting pains and worries for the entire world.

Islamic activism: The concept of actively promoting Islam.

Islamic fundamentalism: Refers to rigid and inflexible interpretation of Islam that puts this religion in conflict with others.

Islamic resurgence: Re-activation of spread of Islam.

Islamic revival: Means revival of old Islamic approach.

Islamic Terrorism: Refers to emergence of a large incidence of terrorist acts by followers of this religion.

Islamophobia: The fear of Islam taking over other religions.

Jaish-e-Mohammad: An Islamic terrorist organization.

Jamaat-ud-Dawa: A front organization of the L-e-T of Pakistan.

Jamiat Ulama-e-Hind: An Islamic body of India.

Janana: A Sanskrit word for knowledge.

Jarasandha: A demonic ruler of the present day Bihar in the Mahabharata times.

Jidda: A commercial town of Saudi Arabia.

Jihadi Terrorism: The form of terrorism, like the Islamic one, that aims at, or perceived to be so, promotion of a particular religion.

Jihadis: A term often employed to describe Muslim terrorists.

Jugaar: Refers to a web of favours and imperfect, improvised less-than-legal solutions through which most things in India still get done.

Kamsa: An ancient demonic ruler of Mathura.

Kandahar: A town of Afghanistan.

Kargil: A hilly region of Jammu and Kashmir.

Karma: Refers to lord Krishna's principle of action without worrying about results.

Kauravas: A dynasty of Mahabharata times

Khadi: A product of Charkha—indigenously prepared hand woven cloth.

Khalistan: Name given by some separatist Sikhs for their imaginary state.

Khilafat: A movement of late 1910s and 1920s for restoration of the institution of Caliphate in Turkey for which Mahatma Gandhi had extended a lot of support to the Muslim community.

Khudai Khidmatgars: Meaning servants of God. A term evolved by the Frontier Gandhi in pre-partition times.

Kshtriyas: Refers to the ruling class as per Sage Manu's division of work in ancient society.

Kuru: A dynasty that ruled the powerful kingdom of Hastinapura in the Mahabharata times.

Kurukchetra: A location 160 km north-west of Delhi where the epic battle of Mahabharata was fought.

Latent tensions: The tensions ready to emerge.

Lord Rama: The 7th incarnation of Lord Vishnu who was born at Ayodhya.

Lord Krishna: The 8th incarnation of Lord Vishnu, the Hindu supreme God.

Madrasa: Traditional schools run by Muslims.

Mahabharata: One of the two great epics of India.

Mahant: A Hindu religious position.

Malegaon: A town in Maharastra infamous for communal riots.

Market meltdown: The term used to denote the international financial crises of 2008.

Medina: A town of Saudi Arabia.

Mental thought process: The process of thought genesis.

Metaphor: Something related yet different; a term employed to describe the Mahatma.

Militant Islam: Refers to the violent form of Islam or its followers.

Mind-set: A particular orientation of mind.

Mis-nomerism: Being wrongly named.

Mohammad: Name of the Prophet, the initiator of Islam.

Molanas: A form of Muslim clerics.

Molavies: A form of Muslim clerics.

Mon-vratas.: Refers to Mahatma Gandhi's famous technique of not speaking for days—a technique for self purification and introspection.

Mughal: A Muslim ruling class that ruled Delhi prior to arrival of British rule in India.

Mujahids: Muslim religious fighters or terrorists as understood currently.

Mumbaikars: A Maharastrian word for the residents of Mumbai.

Muslim Mindset: Refers to the state of mind of the Muslim community not in peace with other components of society.

Muslim Rage: Refers to anger accumulation in the Muslim community on account of the perception of unfair treatment or on being singled out as perpetrators of terrorism.

Naxal violence: Acts of violence committed by Naxal militants.

Naxalites: Followers of a particular variety of violent communist philosophy.

Noakhali: A town in East Bengal which acquired ill-fame on account of Muslim violence against Hindu minority prior to and during the time of the partition of India in 1947.

Non-cooperation: A component tool of the GP.

Nurseries of terrorism: Refers to a place, institution and/or a country where terrorism is actively supported, grown and nursed.

Padyatra: The tool of long march employed by mahatma very effectively.

Pandavas: Decendents of Pandu, a member of the Kuru clan of Hastinapura in the Mahabharata era.

Parivar: Means a family: Often employed to collectively describe the RSS group of institutions.

Perception of superiority: Refers to a situation where a group or community too often talks or thinks of its glorious past and tends to place itself on a higher pedestal.

Perception of unfairness: Developing thoughts of being treated unfairly, collectively or otherwise.

Perpetual denial: A condition in which an accused denies doing any wrong or being associated with anything of that type. He or she tends not to accept proof of any type about his/her culpability.

Political Islam: A term employed to describe the political face of Islam in some countries.

Pot of fermentation: Refers to a society where a lot of unsustaining ideas accumulate and/or churn up creating its internal tensions.

Prakarti: An ancient Indian term employed to describe human nature.

Pujaries: A term used for those who conduct worship in Hindu temples.

Quran: The religious book of Islam.

Rage management: Refers to management of anger.

Ravana: The demonic ruler of Sri Lanka in Ramayana times.

Righteous conscience: A form of mental situation where good thoughts pre-dominate.

Righteous thinking: The process of good thoughts genesis and expression.

Saffron Terror: Refers to acts of terror indulged in by Hindu fundamentalists

Sakuni: A very cunning ruler of Kandhar who had married his sister to the blind king of Hastinapura.

Sakuni: An evil concentrate: The maternal uncle of Duryodhana, the key figure of the epic Mahabharata.

Samvada: A term employed by Mahatma Gandhi for describing political or non-political dialogue.

Sangh Parivar: Refers to a group of Hindu organizations.

Sankaracharya: A high title of Hindu religious leaders.

Sanyasis: Refers to a female Hindu saint.

Sarva-dharma samvada: Collective dialogue of people from several religions or communities employed effectively by the Mahatma to solve important problems.

Sataya: Means truth.

Satayagraha: Means insistence for truth; a term evolved by Mahatma Gandhi during his struggle in South Africa against the discriminative White regime

Satayagraha: Means insisting upon truth.

Swadeshi: Anything that is produced locally—a campaign employed very decisively by Mahatma against the British Raj.

Scholarly Inertia: Refers to scholars inability to be decisive in a community.

Secular Muslim intelligentsia.: Refers to a section of Muslim community where its members do not actively mix religion and politics.

Secularism: Refers to governance or management wherein religion is dissociated from it.

Self-purification: The process of freeing one-self from unwanted thoughts and traits: often practiced by the Mahatma.

Shahadat: A term employed to describe self-sacrifice.

Shiv Sena: A Maharastrian hardline political party.

Siege mentality: Where thinking of a group gets limited to a particular thought process.

Sishupala: A demonic ruler of Mahabharata times who was anti-Krishna in his attitude and behaviour.

Soft state: Refers to a state which is not able to safeguard interests of its citizens—and wherein outside evil elements get a free run.

Song of Wisdom: Another name of Bhagavad-Gita.

Soul-Force: Refers to the energies of heart and mind.

Sudershana: A celestial rotating weapon of Lord Krishna.

Syndrome of inabilities: Refers to development of a mental feeling of incapability or inability to compete.

Taliban: An organized terrorist group originally developed and promoted by Pakistan with US assistance for fighting the Soviet occupation of Afghanistan.

Tallukedars: Refers to a pre-partition Muslim landed community in India.

Terrorism: The act of creating terror—and /or killing innocent and unconnected people.

Terror-neutral: One that does not promote terror.

Thana: The local Indian term for a police station.

Thought warriors: Refers to people who are relatively more active with thought genesis and their expressions rather than taking action.

Tokens of Islamicity: Refers to symbolic expressions of Islam.

Two nations' theory: The theory promoted by the Muslim League and Mr. M A Jinnah to justify their agitation for creation of Pakistan in 1947, with British connivance.

Ugrsena: Maternal grand father of Lord Krishna.

Unholy nexus: Means unjust association.

Universities of Terrorism: Refers to madrasas and other educational institution where terrorism is actively thought to young students.

Vasudeva: Father of Lord Krishna.

Vedic Vishva Kalyan Trust: A mis-nomerism adopted by a Sangh Parivar organization.

Victim syndrome: Development of a misplaced feeling of being a victim, developed individually or collectively.

Vigilante effect: Effect of collective vigilance or efforts by a self-appointed group to reduce crime or terror.

Vishwa Hindu Parisad: A Hindu hard liner organization.

Wahabism: A fundamentalist sect of Islam.

War Against Terror: An anti-terrorist campaign launched by US and NATO forces in Afghanistan and its eastern borders with Pakistan.

Weapon of thought: Refers to usage of energies of thought for a particular objectivity.

Western Imperialism: The western countries' approach of extending their influence over other countries through diplomatic as well as non-diplomatic methods and practices.

Yadava: A ruling dynasty of ancient Mathura in which Lord Krishna was born.

Yoga: Refers to the act of joining or combining.

Yudhistra: The eldest of the Pandava brothers.

REFERENCES

1. Brian Jenkins (1987) quoted in Jacob W.F. Sundberg's, "Introduction to International Terrorism—The Tactics and Strategy of International Terrorism," in Magnus D. Sandhu and Peter Nordbeck, eds. International terrorism: Report from a Seminar Arranged by the European Law Students Association, 1987: Juuristforlager i Lund: Academibokhandeln i Lund, 1989.
2. Lapidus, Ira, M. (1988), "The History of Islamic Societies," Cambridge, UK.
3. Cantwell, Smith, Wilfred (1957), "Islam in Modern History," Princeton.
4. U.V. Singh (2008), Management Wisdom of Lord Krishna," New Century Publications, Ansari Road, New Delhi, India.
5. Delhi Policy Group (2002), "War and Peace in Islam," Harman Publishing House, Nairana Ind. Area, New Delhi.
6. Holyoake, George J. (1896), "English Secularism," The Open Court Publishing Company, Chicago.
7. Abdel Wahab El Messari. Episode 21: Ibn Rushd, "Everything you wanted to know about Islam but were afraid to ask. Philosophia Islamia.
8. Kosmin, Barry A. (2007), "Contemporary Secularity and Secularism." Secularism & Secularity: Contemporary International Perspectives. Ed. Barry A. Kosmin, Ariela Keysar and and Hartford, C.T.: Institute for the study of Secularism in Society and Culture (ISSSC), 2007.
9. Lapidus Ira M. (1975), "The Separation of State from Religion in Development of early Islamic Society," *International Journal of Middle East Studies,* 6(4), pp. 363-385.
10. Munby D.L. (1963), "The Idea of a Secular Society," Oxford University Press, London, pp. 14-32.
11. Huntington P. Samuel (1993), "A Clash of Civilization," Foreign Affairs, Summar 1993 Volume.
12. Sayyed Abdul Hasan Ali Nadvi (1980), "Muslims in India," translated by Muhammad Asif Kidwai, Academy of Islamic Research and Publications, Lucknow.

13. Qutub Sayyid (1978), "Milestones," Kuwait, p. 31.
14. *Ibid.*, pp. 14-16.
15. Osama bin Laden, "Osama bin Laden's Warning: Full Text," Full Text of a recorded statement broadcast on Al-Jazeera Television. BBC News, South Asia, Sunday October 2001.
16. Jonathan Paris, quoted in: America and Political Islam: The Intellectual Context of American Foreign Policy: The University of Cambridge, 1999, p. 25.
17. Jaswant Singh (2006), "A Call to Honour," Rupa & Company, Ansari Road, New Delhi.
18. Nelson Mandela (1994), "Long Walk to Freedom" Published by Little Brown and Company, Lancaster Place, London WC2E7EN.
19. Bidyut Chakaraborty (2007), "Mahatma Gandhi: A historical Biography," Roli Books Pvt. Ltd., GK-11, New Delhi.
20. Harijanbandhu, 19 January, 1936, CWMC, Vol. 62, pp. 142-43.
21. John Dear (1994), "The God of Peace: Towards a Theology of Non-violence," Maryknoll, Orbis Books, New York.
22. David Cortright (2007), "Gandhi and Beyond: Non-violence for Age of Terrorism," Viva Books Pvt. Ltd, Ansari Road, Daryaganj, Delhi.
23. Jim Wallis (1994), "The Soul of Politics: A Practical and Prophetic Vision for Change," Orbis Books, New York.
24. George Orwell (1954), "Reflections on Gandhi," in a Collection of Essays, Ancher Books, Garden City, New York.
25. Reinhold Niebuhr (1960), "Moral Man and Immoral Society: A Study in Ethics and Politics," Scribner's, New York.
26. Dorothy Day (1980), "The Long Loneliness: The Autobiography of Dorothy Day," Harper, San Fransisco.
27. David Delinger (1993), "From Yale to Jail: The Life Story of a Moral Dissenter," Panthion Books, New York.
28. Tariq Ali (2003), "Bush in Babylon: The Re-colonization of Iraq," Verso, London WIF OEG.

INDEX